A Life in the American Century

For family and friends who shared this; above all, Molly

A LIFE IN THE AMERICAN CENTURY

Joseph S. Nye Jr.

polity

First published in 2024 by Polity Press

Polity Press
65 Bridge Street
Cambridge CB2 1UR, UK

Polity Press
111 River Street
Hoboken, NJ 07030, USA

ISBN-13: 978-1-5095-6068-4

A catalogue record for this book is available from the British Library.

Library of Congress Control Number: 2023938122

Typeset in 11.5 on 14pt Adobe Garamond
by Fakenham Prepress Solutions, Fakenham, Norfolk NR21 8NL
Printed and bound in the United States by Sheridan

For further information on Polity, visit our website:
politybooks.com

Contents

Preface

"May you live in interesting times," goes an ancient Chinese blessing and curse. I have. The world has changed dramatically during my life, which has coincided with what is often called "the American century." With poetic hyperbole, in 1983 the American Catholic bishops described our era as "the first generation since Genesis with the capability of destroying God's creation." For better or for worse, for four score years, I have lived in interesting times, and confronted the existential threat of nuclear weapons. The story I am telling is personal, but I hope it helps historians to look back, and our grandchildren to look forward.

My earliest political memories are of World War II, the atomic bomb, and the death of Franklin Roosevelt. From a child's point of view, the war was represented by my parents' concern about rationing coupons, conserving gasoline, and defeating evil people. Dropping an atomic bomb on Japan meant we would win, and the boys would soon come home. Little could I have imagined that I would one day visit Hiroshima as a guest of the Japanese government, or that I would be in charge of President Jimmy Carter's policy to stop the spread of nuclear weapons and would win the State Department's Distinguished Service Medal for my work. Subsequently, when I returned from Washington to Harvard, I tried to think through what I had done and wrote a book with the title *Nuclear Ethics*. During the Reagan Administration, I wrote and commented in national newspapers, magazines, and television on nuclear arms control and our policy toward the Soviet Union.

Nor could I have imagined that I would then work in Bill Clinton's Pentagon and be responsible for an East Asian security policy that the Japanese dubbed the "Nye Initiative," and for which I would one day stand in the Imperial Palace in Tokyo to receive the Order of the Rising Sun from the Emperor of Japan.

As I entered my teens, my political imagination was captured by maps colored for areas representing American troops moving up the Korean peninsula and then being pushed down again after Chinese troops surged across the Yalu River. I did not imagine that someday I would sit in the Great Hall of the People in Beijing and meet General Chi Haotian, the Chinese Defense Minister, who, as a young soldier, had participated in those battles. Or attend a 1995 summit meeting between the American and Chinese presidents and hear Bill Clinton tell Jiang Zemin that the United States had more to fear from a chaotic China than from a rising China, echoing an estimate by the National Intelligence Council that I chaired in 1993. Later, in 1999, I wrote an invited editorial for *The Economist* of London, speculating on whether we were fated to replicate Thucydides' prediction that an established and a rising power were fated to clash. How we handle that relationship is one of the great questions that has preoccupied me, and I will return to it often below. But first, let me go back to the beginning.

When I was born in 1937, one of every four Americans was out of work. War raged in Spain, and Hitler's growing strength portended world war. Mussolini had invaded Ethiopia and Japan slaughtered Chinese civilians in the "Rape of Nanjing." This was also the year Pablo Picasso painted his iconic image of the horrors of the destruction of Guernica, but most Americans, including my family, were strongly isolationist, despite Franklin Roosevelt's efforts to coax Americans to look outward and broaden their horizons.

Today, our nation debates whether we are witnessing the end of the American century in which the United States has been the dominant power. Some believe that we are about to be displaced by China, but I have argued that the future is still open. I have lived through eight decades of an American era that included World War II, Hiroshima, and wars in Korea, Vietnam, Afghanistan, and Iraq. Nuclear holocaust was always a background fear. School children were told that, in the event of a nuclear explosion, they should duck under their desks and cover their heads. The Cold War ended without the nuclear catastrophe that hung over our heads, but it was replaced by a period of hubris as America became the world's sole superpower. That unipolar moment was soon replaced by fears of transnational terrorism and cyber wars and analysts today speak about a new cold war with a rising China and fear of nuclear escalation following Russia's invasion of Ukraine. Our mental maps of the world have changed dramatically over my lifetime.

So has our technology. When I was born, there were no real computers. Today, most of us carry a computer in our pocket that would have required a building to house just a few decades ago. I have an even smaller one implanted in my body that paces my heart. In 1937, transcontinental and transoceanic air travel was barely possible. Over the years, I have logged more than 1 million frequent flyer miles on more than one airline. And then, during the Covid pandemic of 2020, I suddenly stopped traveling. Nonetheless, new technology allowed me to give talks on four continents in the course of a week without spending a drop of jet fuel. At the beginning of the American era, no one considered the impact of humans on the earth's climate: today, it is a major concern as we confront ever more intense wildfires, storms, melting glaciers, rising sea levels, and forced migration of peoples.

My family is a very American mix of immigrants. Benjamin Nye was a Puritan who came to Massachusetts in 1639 and the house he built is still preserved as a museum in the small town of Sandwich on Cape Cod. One of my ancestors fought in the American revolution before moving to Maine. My grandmothers, however, were more recent immigrants from Ireland and Germany. My paternal great grandfather, John Ward Nye, was a farmer from Maine who joined the California gold rush but found no gold. Unlike so many New Englanders, I have a grandfather who was born in California but decided to return East to work for another branch of the Maine family that had prospered in New York. When my grandfather fell in love and married Lillian Spaulding, the artistic daughter of an Irish Catholic family that ran the Brooklyn boarding house where he was staying, the staunchly Protestant family was scandalized, and he was forced to resign from the family company. After his mother died of cancer when he was nine, my father was brought up by two Baptist "old maid" aunts (as they were then called). They told him his mother had gone to hell because she was a Catholic. The little boy loved his caring aunts and loved his mother, so he developed a distrust of organized religion. As an adult, my father refused to go to church but retained a broad belief in God. He sent me and my sisters to Sunday School; I too wrestled with religion during various phases of my life, at one time even contemplating a career as a minister. That was not to be.

Religious intolerance was intense in twentieth-century America, but by 1960 I was able to cast my first vote for Jack Kennedy, an Irish

Catholic. I never knew my Irish grandmother, but I like to imagine her smiling at this vote by her grandson. America has serious flaws, many of which preoccupy us now, but we have also had a capacity to recreate ourselves. Growing up, society told me that homosexuality was abhorrent. Today my wife and I accept and love a transsexual member of our extended family. Racial prejudice was rampant, and I had no African American friends. Now my granddaughters date across racial divides. Our nation is far from overcoming our original sin of slavery, but we have made racial progress, including the election of a Black president. I deeply believe more will come. Without that hope, who are we? As my friend and co-chair of the Aspen Strategy Group Condoleezza Rice said in celebrating Juneteenth 2021, our saving grace as a nation is "that we are always working toward a more perfect union – that we may never get to the 'perfect', but that we are always striving for it."[1]

Americans have worried about our decline right from the start. As a fragment of European society that broke off to worship in a purer way, we have long worried about whether we were living up to those standards. American exceptionalism can blind us, but it has deep roots. Today, both our values and our power are changing. Every modern generation witnesses what it believes to be unprecedented changes in technology and society, but not every generation experiences the rise of a nation to global power and suffers recurrent anxieties about national decline.

For eight decades, we have lived in what *TIME* publisher Henry Luce in March 1941 baptized "the American Century." In the nineteenth century, the global balance of power was centered in Europe, which sent its imperial tentacles around the world. The US was a bit player with a military not much larger than that of Chile. As the twentieth century began, the US became the world's largest industrial power, and accounted for nearly a quarter of the world economy (as it still does today). When Woodrow Wilson decided to send 2 million troops to Europe in 1917, the US tipped the balance in World War I. But afterwards, the US "returned to normal" and in the 1930s became strongly isolationist. It is more accurate to date the American century with Franklin Roosevelt's entry into World War II in 1941. It was in that context, to resist

[1] Condoleezza Rice, "Keeping Freedom Strong," Hoover Institution, Stanford, June 19, 2021.

isolationism and urge participation in the war, that Luce coined his famous term. Some have referred to an American empire, but our power always had limits. It is more accurate to think of the American century as the period since World War II during which time, for better or for worse, America has been the pre-eminent power in global affairs.

With five years as a political appointee in the State Department, Pentagon, and Intelligence Community, I spent enough time in Washington to witness American power up close, and occasionally play a part in it. *TIME* and *US News* described me as a member of the "foreign policy establishment," and I served on the boards of organizations like the Council on Foreign Relations, the Trilateral Commission, the Atlantic Council, and others.

At the same time, my career as a Harvard professor and dean whetted my curiosity about America's role and power in world history, and I have spent a lifetime trying to understand and interpret it. In 1990, while writing a book questioning the concept of American decline, I invented the concept of "soft power" – the ability to get what one wants through attraction rather than coercion or payment. The term has subsequently been widely cited – a quick Google search shows millions of citations – but the most surprising was in 2007 when the President of China declared soft power to be their national objective. That led to countless requests for interviews, including a private dinner in Beijing when the foreign minister asked me how China could increase its soft power. A concept I outlined while working at my kitchen table in 1989 was now a significant part of the great power competition and discourse.

My interest in developing the concept was to explain how American power rested not just on our economic and military might, but also on our values. Historians sometimes divide the American era into four overlapping phases: the postwar liberal order up to the 1970s; the neoliberal market order that began with Reagan in the 1980s; the sole superpower era following the collapse of the Soviet Union in 1991 until the Iraq war and the financial crisis of 2008–9; and now, the fourth phase, which is ongoing and is marked by populist reaction to globalization and the rise of China.

In 1945, the US represented nearly half of the world economy and had the only nuclear weapons. The Soviet Union broke our atomic monopoly in 1949, but it was not until 1970 that our share of the world economy returned to where it had stood before World War II, to one quarter. President Nixon and others interpreted this return to normal as decline and broke the dollar's tie to gold in 1971. The US remained the world's strongest military power as well as the largest economy, but since the 2010s China has become a near peer economic competitor, and large parts of our country have reacted negatively to the disruptions caused by globalization. As yet, this contemporary era has no fixed label. As one author commented: "The order will remain American because of the centrality of the US dollar, but it will become increasingly diverse in the social purpose(s) that it enshrines."[2]

One of the great questions for the future will be what happens to American (and Chinese) soft power. In 2015, I published a book titled *Is the American Century Over?* Will the US still be the strongest power in 2045? After looking at potential challengers – Russia, China, the European Union, India, and Brazil – my guess was a tentative "yes," but with the warning that we should not expect the future to resemble the past, and my optimism has been tempered by the recent polarization of our society and politics. That book was full of facts and figures. This book is about my personal story of what it felt like to live through this American century.

Telling stories is an important way for humans to create meaning in their individual and collective lives, but the audience or reader is at the mercy of the storyteller. Fortunately, I kept diaries for fifty years, including those I spent in government. Diaries help protect against "the rosy glow of the past." Nonetheless, while I have checked memories against my diaries and contemporary accounts, storytellers always resemble people trying to describe an elephant while wearing blindfolds. We touch different parts, and they feel different. It is difficult to describe the whole. Selection is a necessary part of storytelling, but I have tried to tell a true story as best I can.

[2] Mark Blyth, "The End of Social Purpose?" in Peter Katzenstein and Jonathan Kirshner, eds., *The Downfall of the American Order?* (Ithaca, NY: Cornell University Press, 2022), p. 51.

Abbreviations

ACDA	Arms Control and Disarmament Agency
AID	Agency for International Development
AIPAC	American Israel Public Affairs Committee
ANW	Avoiding Nuclear War
APEC	Asia-Pacific Economic Cooperation
APSA	American Political Science Association
ASG	Aspen Strategy Group
CFIA	Center for International Affairs (Harvard)
CSIS	Center for Strategic and International Studies
CTB	Comprehensive Test Ban
DMA	Defense Ministerial of the Americas
DOD	Department of Defense
DOE	Department of Energy
DPB	Defense Policy Board
EASR	East Asia Strategic Report
FCO	Foreign and Commonwealth Office
GATT	General Agreement on Tariffs and Trade
GCC	Gulf Cooperation Council
GCSC	Global Commission on Stability in Cyberspace
IAEA	International Atomic Energy Agency
IISS	International Institute for Strategic Studies
IMF	International Monetary Fund
INF	Intermediate-Range Nuclear Forces
INFCE	International Fuel Cycle Evaluation
ISA	International Studies Association
ISKRAN	Institute for US and Canadian Studies
MFN	most favored nation
NAFTA	North American Free Trade Area
NIC	National Intelligence Council
NIEs	National Intelligence Estimates

NIO	National Intelligence Officer
NPT	Non-Proliferation Treaty
NRC	Nuclear Regulatory Commission
NSC	National Security Council
OES	Oceans, Environment, and Science
PDB	President's Daily Brief
PFP	Partnership for Peace
PLA	People's Liberation Army
PRM	Presidential Review Memorandum
R2P	Responsibility to Protect
ROTC	Reserve Officer Training Corps
SALT	Strategic Arms Limitations Talks
SDS	Students for a Democratic Society
STR	Special Trade Representative
UNCTAD	UN Conference on Trade and Development
UNPROFOR	UN Protection Force
WEF	World Economic Forum
WTO	World Trade Organization

1

The Early Years

Because the local hospital was overstretched as a result of a flu epidemic, I was born at home in South Orange, New Jersey, a leafy suburb of New York. Every day, my father took the train to Hoboken and a ferry boat across the Hudson to Wall Street where he was a junior partner in Freeman and Company, a bond trading firm started by distant cousins and neighbors from the Kennebec valley in Maine. He had started as a messenger boy at age 15 when his family ran out of money at the end of World War I. He never graduated from high school or college, but over the years filled in with evening classes at New York University (NYU). While he was proud when I earned a doctorate from Harvard in 1964, he loved to tease me about how long it took me to get educated. When I later became dean of Harvard's Kennedy School of Government, I donated a tree in his memory in the school's courtyard. My father and I were close, and I was very proud of him. He had an enormous influence on me, but there was always a bit of tension related to competition and independence.

While my father was a natural extrovert, my mother was an introvert, stoical and quietly strong-willed. She grew up in South Orange, one of two daughters of a divorced mother who was the daughter of German immigrants. When my grandmother later came to live with our family, she and my mother would speak German when they wanted to keep secrets from the children, particularly around Christmas time. My mother graduated from Columbia High School and attended Smith College, but had to drop out after her freshman year for financial reasons. She worked as a secretary in New York, where she met my father. They were a loyal couple, but almost polar opposites as personality types. I sometimes think I am more like my mother, but, like all humans, I am a hybrid.

Childhood portrait, age 4

The 1940s: FDR and Truman

During World War II, when I was in kindergarten, my parents moved thirty miles west to New Vernon, a rural hamlet of a few hundred people. My father doubled his daily commute so that my three sisters and I could grow up on a farm. We lived in a white clapboard colonial house across from an old Presbyterian church. Although we were in the center of the town, behind the house we had a 100-acre farm with barns, chicken and pig pens, and flowing fields and deep woods for a child to explore. Dad hired a farm manager, but also insisted that we children work on the farm: picking and storing apples, harvesting and grading potatoes, shucking field corn, helping to take care of the cows, pigs, and chickens. On Saturdays, it was often my job to kill, pluck, and dress a chicken that we would eat for the Sunday noon meal.

Another job I had as a boy in New Vernon was to mow a patch of lawn with an old-fashioned push mower, for which I was paid 25 cents;

if I forgot, I was chastised. Rather than being given an allowance, we children were given tasks to earn money to encourage our independence. Having grown up poor and survived the Great Depression, my parents were quite frugal despite accumulating wealth. My father was not interested in conspicuous consumption or having children who flaunted wealth.

New Vernon was a small community: one stop light, one church, one grade school, one gas station, one small village store which doubled as the post office, and a volunteer fire department where square dances were held on Saturday nights. Our farm manager was the caller and I loved to attend as a kid. Everybody knew each other, everyone was white, and almost all were Republican. One evening, my father warned us that a Democrat was coming to dinner, but not to worry because he was a contractor and they had to be Democrats.

We bemoan our political polarization today, but partisanship was intense where I grew up. FDR was president at the beginning of Henry Luce's American century. He had saved democracy in America during the challenge of the Great Depression, and he had overcome isolationism and led the United States into World War II. But FDR was no hero in rural Republican New Vernon. At the time of his death in April 1945, I was walking home from the township school in our little village when one of my first-grade friends echoed his parents' views of FDR by proclaiming, "The tyrant is dead!"

Similarly, Harry Truman was an important president who launched the 1948 Marshall Plan in Europe and the creation of NATO in 1949, but in New Vernon many people dismissed him as an accidental president who would soon be voted out of power. On the eve of the November 1948 presidential election, my father sent me to bed before the results were known but assured me that, when I awoke in the morning Thomas Dewey would have defeated Harry Truman. (*The Chicago Tribune* made that same mistake with its premature much-photographed iconic headline "Dewey Wins!") Our country is politically polarized today, but extreme partisanship is not new. It goes back to the early days of the Republic.

Beneath the sense of Republican community, there were also severe class and ethnic differences. At our little primary school, Harding Township School, it was more important to be an athlete than to be rich, and if you were from a very poor family or had an Eastern or Southern European name, other kids talked behind your back. Race was not an issue because there were no African American students. Years later, when my wife and I bought a house in a small New Hampshire town, I was fascinated to find a similar social structure. I have always been amazed at the ways in which humans, like the chickens we raised, work out pecking orders. On the surface, rural life may appear to resemble Edward Hicks's famous primitive painting of "the peaceable kingdom," but appearances can be deceptive. A small community has both pluses and minuses.

I came from a wealthier family than the average, but I was not an athlete. I had few neighbors to play with, and I was younger than the other kids in my class, which, at that age, was a disadvantage. I was usually near the last to be picked when sides were chosen for games at school. Unfortunately, this did not drive me to excel in my academic work, which held little status among my peers. Some of the most popular kids had "stayed back" in previous years, and that made them bigger, stronger, and bossier. My academic goal was just to get by, which I did. When a teacher spoke to my parents about underachieving and assigned me extra homework, I treated it as punishment, not an incentive. Kids will only learn when they are ready to do so.

Though I did like to read, my favorite activities involved being outdoors. I loved to hunt and fish. The center of our village had a crossroads with a blinking stoplight. Down the hill from the crossroad was a pond amidst open fields where I would catch sunnies and catfish and bring them home for my patient German grandmother to cook. In an age before cell phones and computer games, radio and television were our other sources of entertainment, but the screens were small, and the programs were few. More often, I played outside, where I crept through the woods and constructed forts of logs and re-enacted the fantasy of defending our farm. Or I would ride my bike to a friend's house, or a few miles further to fish for trout in Primrose Brook in Jockey Hollow, where George Washington's troops had spent the Winter of 1779.

What I learned from growing up in rural New Vernon in the 1940s was self-discipline and self-reliance. I had a few good friends, but there were not many kids to play with. I wasn't a lonely child because I had a large warm family that gave me confidence and my father was generous with praise and strict with criticism when deserved. I learned self-initiative, which served me well during my college years when I had a summer job in a mining camp on the Alaskan border and hitchhiked alone across the country. I benefited from that self-reliance later, too, as a young researcher in East Africa, and when I joined the State Department and felt like the proverbial child thrown into a pool and told to swim or sink.

America today is divided between urban and rural cultures, and while the population trends favor the cities, our federal constitution gives rural areas a persisting political power. Growing up in rural America has helped me appreciate that culture, but even more important it gave me a deep love of nature and the outdoors. In the eighteenth century, the German philosopher Immanuel Kant said that two things filled him with awe – the starry heavens above and the moral law within. When I become too discouraged with my study of the latter and disillusioned by the many terrible ways that humans treat each other, I can always find solace in the former. This came in very handy when the pandemic struck in 2020, when my faith was restored by raising baby chicks and my vegetable garden flourished from the additional attention. I have maintained a vegetable garden all my life. I love watching things grow. Over the years, I have received numerous honorary degrees, but one of my favorite prizes is a purple ribbon I won for a cauliflower that was rated the best vegetable in the show at a local New Hampshire fair.

The Eisenhower years

Dwight "Ike" Eisenhower, the hero of World War II in Europe, was a moderate Republican with broad popular appeal. His victory in 1952 helped to reconcile a large part of the Republican Party (including my parents) with the New Deal. He ushered in what is sometimes portrayed as a "return to normal" in the US. While we were locked in a bipolar Cold War with the Soviet Union, American culture, economic preponderance, and military strength were the foundation of the American century.

Eisenhower came into office with modest objectives. He consolidated Truman's doctrine of containment and made it sustainable by a set of prudent judgments such as avoiding land wars in Korea and Vietnam that later trapped his successors. He strengthened the new alliances with

Europe and Japan and was willing to negotiate with the Soviet Union. While he relied on nuclear threats of massive retaliation to offset Soviet conventional superiority in Europe and to save spending on expensive land forces, he was simultaneously very careful in resisting the actual use of nuclear weapons against North Korea and China.

Eisenhower understood the limits of American power, and managed crises well. Although he used the misleading metaphor of dominoes falling in Southeast Asia, he avoided letting this suck him into major involvement in Vietnam. He considered intervening with air power, nuclear weapons, or ground troops, but finally ruled out acting unilaterally. He kept his emotional needs separate from his analysis and avoided the trap that later destroyed Lyndon Johnson, who lacked Eisenhower's emotional and contextual intelligence. One result of Ike's prudence was eight years of peace and prosperity.

But it was also a period marked by fear of communism, and the demagoguery of Senator Joseph McCarthy, whose career prospered for four years on the basis of his big lies. Fear encouraged conformity. Books like David Riesman's *The Lonely Crowd* and William Whyte's *The Organization Man* were critical of conformity. *TIME* magazine dubbed my college contemporaries "The Silent Generation." There was a great deal of conformism, but that title fails to capture what for many of us was also an age of exploration, at home and abroad, as Otto Butz described in his book *The Unsilent Generation*.

In 1950, I no longer walked up a rural road to Harding Township School but took a school bus to Morristown School in the county seat ten miles away, where I discovered that, in a new environment, with a little effort, I could be first in class and a leader. As I tell my friends who worry about their children, kids learn when they are ready to learn, but a change in incentives and reinforcement can make a big difference. I also learned to play team sports, traveled to Europe with my family, and was introduced by my younger sister to her classmate Molly Harding, who would become the most important person in my life. When it was time for college, I never did the type of proper search with multiple applications that creates anguish for so many young people today. Fortunately for me, competition was not as tough then. I applied to two schools, Princeton and Yale, but growing up in Northern New Jersey, I had my heart set on the former. In my ignorance, I turned out to be lucky.

Princeton

At first, Princeton was something of a shock. At Morristown I was a big fish in a small pond, but among the beautiful gothic spires of Princeton, I was a lonely minnow. I was the only student from Morristown, while students from large prep schools like Exeter, Deerfield, and St Paul's came by the dozen. Now, no one knew my name and I had to find an identity. I tried football and crew, but was outclassed. I often drank too much on weekends to be one of the boys. The social difficulty was reinforced by the unfortunate system of "bicker," or bidding for entry into the eating clubs, where we adolescents were ranked by other adolescents on a social status I barely understood. I was accepted by a good club but was rejected by two higher-ranked clubs. I quietly suffered the blow to my ego.

The following summer, I took a job as a laborer at the Granduc mining camp that was exploring for copper on the border between British Columbia and Alaska. It is a land of breathtaking jagged snow-capped peaks, and our mine was perched above a huge glacier. On the mountain above us was another glacier from which (years later) an avalanche broke off and destroyed the camp. We slept in sleeping bags in shacks perched on the mountain side and donned our gear in a wash shack where we hung our helmets and lights and heavy rubber jackets. The latrine was a large canvas tent over a rushing glacial stream. If I was on the graveyard shift at night, I sometimes drove the little train of ore carts out of the tunnel to dump the rocks down onto the lower glacier, and would be greeted by a spectacular display of northern lights.

At other times, a storm would roll in from the Pacific to fill our valley with fog for a week until it rained itself out. That was not only visually disappointing, but it stopped the planes from landing with our supplies. Two planes crashed during the summer I worked at Granduc. A deHaviland Beaver failed to clear the lip of the glacier face after flying up from the river valley under the clouds. The scar on the ice wall showed where the pilot just missed clearing the lip by a few feet before crashing to his death in the river that flowed out of the glacier. I was part of a crew that went down to find the pilot's body and carry it back to camp. It was my first experience of violent death. The memory often returned to me years later when I flew hundreds of miles in bad weather in Alaskan bush planes during fishing and camping trips.

At Granduc, I again had to prove myself, but this time among rough men who had never heard of Groton or Andover or Princeton, and could not care less about any of them. Now I had to prove myself with the hard work of shoveling muck into ore carts or wrestling heavy creosoted mine timbers into place. Warren Bennis, a leadership theorist who taught at Harvard's Kennedy School when I was dean, wrote about people going through personal crucibles from which they emerge with a better understanding of themselves. The mining camp was that type of a crucible for me.

At the end of the summer, I hitch-hiked back across the country, dependent on the good will of strangers. I spent many hours by the roadside, slept outside, and learned what a large and wonderful country we inhabit. The result of my summer adventure was a new perspective and self-confidence when I returned to Princeton. I often tell students that a gap year or summer job working with people who labor with their hands is as valuable as any course they will take in college, and it has made me an advocate of public service that cuts across classes.

I wrote a regular column for the *Daily Princetonian*, and one of my editorial crusades was to criticize Princeton's practice of compulsory chapel, as I continued to struggle with the role of religion in my life. In New Vernon days, I had wanted to become a minister, but that aspiration died at Princeton. In my freshman year, a philosophy class challenged me to ask how I knew what I thought I believed. I still feel the impact of reading Descartes' "I think; therefore I am." I spent much of freshman year stripping away things I thought I knew; reading and annotating my Bible and questioning my faith until I became agnostic. There is so much in life we can never know. On many evenings, I sat alone in a pew at the back of Princeton's lovely gothic chapel, my favorite building on the campus. l recall the stillness and the soft yellow glow of the chandeliers as I peered into the shadows of the long narrow nave and wrestled with my religious views.

After a brief flirtation with psychology, trying to understand why we humans think the way we do, I decided to major in a program in economics, history, and politics to better understand what we humans have done. I was fascinated by Joseph Schumpeter's theory of capitalism as "creative destruction" and the role of entrepreneurs who took the risks to make it happen. In my senior year, my thesis advisor, the economic historian Jerome Blum, obtained access for me to the files of a failed Philadelphia company, the American Preserve Company, which led to my thesis "Death of a Family Firm." It won a prize. I was also named Class Day Speaker at graduation, and I can remember standing in Alexander Hall and telling my classmates that, while we could not alone save the world, we could each do our small bit to improve it. I learned a lot at Princeton, with Woodrow Wilson's famous precept system and its close attention to undergraduate education, but I disliked the social system.

There were no women and no African Americans in my class. I grew up knowing few African Americans, except for Clara Pearson who helped my mother and whose husband was the foreman at a small construction company where I worked on road building on a high school summer job. Clara and my mother sat together at the kitchen table for lunch, and my Republican father helped Clara with her finances. But I did not have to be acquainted with many African Americans to know that society's treatment of them was not just. Neither Thomas Jefferson nor our nation lived up to his words that all men are created equal and endowed with inalienable rights, but those words had a profound effect on a boy growing up in a Republican family in rural New Jersey. I was not politically active in 1954 – and was attending a de facto segregated school – but I was elated when I learned of the Supreme Court decision in *Brown* v. *Board of Education* to end segregated schools. In 2008, when Michelle Obama, a Princeton graduate, spoke at the Democratic National Convention, tears came to my eyes. Years later, when I had an opportunity to meet her, I told her what her example meant to a middle-aged white man.

At the beginning of my senior year at Princeton, I planned to join the Marine Platoon Leaders' Corps. All able-bodied young men faced the draft in those days, and I was a healthy specimen and looking forward to the challenge. Then in the Fall of my senior year, I bumped into one of my professors, E. D. H. Johnson, in Firestone Library and he convinced me to apply for a Rhodes Scholarship to Oxford. I did so and, to my surprise, I won. The process involved grueling interviews at the New Jersey state competition and then at the regional level in Philadelphia, where Milton Eisenhower chaired the committee. Late that night, after driving home from Philadelphia, I stood on the front steps of our home in New Vernon and paused to stare at the infinity of a Van Gogh starry night and wonder at it all. One result was that, instead of joining the Marines after graduation and winding up as an officer in Vietnam, it took thirty-five years before I saw service with the Department of Defense (DOD), and when I first went to Vietnam it was as dean of the Kennedy School to visit an educational program we had there. Any time I am tempted by hubris, I remember that much of where the roulette ball lands in the wheel of life is outside our hands.

Dreaming spires

Oxford was a new type of learning experience. At first, the common English language fooled me into thinking that British culture and education was like ours, but it is not. With my Rhodes group, I sailed from New York to Southampton on the *Queen Elizabeth*, a nice way to get to know the others before we split up into the various colleges that comprise the University of Oxford. We were a geographically diverse group chosen from competitive districts around the country, but there was no diversity in terms of race or gender.

Exeter, one of the oldest but not richest of Oxford's colleges, was founded in 1314 in the center of the city. Rector Kenneth Wheare thought that the best way to integrate the Yanks was to match them with a British roommate. I shared a wonderful eighteenth-century paneled suite with high ceilings and leaded windows, but there was no central heating and the original fireplace had long ago been blocked up and replaced by a little electric coil with a meter into which you fed a shilling to produce an hour of warmth. My British roommate Richard Buxton (who later became Lord Justice Buxton) was a graduate of a private school who had done his national service as an army officer in the British colony of The Gambia. He believed in the bracing value of fresh air and would return to the room and throw open the windows. As I watched my shillings fly out the window, I almost relaunched the American revolution, but eventually we became friends.

Like many Americans, my memories of Oxford are steeped in cold and damp. One winter, I kept a paper clip chain of the number of days without sunshine and got to twenty-one. I joined the college rugby team where I was tolerated not for any skill but for my temerity and strength in tackling as though I was still playing American football, albeit without pads. After a muddy practice, we would retreat to the college cellar where there was hot water for eight bathtubs, but by the time my turn came I often wondered whether there was more mud on me or on the rim of the tub. Fortunately, Oxford has since discovered central heating and plumbing.

Stroke of the rugby boat, Exeter College, Oxford, 1959
Source: B. J. Harris

We ate dinners at long benches and wooden tables in a great seventeenth-century hall with a vaulted ceiling, overseen by massive portraits of long-deceased bishops and nobles, and a platform at the end where the dons dined in black gowns at high table. There were two large fireplaces on either side in the middle of the hall. One night, I had tarried in my room and rushed in after the dinner bell. Searching for a seat, I remarked on my good fortune that one remained next to the roaring fire. I should have known better. Soon after I seated myself, someone passed me a note saying I was "sconced" for taking the seat of the senior scholar.

Sconcing meant I had to order a silver pint tankard of beer. If I emptied it without taking it from my lips, I could sconce my challenger back with a two-pint tankard. For the sake of deterrence, I decided to do so, but when my opponent downed the two pints without taking it from his lips and challenged me again with a huge three-pint silver tankard, I capitulated. This was tougher than the mining camp!

My two years at Oxford provided an opportunity for a tremendous deepening of my education. At that time, the Rhodes Trust encouraged us to forswear pursuit of a graduate degree and instead take a second undergraduate degree and plunge into college life. I learned a great deal from my immersion in British college culture. Social class is ubiquitous in America, but somewhat less obvious than in Britain. For instance, at Oxford, I had a "scout" or servant who cleaned my room and brought me a pint of milk every morning. At Princeton, I had to clean my own room and go to the store for milk, but had a refrigerator to keep it fresh. Oxford taught me the difference between a capital-intensive and a labor-intensive class-ridden economy.

In terms of formal education, at Princeton I had taken four or five courses a term and received grades at the end of each. At Oxford, there were no courses and attending lectures was purely voluntary. Three times a week I would write an essay and discuss it one-on-one with my tutors in philosophy, politics, and economics. My philosophy tutor, William Kneale, taught me the importance of precise definition, which was characteristic of linguistic philosophy prevalent at that time. I remember my first essay, in which I thought I had proven the impossibility of altruism because even a donor who gives a coin to a beggar does it out of self-interest. Kneale dryly pointed out that I had not answered the problem but simply defined it away. My politics tutor, Norman Hunt (later Lord Crowther Hunt who became an important figure in Harold Wilson's government), would patiently explain that in parliamentary systems power was tamed by civilizing it rather than through the checks and balances that the Americans practiced. He also proclaimed that Britain sent its best students into government, while the US sent them into business. Wilfred Knapp, my tutor in international relations, explained the weakness and folly of British foreign policy between the two world wars.

There were no grades awarded until the end, when one sat for six three-hour exams in the cavernous nineteenth-century Examination

Schools. One day, after lunch, I was in my room in college boning up for an exam when I suddenly realized I had lost track of the time. I flew down the High Street to the Schools, my robe flapping, arriving half an hour late and realized with horror that, in my haste, I had forgotten my pen. The examining don, regaled in black robe and white tie, interrupted the hall of bowed student heads and asked if anyone could help this poor American with the loan of a pen. The loaned fountain pen leaked, and it was not my best exam.

Fortunately, I was looking for education rather than grades at that point. I was more interested in self-exploration. I tried and failed to write a novel (though I eventually published one four decades later). In the Exeter Fellows Garden, staring up at the gothic spires of the ancient Divinity School and Bodleian Library and wondering what I would become, I read books on a wide variety of topics ranging from art, theater, and ballet, to history and novels.

This is not to say I did not learn an enormous amount from my studies at Oxford, but it did not come in packaged courses like Princeton. I learned even more from travels during the long vacations in Western and Eastern Europe, and in Morocco. Visiting Auschwitz deepened my revulsion at anti-Semitism. I still vividly remember the bins of spectacles, clothing, and other personal belongings, each representing the destruction of a human being. My most remarkable trip was behind the Iron Curtain to the Soviet Union, Poland, Hungary, and Czechoslovakia in the summer of 1959 with two other Rhodes Scholars, John Sewall and Sam Holt. We drove a small British Sunbeam Rapier car from Finland to Leningrad, Moscow, Smolensk, Minsk, Warsaw, Budapest, and Prague. At the time, Western visitors were very rare behind the Iron Curtain.

Whenever we pulled into a city, we were greeted by large crowds who treated us as though we had arrived from Mars. We were surrounded by people asking questions ranging from "Do you believe in God?" to "Why do you have so many hostile missiles aimed at us?" We were accompanied by an official "Intourist" guide who made sure we visited the obligatory sites in the daytime, but in the evenings, young people would often invite us to "parks of culture and rest," where the girls would ask us to dance and the boys would challenge us to feats of strength like swinging a hammer to drive a weight up a pole. (Fortunately, Sewall, who rowed on the Oxford crew, could always win.) As we were leaving to return to our hotel after one such episode, we were stopped by a Soviet militiaman in uniform, who pulled out his revolver. I thought he had discovered that Sewall was a commissioned second lieutenant and that we would be arrested. Instead, much to our relief, he slipped the bullets from the chamber and said, "Here, throw these away for peace and friendship."

Before our trip, the Soviet empire had seemed mysterious and foreboding. After the Soviets launched their Sputnik satellite in 1957, there was a widespread belief that they would surpass us and that we were in decline. In 1959, Vice President Nixon and Nikita Khrushchev engaged in a much-publicized debate about which system was superior, with Khrushchev proclaiming that the Soviets would own the future. Our visit made me doubtful. Close-up, the much-vaunted empire looked far less foreboding.

I learned an enormous amount from the large number of friends I made at Oxford, both Rhodes Scholars, British students, and foreigners. My experience later led me to advise many of my Harvard students to take time to study abroad. One discovers what it means to be an American by meeting and understanding non-Americans.

Of all the many long conversations I had at Oxford, perhaps the most consequential were those with Kwamena Phillips, a college mate from Cape Coast, Ghana. At that time, African countries were becoming independent and the many debates about the future of the continent fascinated me. Kwamena thought that Africa would pioneer a new form of democracy; Ghana's president Kwame Nkrumah was preaching African unity through Pan Africanism. I wondered about that future, and I am sure that it was those Oxford conversations that encouraged me to spend time in Africa and witness Uganda and Kenya become independent countries in 1962 and 1963. Watching the British flag come down and the new flags rise was a moving experience. Kwamena visited my family in the US before he went home to Africa, but unfortunately he died after returning to Ghana, so we never were able to discuss together the answers to his questions or to finish our conversation.

The Kennedy years

The long 1960s was a turbulent decade, which many scholars see as a turning point in modern American history. My colleague Robert

Putnam refers to two 1960s – "rather like a swimmer making a flip turn, Americans entered the 1960s moving toward community, but midway through the decade abruptly changed direction and left the 1960s behind, moving toward individualism."[1] In terms of a balance between our basic values of liberty and equality, the pendulum was swinging back in a libertarian rather than the communitarian direction that had marked the Progressive era, the Depression, and World War II.

John Kennedy campaigned on restoring vigor in government, but his practice was more moderate than his campaign. In terms of our role in the world, Kennedy failed in his efforts to overthrow Fidel Castro with the Bay of Pigs invasion, but he avoided a crisis in Berlin by tolerating the Soviet construction of the Berlin Wall in 1961, and then managed the Cuban Missile Crisis in 1962, when the country came closer to nuclear war than ever. In 1963, Kennedy negotiated the first major arms control treaty, the Limited Test Ban Treaty. Two years later, the US became deeply entangled in the disastrous Vietnam War that ended in defeat and tore us apart at home. Kennedy had limited American troops to 16,000 "advisors," but in 1965 Lyndon Johnson decided to change the role to combat troops and eventually increased the number to more than half a million.

In 1967, I remember sitting on the front porch at my wife Molly's family farm in Clinton, New York, gazing over the pastoral landscape of gentle green hills and dairy farms, wondering what was happening to our country. The decade had begun with Kennedy's soaring rhetoric about asking what you could do for the country and the world, but by the end it was marked by riots in the streets, cities on fire, three major political assassinations, two failed presidencies, and crowds marching in the streets around the world protesting American policies in Vietnam. It was not a great era for America's soft power of attraction.

At the same time, the 1960s also saw positive changes, such as the first major civil rights legislation since the Civil War era, the development of the women's movement, and the landing of humans on the moon. In the 1950s, Eisenhower had represented stability, but by 1960 many saw that as stagnation. I remember the shock of learning that the

[1] Robert Putnam, *The Upswing; How America Came Together a Century Ago, and How We Can Do It Again* (New York: Simon and Schuster, 2020), p. 301.

Soviet Union had beaten the US to space with its launch of Sputnik in 1957. Americans took it seriously when Nikita Khrushchev banged his shoe on the table at the UN in 1959 and falsely claimed that the Soviet Union would soon surpass a declining United States. Kennedy called for a renewal of American vitality, and I became swept up in his Camelot myth.

Harvard

I did not have a career plan when I left Oxford. My father suggested joining him in the financial business, but I was more interested in international affairs. I thought I might possibly join the Foreign Service, but also that it would be a good insurance policy first to earn a doctorate. I applied to the government department at Harvard, following in the footsteps of my Rhodes friend Roy Hofheinz.

Unlike the freedom I enjoyed at Oxford, I now had to buckle down and take my studies seriously, with required courses and the looming hurdle of written and oral general exams at the end of two years. My examiners were the brilliant but erratic theorist Louis Hartz; my gentle mentor and thesis advisor Rupert Emerson; Suzanne Rudolph, a smart expert on India; and the gruff Henry Kissinger. They grilled me for two hours.

The most senior professors in the government department were like feudal barons with little fiefdoms which I tried to avoid joining. The sharpest division was between the famous theorists Carl Friedrich and William Yandell Elliott. Students were invited to dinners and lunches at their houses, and many became identified with one or the other. I was more impressed by the sharp conservative urbanist Ed Banfield, but my main interests were international. I audited courses by Henry Kissinger, Stanley Hoffmann, and Ernest May on foreign policy and nuclear weapons. I was strongly influenced by Hoffmann and Kissinger. Their backgrounds as children of European Jewish refugees initially made them close friends at Harvard, but their friendship was destroyed by differences over the Vietnam War.

I also enrolled in seminars by John Kenneth Galbraith, Edward S. Mason, and Rupert Emerson about the challenge of nationalism and economic development in newly independent African nations. Mason, an economist who chaired the World Bank team charged with helping Uganda prepare for independence, told our seminar one day that his mission had been puzzled by whether to plan for a Ugandan market of 8 million people or for an East African Common Market of 30 million, which made more economic sense. He said the answer was outside his competence as an economist and would require a political scientist. I immediately thought to myself: "There's my thesis project!"

I developed a proposal and won a grant from the Ford Foundation, which had created a foreign areas training program to encourage young Americans to learn more about the rest of the world. Molly and I went to live in East Africa for a year and a half to research my thesis on whether the professed pan-Africanist leaders of Tanzania, Uganda, and Kenya could preserve the common market they had inherited from the departing British colonialists and forge an East African federation as they promised they would. The story of their failure to do so is told in my thesis, which eventually became the first of my published books.

In Robert Frost's famous poem, "two roads diverged in a wood and I took the one less traveled on." I started out in one direction, but ironically my later career wound up on the other road as I ended up focusing on international relations rather than the comparative politics of African development – but this path brought me to world politics through a side door rather than a front door. Although I had taken a course from the great realist scholar Hans Morgenthau (who was visiting Harvard at the time), I felt that the dominant realist approach, which focused on balance of military power among states, was valid but too narrow, and did not take sufficient account of ideas, social processes, and economic integration. Studying those aspects of relations between new states from the local to the national level gave me a different perspective on my eventual field of study.

Other than voting for JFK in 1960, I felt too junior to participate in politics. I was preparing to marry at the end of the Spring term. I focused on my studies and after receiving A grades on all my Fall courses, I felt able to go to the department office to ask for the renewal of my graduate fellowship. I was stunned to learn that this was impossible because I had missed the deadline and the funds were fully allocated. It was the calendar, not my grades, that determined renewal. Bob McCloskey, the genial department chair, said he would allow me to earn money by teaching a sophomore tutorial before my general exams and would help me become a research assistant to Robert R. Bowie, Director of the Harvard Center for International Affairs (CFIA). That solved my immediate financial problem, but meant a lot of work pressure for the first year of married life.

I married Molly Harding in 1961, a decision that turned out to be the most important event in my life other than being born. We set up home in a tiny, rented house near the Charles River, which has long since been torn down and replaced by Harvard's gigantic Mather House (where our granddaughter Sage lived as a student decades later). During that hellish first year of our marriage, Molly pursued her interest in art and provided an income by working as an assistant at the Fogg Art Museum.

I enjoyed teaching sophomores and working for Bob Bowie was very challenging. He was a tough lawyer with a shock of white hair, rimless glasses, and a steel-trap mind who had been Director of Policy Planning in the Eisenhower State Department before coming to head the Harvard Center. The CFIA was a new venture created by the Ford Foundation to help scholars better understand the world in which the US found itself. It cut across disciplines with an all-star faculty from political science, economics, and sociology.

Each week, the Center held three faculty seminars on Europe and Atlantic relations, nuclear weapons and arms control, and political and economic development. As Bowie's assistant, I could sit in, take notes, and learn. At the same time, Bowie had me researching and drafting articles and speeches about the policy problems caused by Khrushchev's increasingly aggressive actions toward Berlin in the year before the Wall was erected. The Soviets regarded the Berlin enclave deep behind their Iron Curtain as an impediment that had to be removed in order to consolidate their position. Was he bluffing? How far would he go? Could we defend West Berlin? I had to try to draft answers to these unanswerable questions. Bowie was a formal and meticulous taskmaster, returning draft after draft until it met his approval. Praise was scant, but I learned a great deal from his criticism, and we later became friends. Despite the fascination of the Cold War events, however, my attention was being increasing drawn to the next steps of traveling to East Africa to research my thesis.

Uganda, Kenya, Tanganyika

Molly and I flew up the Nile from Cairo to Khartoum to Kampala with a mixture of trepidation and anticipation as we watched the shadow of our little Fokker Friendship turbo-prop trace its way across the vast swamplands of Sudan. We landed in Entebbe, a peninsula jutting into Lake Victoria, and then drove through palms, banana trees, and small villages. We marveled at trees covered with red tulip-shaped flowers and purple vines of bougainvillea as we approached our new home at the East African Institute of Social Research on a hill dominated by Makerere University College. As we unpacked our suitcases in our simple cinder-block flat, lizards scampered up the bedroom walls. When I tried to catch one in a shoebox to take it out, we were shocked to see its tail fall off. Later we learned that shedding a tail was a natural defense against predators and it would soon be regrown. We had much to learn.

While Uganda straddles the equator, the capital is spread over a number of lush green hills that rise to 4,000 feet above sea level; the temperature is mostly warm and humid but rarely uncomfortably hot. Three of the hills are crowned, respectively, by an Anglican cathedral, a Catholic church, and a grand mosque, while another marks the palace of the Kabaka, the hereditary monarch of the Baganda people, the ethnic group that surrounds Kampala. The views from the hills were impressive, but the streets of the city were dusty and lined with low shops and people cooking at fires by the side of the road. Few tall buildings existed, and the colonial Grand Hotel was a misnomer.

We soon got used to lizards and cockroaches and the need to boil water and live on antimalarial pills in our little flat at Makerere, and we came to love Kampala. Swarms of fruit bats took wing at dusk, while women in voluminous Basuti dresses (originally designed by Victorian missionaries) had babies strapped to their backs while they balanced baskets of plantains on their heads. As they sidled by us, they would murmur wonderful melodious greetings in Luganda. We shared a kitchen and bathroom with Okot p'Bitek, a talented Oxford graduate from the Acholi region of northern Uganda who became a noted writer and a good friend.

Later, when we moved to a bigger flat, a large friendly woman in a Basuti knocked on our door and explained in minimal English that she had worked for the previous tenants and needed employment. Though we were reluctant to have a servant, we succumbed. Dolisi took wonderful care of us, but, no matter what we said, she always laid out formal place settings at mealtimes, with several forks, several knives and spoons, and several glasses. When I walked home from the Makerere library for a simple lunch, my grilled cheese sandwich was elegantly placed. Dolisi knew how Europeans were supposed to behave even if we Americans did not!

We loved Uganda, traveling all over the country. Molly worked with an educational psychologist visiting rural schools. I studied the politics of Uganda, Kenya, and Tanzania (then Tanganyika) to understand the forces holding the countries together as well as pulling them apart. On the positive side were two very different forces: economic rationality and pan-African ideology. The British had bequeathed the newly independent countries a common market – a common currency, and an East African Common Services Organization that made good economic sense for developing countries. In addition, the leaders of the independence movements were adherents to a pan-African ideology who proclaimed that their next step was to create an East African federation as a step toward uniting Africa. Some, like Julius Nyerere, a former teacher who had translated Shakespeare into Swahili, were dedicated to the ideology; others, like Milton Obote in Uganda, paid it lip service only.

On the side of disintegration was the fact the leaders had to build nation-states that could govern and hold power. Despite the arbitrary nature of colonial boundaries, the instruments of budgets, civil service, police, and armies that the leaders had captured from their colonial rulers were the tools at hand, and they reflected those colonial boundaries. Moreover, the leaders were trying to use those instruments of the state to build nations. Pan-Africanism and nationalism were expressed by some elites, but most ordinary citizens felt a sense of community in terms of their tribe and language. In Tanganyika, with many smaller tribes and the lingua franca of Swahili, Nyerere's task was less difficult than that of Obote in Uganda or Jomo Kenyatta in Kenya, where there were greater disparities of power and deeper rivalry among tribes and where Swahili was less widely spoken. The problem was not hypocrisy of the leaders, but a context in which they were trapped in the colonial cages they had captured.

In those early days it was still possible for a mere graduate student to interview leaders like Nyerere (who came across as the teacher he was), Obote (who was self-important and evasive), and Tom Mboya (the enthusiastic trade unionist whose assassination was such a loss for Kenya). In addition to political leaders, I interviewed civil servants and local party officials. While I sometimes encountered suspicion and skepticism, particularly among some party officials and intellectuals, there was surprisingly little anti-Americanism or evidence of the Cold War in East Africa at that time. I generally felt welcomed. Security was not a problem.

We purchased a VW Beetle to travel across East Africa as I conducted interviews for my thesis, setting up temporary residences in Nairobi and Dar es Salaam, with side trips to the islands of Zanzibar. Driving in East Africa was something of an adventure as few roads were then paved. On one trip to Northern Uganda a loose stone shattered our windshield and we drove ninety miles to Kampala, covered in red dust. On a trip from Nairobi to Dar es Salaam across the magnificent plains of northern Tanzania where giraffes and gazelles grazed near the road, we struck a rock and blew out our tire.

Today, Dar is a busy Indian Ocean port of some 5 million people, but in those days it was a rather sleepy capital showing some remnants of the architecture from when Tanganyika was a German colony before World War I. A friend arranged for us to stay for free at Kivukoni, an adult education college based in a former hotel across the harbor from the city. After visiting government offices in the city for interviews (and interminable cups of milky tea), I would take a small ferry across the inlet of the harbor and trudge through sand and coconut palms back to Kivukoni, where I could shed my city clothes and plunge into the salt water for a refreshing swim.

Nairobi was large and bustling, and showed signs of its British settler elements with fancy hotels like the Delamere and the Stanley. Sitting a mile above sea level, the city was quite cool during the rainy season. It was in Nairobi that we learned of Kennedy's assassination in November 1963. The shock was enormous, and our dream was dying. My research was showing that the East African Common Market was likely to collapse; corruption and political violence were growing, and in January 1964 army mutinies challenged the new governments in Kenya and

Uganda before they were put down. While I had been staunchly anti-colonial and critical of the British, I was dismayed to see leaders like Obote use racial charges to fire white civil servants who resisted corruption or told the truth about what was happening.

But I faced a dilemma. I had gone to Africa with deep sympathies, which I now realized were naive. I was not willing to become an apologist for what I knew was wrong, but I did not want to become a carping critic of African leaders for the rest of my life. My Harvard colleague Albert Hirschman once wrote a book about choices, calling it *Exit, Voice, and Loyalty*. Much as we had loved our time in Africa, I gradually chose exit, and eased myself away from what might have become a career as an Africanist. It is telling that one of my first articles in a peer-reviewed journal was titled, "Corruption and political development: A cost-benefit analysis."[2]

The choice to broaden the scope of my work looks clearer with the perspective of 20:20 hindsight than it did at the time. I still had a thesis to write and was trying to make sense of what I had observed on the ground in East Africa. In the thesis I quoted the great German theorist Max Weber, who wrote: "Not ideas, but material and ideal interests, directly govern men's conduct," yet ideas have, "like switchmen, determined the tracks along which action has been pushed by the dynamics of interest."[3] Unfortunately, pan-African ideas proved to be less powerful switchmen than emerging national interests.

I wondered if this was a universal truth, and how it was that the uniting of Europe seemed to be helping that continent overcome its history of world wars and the horrors of the Holocaust. I discovered the writings of Ernst Haas and the new theorists of functional integration who argued that world peace would not emerge from world federalism but from regional integration – a "peace in parts" (to anticipate the title of a book I published years later). But I wondered if that was consistent with the political pressures in developing countries. The American government and the US Agency for International Development (AID) was promoting the idea as I discovered one night when we went to the movies in Kampala. In addition to the main feature, the cinema played a

[2] *American Political Science Review*, June 1967.

[3] Hans Gerth and C. W. Mills, eds., *From Max Weber* (New York, 1946), pp. 63–4.

short AID documentary describing the success of the Central American Common Market. I wondered how those five countries had succeeded when East Africa did not. That anomaly was the pull that helped widen my intellectual horizon beyond Africa to regional integration theory in general.

In any event, I was standing on the lawn of the East African Institute of Social Research at Makerere when I opened a letter from Harvard inviting me to instruct introductory courses on government for a modest salary of $6,000 a year. I decided I would try it for a while. The while turned out to be long.

2

The Vietnam Years: Johnson, Nixon, Ford

Decades are not purely chronological. As we have seen, there was a major difference between the first and second half of the 1960s, with the first a continuation of the '50s and the second spilling into the '70s. To illustrate: in the early 1960s, three-quarters of Americans told pollsters that they had a great deal of confidence in government. In the early 1970s, after Vietnam and Watergate, that number had declined to one-quarter, and it never recovered the level of the early 1960s.

The 1960s experienced a generational revolution as postwar baby-boomers put a strain on the existing institutions. Progress on civil rights and feminism brought important positive social changes, but the late '60s also saw an increase in violence and destruction. In France, the events of 1968 brought down the presidency of Charles de Gaulle. Germany, Italy, and even Japan saw the rise of the "red brigades," who kidnapped and killed government and corporate leaders. Violence occurred both in America and in other developed countries, but the real cloud hanging over the US in the late '60s and early '70s was the terrible problem of the Vietnam War.

Not only did the Vietnam imbroglio undercut the soft power of the American century overseas, but it tore apart society at home. I remember wondering how men like McGeorge Bundy (former Harvard dean and Molly's distant cousin) and Robert McNamara could be so blind. I despised them. Two decades later I spent time with them during a Harvard Kennedy School oral history project about how we survived the Cuban Missile Crisis (which I will describe below). To my surprise, I came to like them as I realized how multidimensional they were as human beings, but I never forgave them for Vietnam. It was hard to understand how men who had saved us from nuclear war by their skillful handling of the Cuban Missile Crisis could be so rash in plunging us into the swamps of Vietnam just a few years later.

Although I was interested in politics, it was as an observer and voter rather than as a participant. Shocked and saddened by Kennedy's assassination, I supported Lyndon Johnson, particularly as he promised to continue Kennedy's policies and retained much of his administration. The 1964 election was cast as a contest between the continuity Johnson promised and the radical approach of Arizona Republican Senator Barry Goldwater, who proclaimed that extremism was justified in the defense of liberty. Vietnam, where the Communist insurgents were doing better than expected, played a major role in the election, with Johnson casting Goldwater as a dangerous warmonger who would get us into a nuclear war over a remote country in Southeast Asia. A famous election advertisement showed a countdown with a little girl counting as she plucks petals from a daisy; as she gets to the end, a missile launch countdown starts, at the end of which a nuclear mushroom cloud erupts.

Although Kennedy had placed 16,000 American troops in Vietnam, he had restricted their role to advisors and US casualties were limited. Johnson had promised to continue JFK's legacy, but little did we know when we voted that, shortly after his election, LBJ would go beyond Kennedy to make two crucial historical decisions. The good one was the Voting Rights Act, which did more to ameliorate civil rights injustices than anything since the Civil War. The bad one (following the advice of Kennedy advisors like Bundy and McNamara), was to try to stave off defeat in Vietnam by a bombing campaign followed by sending combat troops into the region.

Guatemala

In the mid-1960s, however, I was not focused on Vietnam. Instead, my academic curiosity led me to explore the Central American anomaly. Why were those five small poor countries able to sustain a flourishing common market when the three in East Africa were not? Molly and I had our third son in three years, which was quite a handful to manage when, in 1966, we moved the family to Guatemala City to do research for six months.

Like East Africa, Central America is strikingly beautiful. Also like East Africa, Central America was poor – though not for everybody. Those with money lived in houses with walled gardens and bars on the windows to prevent theft. We rented such a house in Guatemala City. Many households hired sentries at nighttime. And over the centuries these disparities created a caste system with descendants of Europeans at the top, mestizos of mixed ancestry in the middle, and people of indigenous culture at the lowest level. This system was reinforced by the brutal use of police and military power to put down indigenous and leftwing revolts, sometimes with American support. In 1954, the CIA had helped to overthrow an elected leftwing government. Some referred to Central America as part of a US empire, though the degree of control was not as great as that of Britain in East Africa.

During our time in Guatemala, the government declared a state of siege, which meant that when we drove at night, we had to keep our interior car lights on as we approached military checkpoints. Our neighbor showed us bullet holes in his car from an occasion when he had startled the (possibly sleeping) soldiers at a checkpoint. A more lighthearted illustration of the social structure came in the form of Irma, the mestizo maid we inherited with the house. One day, a young girl dressed in indigenous clothing and with bare feet appeared at the door asking for work. Irma insisted we hire her as an assistant maid. It seemed easier to do so than to resist, but it turned out that Esperanza, who became Irma's assistant, had an even more rudimentary command of the Spanish language than we did.

I conducted my interviews with officials and business leaders mostly in Spanish, flying to El Salvador, Honduras, Nicaragua, and Costa Rica. Before each interview, I carefully prepared my questions based on the written records, making sure to start with questions that only that official could answer just in case our session was interrupted before the end. Most people were generous with their time and answers. I encountered little explicit anti-Americanism, and, overall, our time in Central America was both productive and enjoyable.

Times of upheaval

Returning to Harvard, I wrote up the results of my Central American study. But the place was rapidly changing as the world around it changed. And so was I. The optimism of the civil rights sit-ins and Martin Luther King's "I have a Dream" speech and the 1965 Voting Rights

Act was giving way to urban riots, Black Panthers, and Students for a Democratic Society (SDS) demonstrations. As LBJ increased the number of Americans in Vietnam, casualties mounted, and protests culminated in the convulsions of 1968 that included Johnson's announcement that he would not run for re-election. That was followed by riots at the Democratic convention in Chicago, Nixon's Southern strategy, and George Wallace's open appeal to racism that led to the defeat of Vice President Hubert Humphrey (for whom I had voted).

I was deeply shocked and depressed by the assassinations of Martin Luther King and Bobby Kennedy in April and June 1968, respectively. It felt like being punched in the gut. King represented the promise of progress on race, and Kennedy dangled the promise of change on Vietnam. I wept when our First Parish Church choir sang Fauré's requiem after King was killed. I was celebrating my tenth reunion at Princeton when Kennedy was killed. I remember sitting on the stone steps under Blair Arch knowing that the train bearing his casket was passing through Princeton and feeling too depressed to join the parties with my classmates. The world was changing for the worse.

In the first half of the 1960s, Harvard faculty meetings were lightly attended. They were held in the great faculty room in University Hall, a building dating back to 1820, where tea was served, a grandfather clock chimed, and portraits of early notables looked down on the assembled faculty. By 1967, the meetings had become so contentious that they had to be held in large theaters. Political differences often followed generational lines. Student protesters had already blocked some visitors and in 1968, SDS occupied University Hall and had to be removed by the state police.

I turned 30 in 1967 and was alert to the popular phrase "don't trust anyone over 30." As a young faculty member, a husband, father of three little boys, and a patriotic American, I was trying to weave the three strands – family, profession, citizen – into a rope of life. Braiding makes a stronger rope, but it is not easy when some strands stick out or resist being woven together. My family was the most important strand, but there was also constant tension about how much time to devote to my work. With a tenure decision looming, I knew the rules were "publish or perish." I planned a book on comparative regional integration to pull together my previous work, but was uncertain whether I had anything new to say. As I wrote that Spring, "One thing that haunts me is the idea of being 50 or 60 and having young scholars asking, what did he ever contribute to the field?" Family provided joy, but also anxiety about time.

Molly was a great partner, not only as a parent, but also helping me to maintain balance in my life, with skiing trips to New Hampshire, fishing and camping in Maine, visiting museums, or simply dining and playing poker with friends. I also really enjoyed my work. Though I sometimes wondered about taking leave and working in government, experienced colleagues like Richard Neustadt advised me to take my time and produce good publications first. Moreover, I was enjoying teaching and getting better at it over time. My first lecture was a disaster. I had overprepared, typed it all out, and nervously read it to the assembled students at a staccato pace. After reaching the conclusion, I looked down at my watch and it was only twenty-five minutes into the hour. The students seemed stunned, as if someone had fired a machine gun over their heads. All I could do was say, "class dismissed." Gradually I learned to slow down, focus on a few main points, read the faces of the audience, and allow some time for feedback. Eventually, decades later, I wound up lecturing to 600 students in Sanders Theatre and being rated as one of the top teachers by the *Harvard Crimson*'s *Confidential Guide*. But it took a while to get there!

There were also invitations to join the faculty at other universities, some of which were tempting. I knew that Harvard promoted fewer than 20 percent of its junior faculty and I vowed to avoid the fixation of "Harvarditis" or the irrational exclusion of alternatives. I rated my probability as less than 50 percent – maybe three in seven if I were lucky. Behind it all lurked the question of whether I really had "an original mind" and could make what others would consider a "major contribution" to the field. I certainly wasn't convinced.

Losing faith

As a citizen in a democracy, I could not avoid the social turmoil of the 1960s, though I had doubts about the growing practice of academics signing public statements and petitions about subjects outside their expertise. Maybe my view of the university was naive, but it seemed to me that society would be poorer if academics debased their search for truth and universities became just another pressure group. As I wrote after a conversation in my house with Ted Marmor (who became a professor at Yale), Doris Kearns (who became a distinguished historian), and Rogers Albritton (a Harvard philosophy professor), I believed that "the university is a place for analysis of ideas on their own merits – a free market place of ideas – one of the few in society, and thus academics should rarely try to act as a pressure group. Of course, this value of a university has limits and assumes no 'Nazi Germany' societal setting. But I don't see that Vietnam has come to this. Curious that Albritton does and feels Johnson is pathological." Over time, I moved somewhat closer to Albritton's position, and eventually joined a group of Rhodes Scholars on a trip to Washington to lobby Speaker of the House Carl Albert to openly oppose the Vietnam War (we failed).

None of us could escape Vietnam. Sam Huntington, chair of the government department, asked me to take on the role of graduate student advisor, and Bob Bowie asked me to direct student programs at the CFIA. These tasks brought me face to face with the problem of how to counsel young men who faced either being drafted into the war or moving to Canada. As a young father, I had a de facto draft exemption, but that just made advising others about Vietnam more agonizing.

My views on the war changed gradually over the course of 1967. At the beginning, after listening to an antiwar sermon in our Unitarian church, I wrote: "Am I pro or anti? Somewhere in between where either label would oversimplify. I vacillate from one to the other depending on the facts of the battle, visions of the end, and visual stimuli of the moral horror. I don't like to think about it but can't escape it. I wouldn't have gone in in '64 or escalated on the ground last year. My concern is what you do from where we are. A main problem is lack of facts – of feeling I don't know what I'm talking about. But then how does the layman ever judge foreign policy in a democracy?"

By April, there was a definite downturn in my views on Vietnam. There seemed to be no end to escalation. By December, I was in a debate at West Point representing the side opposing the war. At lunch the next day, with my Rhodes friends John Sewall and Pete Dawkins, who went on to serve in Vietnam and later became generals, I noted that both were concerned about further escalation.

Vietnam was not the only problem facing American citizens in 1967. Cities were also in flames. I wrote that I was "depressed about the riots in Roxbury – or more accurately about the conditions and white attitudes that cause them. When will this change? Should I ask will this change? Racial equality is a matter of faith (but reasoned faith and based on experience) with me. It is one of the few political attitudes I can remember strongly in high school, one of the first things I asked Molly about when I met her."

Still, some things in politics provided a glimmer of hope. Politicians like Nelson Rockefeller and Bobby Kennedy hinted at possible new paths. On November 30, Henry Kissinger asked me to join George Lodge and Lincoln Gordon in briefing Nelson Rockefeller in New York. I found Rockefeller to be a "pleasant political man whose questions were intelligent but not profound." In any event, early in 1968, my fishing buddy Graham Allison and I took bets on who would be elected president at the end of the year. I bet on Rockefeller and he bet on Bobby Kennedy. Of course, neither of them even made it to the final round. Over the half century of our friendship, Graham and I have often reminded each other of that lesson in humility.

Peaceful interlude in Geneva

In 1968, I escaped the political hurricane at home and became the Carnegie Endowment International Peace Scholar in Geneva, teaching at the Graduate Institute of Higher International Studies, and doing research which was published in 1971 as *Peace in Parts*. I had published journal articles with titles like "Comparative Regional Integration: Concept and Measurement," and I wanted to learn more about how the European Economic Community had succeeded in taming the deep rivalry between Germany and France that had led to three wars in seventy years.

Although I had often been to Europe, I had never lived there, and Geneva proved delightful. We were fortunate to rent a summer house on the south shore of Lake Geneva, with a magnificent view of the Jura mountains. A short drive along the lake was the beautiful medieval walled town of Yvoire, which was like a fairytale for the boys. In the other direction we crossed the border from Chens in France to Hermance in

Switzerland, stopping for the customs officials to look into the car. Given their impressive uniforms and polite manner, 4-year-old Ben announced he wanted to be a *douanier* when he grew up.

From my office in Geneva, near the Palais des Nations and the UN European headquarters (formerly the headquarters of Woodrow Wilson's League of Nations), I could look across the lake in the other direction, admiring the Jet d'Eau fountain in the town and the glaciers of Mont Blanc in the distance. In the winter, we were ideally located to ski every weekend at different resorts, from Swiss Gstaad to French Val-d'Isère. But not everything was so idyllic. When we first arrived in Geneva we lived in a cramped apartment in a small hotel while we searched for housing. One day, as Molly was taking the boys for a walk on the quay by the lake, Ben got too close to the edge and fell in. Without a thought, Molly jumped in after him when his head went under water. She was rewarded for her heroic behavior by a scolding from a well-dressed Swiss woman who reprimanded a soaked Molly for letting the boys walk so near the water. At that time, I was taking French lessons to improve my college level to conversational. A Swiss television station had learned that a Harvard professor was at the Institute, and I was asked to comment on the 1968 election, which looked as if it would be very close between Nixon and Humphrey. I rashly accepted the invitation on the theory that it would make me work extra hard on my French.

My lasting memory of life in Geneva was a relaxation from the pressure I had felt at Harvard. Geneva had some protests, but not like the political cauldron back home. Even simple things like lunch were more civilized. At Harvard I would grab a quick sandwich in the cafeteria. In Geneva, lunch in the simple restaurant near the office meant a tablecloth, a leisurely plate of "steak, frites, salade," and a glass of red wine. There was a lot of talk in Europe about the economic threat from American companies. Jean-Jacques Servan-Schreiber's best-selling book *Le Défi Americain* warned against "the American challenge." I joked that the real threat to Europe was the European lunch. But there is a lot to be said for a more civilized life.

Seen from Europe, the American century was a mixed blessing. Europeans expressed concern about American economic domination. At the same time, they wanted American military protection through NATO, yet were highly critical of American actions in Vietnam. We were hard to live with, but they could not live without us. The 1969 landing on the moon illustrated America's unique role. Molly and I watched with the boys as Neil Armstrong took the famous "one small step for man: one giant leap for mankind." No other country had done this, and it was hard to believe that it was only twelve years after the shock of Sputnik had suggested that the Soviets had won the race for space. The year before the Sputnik launch, Soviet troops had crushed a revolt in Hungary, and a year before the moon landing, Soviet troops had invaded Czechoslovakia to crush "the Prague Spring." As a result, the Soviets lost a great deal of their soft power in Europe. Kennedy's investments, such as the Peace Corps and the Apollo program, increased American soft power at the same time that our war in Vietnam and our racial problems at home undercut it.

From tranquility to turmoil

When we returned to the US in 1969, Harvard was in turmoil. Three years earlier, students had blocked Robert McNamara's car during a visit, and had protested the presence of members of ROTC (Reserve Officer Training Corps) on campus. In April 1969, several hundred students occupied University Hall and were removed by city and state police. Numerous protests followed, including a large and destructive riot in Harvard Square, where it was not clear who were students and who were fringe radicals attracted to the area. The faculty was deeply divided and meetings on issues like ROTC and African American studies were acrimonious.

My office was in the CFIA, which was temporarily housed in the underutilized old Semitic Museum. As director of student programs, I soon had my hands full. False rumors abounded that the Center was organizing the Vietnam War. Our building was occupied a number of times; an attack by a Weathermen fringe group (a faction of SDS) sent a staff member to the hospital; in another attack a bomb was exploded in an office. To quote a Weathermen pamphlet I kept from November 1969: "The people who run the CFIA are hired killers. They write reports for the government on how to keep a few Americans rich and fat. Professors who help the government are pigs. Isn't there a pig you'd like to get?" They boasted that they broke into the building, hung the

Viet Cong flag, "kicked the swine down the stairs, and broke all the windows." On another occasion, as I was briefing our visiting committee of distinguished outsiders about our programs, I heard a commotion in the hallway and protesters broke into the room. They picked up pitchers of water from the table and poured them on the seated guests, who included the elder statesman John McCloy, sometimes known as the chairman of "the Establishment."

Since Kissinger had gone to Washington, I was put in his empty office. I placed a peace sticker in the window, but to no avail. Coming back to my office after a seminar one afternoon, I heard a dull roar as a mob chanted its way toward our building. Bob Bowie came out of his office and told me to call the police. I crawled to my desk as bricks came through the window, despite my peace sticker. The police said they were aware of the situation but there was nothing they could do about it. When the mob broke into my office, they pulled down all my bookshelves and threw typewriters against walls. So much for the ivory tower!

As a young assistant professor, I shared some of the students' views on Vietnam, if not their methods, and I remember talking to some who were holding a sit-in in our library and finding them quite reasonable. But the concerns had spread beyond Vietnam to systemic critiques of capitalism and imperialism. I spoke at large meetings to defend the Center and debate whether it was imperialistic for our economists to advise poor countries on their economic development. I joined the distinguished economist Albert Hirschman and several younger Marxian economists like Art MacEwan and Steve Marglin in teaching a course on imperialism, where at least we could disagree but have serious discourse.

Large rallies were different. I defended the CFIA at mass meetings organized by students. The mood of a large crowd is volatile, and with violent rhetoric whipping up the audience, I always felt an undercurrent of fear and anxiety. After Nixon invaded Cambodia, the National Guard was mobilized and in May 1970 killed four students at a protest at Kent State University. Harvard students called a protest meeting with a number of demands, including the closing of the CFIA. I spoke at a mass rally of students, pleading with them not to attack our Center. To my pleasant surprise, they voted down a resolution to attack us. But the next morning, the *Harvard Crimson* did not report that vote in its news story, instead publishing an editorial urging closure of the Center and arguing that the only reason not to bomb it was that it was housed in the Semitic Museum. In an amusing sequel, many years later I met the student who wrote that editorial: by then he had become a professor of law and was duly apologetic.

Power and interdependence

Oddly, despite the political turmoil, this was a highly productive period in my professional life. I was finishing my book on comparative regionalism, which I had started in Geneva as the necessary prelude to a tenure decision in 1971. But I had also become fascinated by the increasing role of economics and trade in world politics. Partly this was stimulated by a study of the UN Conference on Trade and Development (UNCTAD) I undertook in Geneva, but also by my friendship with Stuart Robinson and Gerard Curzon, who were both deeply involved with the GATT (General Agreement on Tariffs and Trade). Under Jacques Freymond, and with the help of Jean Siotis, the Graduate Institute in Geneva had a culture that valued international institutions. Most important, the world was changing. Increasingly, "geonomics" was intruding daily into the geopolitics that dominated during the early Cold War years.

I also had the good fortune to strike up what became an intellectual partnership and lifelong friendship with Robert Keohane, a brilliant scholar a few years younger than me. He and I are listed in Wikipedia as cofounders of a school of analysis of international affairs known at "neoliberalism" (which both of us regard as an over-simplified label). People sometimes look at our biographies and note that we both earned a doctorate from Harvard in 1964 and assume we were friends in graduate school. The fact is we did not know each other, which tells you something about Harvard in those days, though it was also due to my absence in Africa. But we came to know and respect each other when the Social Science Research Council added a few young scholars to its commission on international institutions.

Slightly later, Keohane, then at Swarthmore, and I were added to the board of the professional journal *International Organization*, published by the World Peace Foundation from its paneled offices on Mt Vernon Street in Boston. As young Turks we criticized its narrow focus on formal intergovernmental institutions. We argued that the field should be understood with a "small i" and a "small o." We were both struck by the increasing role of transnational actors such as multinational corporations, foundations, terrorists, religious groups, and nongovernmental organizations. Much of what was happening in world politics crossed borders outside the control of governments and was ignored by the traditional realist models that focused solely on states and military power that dominated the focus of both scholars and practitioners. The world looked different when seen through the lens I had developed through my study of theories of integration, and Bob had written his thesis about the politics of the UN.

The older members of the board invited us to demonstrate what we meant, and together we assembled a group of scholars at the CFIA and edited their essays in a special issue of *International Organization* on "Transnational Relations and World Politics" (which Harvard published as a book in 1971). Eventually, Bob Keohane became editor of the journal and I was chair of the editorial board. Working with Fred Bergsten and Lawrence Krause, *International Organization* published special issues on the politics of trade and economics. Scholars like Richard Cooper at Yale, who later became a good friend and colleague at Harvard, were also publishing important work on the subject. Dependency theorists like Johan Galtung in Norway and Fernando Henrique Cardoso in Brazil were writing about a new imperialism whereby the center controlled the periphery. At the UN, developing countries demanded a new international economic order. The American century was being challenged.

The postwar world was indeed changing. America's share of the world economy declined from nearly half in 1945 to roughly a quarter by 1970. America was suffering from inflation and balance-of-payment problems, and in 1971 Nixon precipitously took the dollar off the gold exchange standard. Then in 1973 came the oil shock, when the Arab oil-exporting countries cut back production and exports, particularly to the US and the Netherlands because of their support of Israel in the Yom Kippur War. Oil prices quadrupled, long lines developed at gasoline stations, and huge sums of money flowed from the West to oil-exporting nations. Hans Morgenthau proclaimed that never in history had such a transfer of wealth taken place without the use of force. Part of the explanation lay in the mediating role of the transnational oil companies.

Bob and I realized that pointing to neglected areas of world politics like transnational relations was not the same as integrating them into a theoretical framework, and we turned to that task. I was able to get a foundation grant to bring a group of young scholars to the Center to work on new approaches to world politics and we interacted with established business school scholars like Ray Vernon, Robert Stobaugh, and Lou Wells, who had deep knowledge of multinational corporations, as well as sociologists like Alex Inkeles and Martin Lipset. It was a great example of how interdisciplinary centers can promote exploration of the borders and intersections of different fields.

This setting had a strong influence as Bob and I coauthored a number of articles on transnational and transgovernmental relations in world politics. In 1976, we finished *Power and Interdependence*, a book which was still being used in graduate courses in international relations four decades after it was first published. It was "neo-" liberal in the sense that we wanted to show that economic interdependence can be used as an instrument or weapon in power struggles in addition to the traditional liberal view of it as an instrument of peace. But under some conditions of what we called "complex interdependence," political processes change so much that, contrary to realist assumptions, states are not the only important actors, military force is not the most useful instrument, and military security is not the most important goal. Rather than replacing the traditional theory of realism, we supplemented it by showing how to integrate the new elements and actors in world politics. To this day, we argue that in international relations analysis, one should start with realism anchored in the realities of an anarchic world of states balancing power. Our complaint is not about where realists start, but about the fact that they then often stop too soon.

As it turned out, I found this theoretical work useful for policy when I joined the State Department in the Carter Administration a few years later. I was also helped by my participation in the Council on Foreign Relations "1980s Project," which tried (with mixed success) to look ahead to changes in world politics, and by work for the Murphy Commission on the Organization of the Government for the Conduct of Foreign Policy.

In 1975, the US withdrew from Saigon, four years after Molly and I had marched around Lexington Green in front of our house when a young John Kerry led a protest of Vietnam Veterans Against the War. In 1972, Kissinger had negotiated the Paris peace accords that delayed the inevitable defeat and (along with ending the draft) lowered the temperature of the Vietnam issue in American politics. I voted for George McGovern in his forlorn effort to unseat Nixon in 1972, in what turned out to be a landslide election, yet, within a year, the political climate changed as the Watergate scandal came to light. In 1974, Molly and I were transfixed by the congressional hearings into the break-ins into the Democratic Party offices, and elated by Nixon's resignation. At that point I considered him pure evil. Two decades later, when he invited me to dinner at his home in New Jersey to discuss one of my books, I realized he also had redeeming features as a thoughtful and perceptive analyst of international relations. Pure evil and pure good are rare in this world. The Ford Administration came as a relief, but Nixon had destroyed any residual faith I had in the Republican Party.

Historians have a hard time summing up the 1970s. Some describe it as "an untidy interregnum"; others call it "an interesting puzzle."[4] It was a period of international change following the defeat in Vietnam, the oil crises that accompanied the Yom Kippur War of 1973, the fall of the Shah of Iran in 1979, and the Soviet invasion of Afghanistan later that year. At home, the combination of inflation and economic slowdown were labeled "stagflation." In the aftermath of Vietnam and Watergate, polls showed a dramatic loss of trust in government. There was widespread pessimism, malaise, and concern about American decline. *Businessweek* magazine had a cover that portrayed the Statue of Liberty with a tear running down her cheek. It looked like the American century was coming to an end.

[4] Francis Galvin, "California Dreaming: The Crisis and Rebirth of American Power in the 1970s and its Consequences for World Order," in Peter Katzenstein and Jonathan Kirshner, eds., *The Downfall of the American Order* (Ithaca, NY: Cornell University Press, 2022), p. 89.

3

The Carter Years: The State Department

Jimmy Carter had little experience of Washington or world politics, and, as an engineer, he often became immersed in details rather than strategy. He wanted to change America's role in the world but had the bad luck to inherit the remnants of Brezhnev's Cold War Soviet leadership rather than the new Gorbachev generation that Reagan was dealt five years later. And the collapse of the Shah of Iran in 1979 proved fatal to Carter's re-election. Nonetheless, he made important and bold foreign policy decisions on the Panama Canal and on Middle East peace, and he pushed hard to enhance the role of human rights and to slow the proliferation of nuclear weapons. For the first half of his presidency, I was in charge of the latter policy.

The proliferation problem

Following the oil crisis of 1973, conventional wisdom was that the world was running out of oil and needed to turn to nuclear energy. (Ironically, the case for nuclear energy today is too much oil for the climate to bear, not too little.) It was also widely (and wrongly) believed in the 1970s that the world was running out of uranium. Thus, it would be essential to use reprocessed plutonium that was created by burning uranium in nuclear reactors. At the time, by some estimates, some forty-six countries were forecast to be reprocessing plutonium by 1990. The problem was that plutonium is a weapons-usable material. A world awash in plutonium commerce risked nuclear proliferation and nuclear terrorism. Already in 1974, India became the first state beyond the five listed in the 1968 Non-Proliferation Treaty (NPT) to launch what it euphemistically termed a "peaceful nuclear explosion."

France agreed to sell a plutonium reprocessing plant to Pakistan, where Prime Minister Ali Bhutto had said the country would eat grass before letting India develop a nuclear monopoly in South Asia. In

Latin America, Germany was selling a uranium enrichment plant to Brazil, and Argentina was exploring plutonium options. Other countries were quietly exploring options, and an incipient nuclear arms race was developing. A decade earlier, John Kennedy had predicted a world of twenty-five nuclear powers by the 1970s, and, despite the signing of the NPT in 1968, it began to look like his prognosis might come true.

Carter, who had experience as a nuclear engineer in the navy, was determined to prevent this. Before joining the transition team for the State Department, I had participated for more than a year on a Ford Foundation and Mitre Corporation commission on nuclear energy and non-proliferation, which included a number of eventual members of the Carter Administration, including Secretary of Defense Harold Brown and Arms Control Director Spurgeon Keeney. McGeorge Bundy, president of the Ford Foundation, was also an active player.

The world seemed headed for a plutonium economy and the spread of nuclear weapons. The Ford–Mitre Report called this conventional wisdom into question and argued that the safest way to use nuclear energy was an internationally safeguarded "once through" fuel cycle that left the plutonium locked up in the stored spent fuel. Carter accepted our report when we met with him in the cabinet room in the White House, but the conclusion was wildly unpopular with the American nuclear industry and with senators from western and southern states whose facilities would be closed. It was also anathema to allies such as France, Germany, and Japan, whose energy strategies (and exports) would be undercut. My job was to implement Carter's policy, and, needless to say, I was heavily criticized by all the groups mentioned above. As an academic, it was a new experience to see my name in critical editorials and headlines, or to be hauled before a Senate committee for a hostile grilling. When constantly told you are wrong, it is sometimes hard to remember that you might be right!

The other thing that was new for an academic was the experience of managing a large number of people and a complex multiagency process. At Harvard, I had managed one person – my secretary – and in truth it was probably the other way round. In Washington, there was no shortage of bureaucrats and rival political appointees eager to take my job – or leave me with the title but empty it of substance. I had been issued a hunting license, but there was no guarantee I would bag any game. My first instinct as an academic was to try to do things myself, but that was impossible, and, after a few weeks of staying up until midnight and rising at 5 a.m. to be ready for Secretary of State Cyrus Vance's morning staff meeting, I realized I was drowning. I discovered that, unlike academia, politics and bureaucracy comprise a team sport. The secret to success was to attract others to want to do the work for me. In that sense, I learned soft power the hard way.

The first hundred days

In 1976, I had written a few minor papers for the Carter campaign and it was in December of that year that Tony Lake (later head of policy planning in the State Department) asked me to go to DC to be an advisor on the transition team. The group shared cramped offices on the ground floor of the State Department, and I was tasked with the problem of non-proliferation. It was a good group and their work was serious, but so were the anticipation and the jockeying about positions in the new administration.

On Thursday December 30, after Representative Patsy Mink of Hawaii had been named Assistant Secretary for Oceans, Environment, and Science (OES), which included nuclear energy, I concluded that there was no place for me, but that evening Vance, a gentlemanly lawyer, invited me into his office and asked me to join his team and handle proliferation. "Write me a memo on how to do it, and we will discuss it tomorrow." When I left his office, I was not sure what I had been offered. Don McHenry (later UN Ambassador) suggested using the vacant position of deputy to the Undersecretary for Security Assistance, and Dick Holbrooke, at whose apartment I was staying, helped me write a memo defining my role in relation to the whole government, not just the State Department. I showed it to Vance the next morning and he agreed, but it still felt slightly unreal when I described it to Molly on my return to Boston that weekend.

A few days later, I met Lucy Benson, a wonderful strong-minded woman who had been head of the League of Women Voters and was slated to be undersecretary. We hit it off well, and I described my work for the Murphy Commission about strengthening the role of science and technology in the State Department by expanding the undersecretary's role. Within that framework, the deputy could be primarily responsible for non-proliferation. She told me to work out a memo, which we took to Vance and he agreed. After years of academic work, I had implemented my Murphy Commission recommendation in four hours. The moral of the story is the fluidity of transitions and the importance of being in the right place at the right time.

As an illustration of my naivety, however, when Vance offered me a ride to the airport the next day, I assumed he meant a shared taxi, but of course we were soon enveloped in a black secret service limousine and whisked from the basement of the State Department to another basement at National Airport. I had a lot to learn. A few days later, when Henry Kissinger heard of my appointment, he summoned me from the cramped ground floor of the transition team to his palatial office on the seventh floor. He turned on his charm to tell me that I was still one Harvard professor he respected. I decided that in all honesty I should let my former teacher know that I had just published a piece in the *Boston Globe* summarizing the pros and cons of his tenure as Secretary of State. Henry's brow furrowed as he focused on my criticism and warned me not to believe the press, which fixates on tactics rather than strategy.

On January 13, 1977, I met with Zbigniew Brzezinski, David Aaron, and Jessica Tuchman of the incoming National Security Council (NSC) about how my new office would relate to the rest of the government. Zbig said he would issue a request for a Presidential Review Memorandum (PRM) which would name me as the coordinator of a new "NSC Ad Hoc Committee on Non-Proliferation." This was important because it gave a State Department official authority to convene meetings across all agencies. On this request, at least, I was not naive.

Back in the State Department, Leslie Gelb, an experienced Washington hand who had been named head of the Bureau of Politico-Military (PM) Affairs, suggested that the nuclear technology team that I had put under Deputy Assistant Secretary Lou Nosenzo be taken out of OES and instead report to his PM bureau. Gelb promised he would keep me informed. While I was pondering that change, my special assistant Edward McGaffigan (whom I had known as a Kennedy School student) came across a memorandum of a conversation between Gelb and a British official in which the former implied he would represent the US at the Nuclear Suppliers Group. In fact, he knew Vance had promised this to me, but when I asked him about it, he said he had forgotten. I decided to leave Nosenzo's group in OES and have it report directly to me.

During the transition, I had written memos recommending great care in trying to cancel the dangerous deals between France and Pakistan and between Germany and Brazil. I warned that we should approach each one quietly to avoid stirring up nationalism in all four countries. But that was not to be. On January 15, well before the Inauguration, Germany sent Peter Hermes, a top official, to call on Vice President Mondale and Vance and to warn them that Germany was about to send blueprints for the uranium enrichment plant to Brazil. The Germans may (or may not) have intended it as a friendly heads up, but the White House interpreted it as pre-emptive hardball. Hermes's visit made things worse and engendered a flurry of meetings at our end.

On my fortieth birthday, I returned to Massachusetts to drive my family to Carter's Inauguration. I wanted them to develop a sense of excitement for the impending move to Washington about which the three boys were skeptical. As I had noted earlier, "if this job spoils my family relationship, I will have been a failure." January 20 was clear and crisp in DC, and walking with the crowd to the gleaming white Capitol in the cold sunshine had the aura of going to a football game. We had good seats, and I was impressed by the humility of Carter's speech and was struck by his discussion of nuclear weapons.

The next day was my first formal day on the job, and also the occasion of my first political gaffe. I gave an interview to a Brazilian journalist I had known at Harvard, and I wanted to use it as background to calm the waters. Instead, the headlines in Brazil treated my comments as a major new policy initiative in which the US was offering assurances of a supply of uranium fuel if Brazil would give up its quest for the sensitive German technology. Of course, there was no policy yet, and I was criticized by the White House. It was "Flap #1" and I felt sick about it. I apologized to Vance, who graciously said: "We all make mistakes."

The more serious problem was how to organize the work of PRM15 on proliferation policy. We had to hammer out different views on how restrictive to be about reprocessing, breeder reactors, and exports. The outside world, however, could not wait for a dozen differing government agencies to agree on a new policy. Dangerous deals were progressing;

eighteen nuclear export cases had backed up in the pipeline; allies were clamoring for bilateral negotiations; intelligence reported that a number of countries (including Korea and Taiwan) were exploring nuclear weapons options; and the Office of Management and Budget wanted guidance on big budget items related to reprocessing and breeder reactors. In addition, Congress was demanding briefings and hearings aimed at new legislation. As Bob Fri, the genial holdover head of the Energy Research and Development Administration remarked to me on February 24, "How can you work out a detailed new policy in one month?"

In the meantime, on February 10, Germany sent another high-level delegation for two days of negotiations with Deputy Secretary Warren Christopher; the French followed a week later, and Japan a few days after that. In each case, we pleaded for delay. On February 16, I gave a speech at the Council on Foreign Relations in New York about the general direction of policy and was afterward told by an industry representative that I was wrong about reprocessing and he would get me fired. The industry press echoed such attacks, and they reverberated in the halls of Congress where representatives like Mike McCormack (D. WA) told me reprocessing was essential and plutonium was safe.

Strategic experts like Herman Kahn said we should reconcile ourselves to inevitable German and Japanese nuclear weapons. Paul Nitze, the grand old man of Cold War strategy, told me that he was not interested in proliferation, because the only meaningful thing was American strength. Other hawks like Albert Wohlstetter and Harry Rowen urged me to stick to my guns because there was ample uranium in the ground to support a once-through-the-reactor nuclear fuel cycle without exposing the plutonium. There was no consensus among experts.

We had promised the Germans that we would talk soon to the Brazilians, so on February 27 I found myself accompanying Warren Christopher to Brasilia, an odd new city of monumental scale, modern buildings, empty spaces, and wide vistas. In talks at the Itamaraty Palace of the foreign ministry, I outlined my proposal of assurances of fuel supply and a prominent Brazilian role in an International Fuel Cycle Evaluation (INFCE). The response was noncommittal and the communiqué merely referred to further consultations. The Germans requested that Christopher come to Bonn for two days of negotiations a week later, but all we got from that difficult transatlantic trip was another communiqué about "staying in close contact."

In the midst of these tense trips to Brazil, Germany, and Capitol Hill, I was trying to shepherd the interagency meetings to produce PRM15, but the meetings produced consensus policy drafts that were unimaginative and written in turgid bureaucratese. At first, I tried rewriting the drafts, but I found myself working late and still not slaying the beast. I knew I had to learn to delegate better.

I also had to give up my academic habits, though I made some exceptions. When Henry Owen, Director of Foreign Policy Studies at the Brookings Institution, asked me to write a few pages to prepare for Carter's proliferation discussions at the Group of 7 Summit (for which he was the coordinator), I got up early and spent two hours writing at the kitchen table. Owen said it was the clearest memo he had seen on proliferation and asked how I had done this. I told him it was a personal note not cleared by other agencies. I later found that I could often steer policy by occasionally blocking out time and writing a major speech myself. Even when cleared by the White House, they had more coherence than the interagency products.

By March 16, we finally had an agreed interagency response to the PRM request that we could take to a Policy Review Committee in the Situation Room in the White House. The small, paneled room in the basement of the West Wing crowded principals around a small table with electronic screens above showing global time zones, while a few support staff sat along the walls. The room was cool, but I could feel sweat trickle down my chest inside my shirt. When I made the presentation about the limits we were trying to impose on foreign countries, Defense Secretary Harold Brown and Energy Czar (and later Secretary) James Schlesinger asked why we allowed any reprocessing of plutonium at all. My reply was to ask them how they expected to turn off longstanding breeder reactor and reprocessing programs in France, Britain, German, and Japan all at once. I said our plan was to buy time by creating an international nuclear fuel cycle evaluation program to study the issue for the next two years. In the meantime, we would slowly eke out permissions to reprocess spent fuel from American uranium as a means of slowing things down. After the meeting, I called Harold Brown to plead for DOD support of my moderate strategy. I think he responded to the call of a lower official from another department because we had served together on the Ford–Mitre Commission.

When the policy memo summarizing the meeting went to the president, Carter seemed to want a clearer and tougher policy. The State Department never saw the cover memo that the NSC staff prepared for him, but they told us that Carter had decided he wanted a tough response and would announce his proliferation policy at a news conference the following day. I called Brzezinski to warn him that the absence of consultations would undercut our "go-slow" strategy by alienating the countries whose cooperation we needed most. Dick Holbrooke, Assistant Secretary for East Asia, and I went to the White House and warned of a possible "Carter shock" in Japan and were able to obtain a week's delay for consultations, but Brzezinski said the president was not pleased. Carter was later persuaded to focus his announcement on the domestic decisions to close down our reprocessing plant in Barnwell, SC, and downgrade the Clinch River Breeder in Tennessee to a research program.

Senator John Glenn wanted me to testify about the new policy but agreed to hold off if we would give him a date for its announcement in early April. That led me to make a one-day trip to Paris. France was crucial to my strategy not only because of its pending deal with Pakistan, but because, underneath its commercial interests, it was deeply concerned about the spread of nuclear weapons and was leery of the German/Brazil enrichment deal. Moreover, France was the country with the most advanced civil nuclear program and if my INFCE idea was to take root it would require French cooperation. I flew overnight and spent all the next day in negotiations at the elegant Quai d'Orsay. They warned me that France would not stop reprocessing at La Hague and we reached an agreement on the general shape of INFCE and further delay of the transfer of equipment to Pakistan. That evening, the French entertained me in the private apartment of Bertrand Goldschmidt, a genial veteran of the French nuclear program. He opened a fine bottle of Lafite Rothschild, but I was too exhausted to really appreciate it. By that point I was happy just to stay awake and avoid drowning in my soup.

Carter made his announcements at a press conference on April 7, but he also implied to a Japanese reporter's question that we might take a permissive stance toward their reprocessing of American spent fuel at their Tokai plant – but that would undercut the policy by giving away too much leverage too quickly. I was scheduled to give a press conference at the State Department that morning and I received a call from the White House saying that the president had mis-spoken and I should walk it back without seeming to contradict him. How do you do that? I answered the many Japanese reporters' questions by saying that an important Japanese delegation was about to arrive in DC, and the president would surely not have wanted such important people to waste their time on travel from Asia if the matter did not still require negotiation.

Every country has its internal divisions. When the Japanese delegation arrived, they all read from the same formal position papers when we met across a big table in a conference room in the State Department, but one member (Imai) told me he was authorized to meet with me privately to discuss ideas for a compromise. At the same time, he cautioned that I should not discuss them with the rest of the delegation. Instead, I should take a tough line because my opposition would help him sell his approach to his delegation. Later, I talked with Joseph Kraft, Meg Greenfield, and other editorial writers to give them background on the American position. What looks like a bilateral international negotiation is often a multiparty-political game.

When I was at Harvard, Bob Keohane and I had written about transnational and trans-governmental politics that are outside the central control of governments. For example, in April 1977, the transnational nuclear industry held a conference in Persepolis, Iran, that condemned the Carter approach. I called it "the international nuclear mafia." I hoped that by creating INFCE, we could organize a set of international meetings that would include them but also dilute them by including "minders" from foreign ministries. In addition to my talks with Japan, I later encountered an amusing effort to create a trans-governmental coalition against me when Undersecretary of Energy John Deutch called to tell me the German undersecretary had just been in his office asking how they could work together to "control Nye." He had not realized John and I had been neighbors and close friends before Washington.

In late April, I flew to London for meetings at the Foreign and Commonwealth Office (FCO) with Undersecretary Patrick Moberly. The British agreed to participate in INFCE, but wanted our reassurance that we would not try to stop their reprocessing plant at Windscale. We also held bilateral meetings with four other countries including France, Germany, and the Soviet Union.

The next day we went to Riverwalk House along the Thames for a meeting of the Nuclear Suppliers' Group. If the FCO, with its vaulted ceilings and giant Victorian paintings, spoke of an age of empire, Riverwalk House was modern drab. We met at a long table with little flags in front of our name plates and more than 100 people in the big room. As we haggled over amendments to the draft guidelines of rules to govern nuclear exports, I was struck by how helpful the Soviets were. I was particularly impressed when Roland Timerbaev, an experienced Soviet diplomat, came over and showed me how moving a comma and changing it to a semicolon could change the meaning of a sentence and allow us to reach agreement. After hours of negotiation, the group finally reached a compromise by agreeing that suppliers would "exercise restraint" in the export of sensitive facilities rather than try for an absolute ban. It was felt that this formulation was more compatible with the obligations to cooperate under Article 4 of the NPT, which was up for review in 1980. And it allowed us to agree on guidelines for nuclear supply.

With agreement achieved, I flew to Austria where the International Atomic Energy Agency (IAEA) was sponsoring a conference at Salzburg and I was giving a speech on our new policy. I met with the Director, Sigvard Eklund, to explain INFCE and how it would relate to the IAEA in a way that would be good for them and good for us. I knew of course that our policy was unpopular, but when I conducted a press conference, I was hit with questions from all directions. And of course, we spent hours in the inevitable series of bilaterals with various countries. I was pleased when André Giraud, head of the French Atomic Energy Commission (later to become Minister of Defense), told me that the French shared our views of proliferation rather than our policy, "but because you had consulted so much, we kept quiet." The press reported my speech fairly, but noted that many countries disagreed with it.

When I returned, I wrote a memo for Vance on May 4 that said our policy was bound to be unpopular, but it was coherent and viable if we provided incentives, remained flexible, and INFCE was open-minded, and we were careful to make sure the Nuclear Suppliers Group and the NPT did not unravel. One afternoon, I bumped into the journalist Marvin Kalb coming out of the elevator in the State Department, and he said: "I hear you're the guy in the building who knows the most about this issue." The next day, Bob Fri and I testified for three hours before Senators John Glenn and Charles Percy about the importance of flexibility and multilateralism as they began to craft what became the Nuclear Non-Proliferation Act that Carter signed in March 1978.

In early May, the *New York Times* ran a story from Tokyo saying that Minister Sōsuke Uno accused me of negotiating in bad faith, because Carter wanted to be forthcoming, but I prevented it. Secretary of the Treasury Mike Blumenthal called to say he had told the president about the Japanese desire to use their Tokai reprocessing plant, and Carter had replied: "All I said was that I understood they had a special problem. They misunderstood. But something can be done about the quantity of material and international supervision. Talk to Nye about it." I also learned from other sources that Japan had sent lobbyists to Congress to see if our policy was reversible; they concluded it was not and decided not to try to make a coalition with Europe against us. We had come a long way since January!

Concentric circles

Managing the political domestic process was complicated because some people and organizations thought our policy was too tough, and some too lenient, and each had their allies on the Hill as well as in the administration. Part of our leverage was granting permits for export of reactor parts and uranium as well "MB-10" licenses to allow the reprocessing of spent fuel overseas that had originated in American uranium. Some White House staff on the Council of Environmental Quality, and others, thought we should cease issuing permits and try to halt all foreign programs. Others in Commerce and Energy pressed for more permits. I found that when I convened meetings of the NSC Ad Hoc Committee on Non-Proliferation, more than a dozen agencies around the table contested each issue. It was important that all voices be heard, but it was not a very effective way to coordinate the day-to-day business of government.

I developed a pattern of using three concentric circles of meetings: a morning staff meeting for those in our building; bi-weekly interagency lunches with undersecretaries of Energy, Arms Control, and occasional others; and monthly meetings of the full NSC committee. Since I met each morning with Vance or Christopher, other state bureaus were eager to be invited to the meetings in my office, which brought them timely information from above. Information was power, and others got the point that if they hoarded rather than shared, they would be invited to my office less often. As for the bi-weekly lunches, we used the time efficiently to coordinate policies among the key departments. Energy controlled the big budgets, but they often needed the State imprimatur for support. And it helped that Deutch shared my views on the dangers of proliferation. I remember trips to the impressive reprocessing facility in Barnwell, South Carolina, and the enrichment and breeder plants in Oak Ridge, Tennessee, in which the local technicians wondered why the State Department was represented – but our voice turned out to be important.

Congress was deeply divided on nuclear issues. At the end of the Ford Administration, the Democratic Congress had abolished the Atomic Energy Agency and the Joint Congressional Committee on Atomic Energy, but Congress remained deeply split on nuclear issues, and not just on party lines. Staff played a large role, but they reflected their members' positions. At a hearing chaired by Representatives Clement Zablocki and Jonathan Bingham on May 19, 1977, John Glenn came over from the Senate to testify in support of the administration, but Representative Mike McCormack lectured him that the country had only half the uranium needed for the 600 reactors we would have at the end of the century and plutonium had to fill the gap. A few weeks later, I was grilled for three hours at a hearing by Senator Frank Church of Idaho, who led the 49–38 Senate vote to overrule Carter's decision to stop the Clinch River Breeder Reactor. Resistance to closing the Barnwell plant in South Carolina was led by Senator Fritz Hollings. All were Democrats.

Each faction tried to sway the press with varying degrees of success. Some reporters were usually accurate, but others less so. After one misleading story in the *New York Times*, I called the reporter and told him his story was nonsense. He said he had three sources. I replied that if they all came from certain staffers on Capitol Hill, he really only had one (biased) source. I learned that if I backgrounded reporters like Don Oberdorfer of the *Washington Post* or Rick Burt of the *New York Times*, who understood the issue, I did not necessarily get a favorable story, but at least a more accurate one.

To be fair, high-tech issues tend to be esoteric and difficult to explain to the public. Personal issues and conflicts are much more dramatic and easier to understand. I remember debating with Mike McCormack on the *MacNeil/Lehrer NewsHour*, one of the most serious channels of journalism. I thought I succeeded, but was struck by my father's comment afterwards: "It is hard for the public to understand these issues, but at least you appeared well." Ah well! It was therefore not too surprising when my friend and squash partner, Undersecretary for Economic Affairs Dick Cooper, described the confusing nature of the discussion of nuclear issues at the Group of 7 Summit among leaders with many other things on their minds. A high-level White House staffer warned me that even Carter, with his nuclear background, did not understand proliferation issues as well as people thought, and that led to occasional flip-flops that we had to manage. The same was true for Vance and Brzezinski. Given the wide range of issues on their plate, that was not too surprising.

Sometimes, the ability of the technical community to communicate was not much better. When I went to Oak Ridge National Laboratory to explain the administration position, one of the scientists stood up and asked me what right Carter had to truncate the nuclear fuel cycle. To the nuclear priesthood, the fact that he had been elected was much less important than what they saw as the natural evolution of their technology.

A dramatic example came when Harold Agnew, the perceptive and witty Director of the Los Alamos National Laboratory, invited me to ten hours of briefings. I toured a room with models and films of all our nuclear weapons (some surprisingly small), held a warm nickel-coated hemisphere of plutonium in my hands, watched pouring and milling in a building with glove boxes, and saw conventional explosive lenses being shaped for bomb assembly. I was amazed at what humanity could invent. But I worried about our capability to control it.

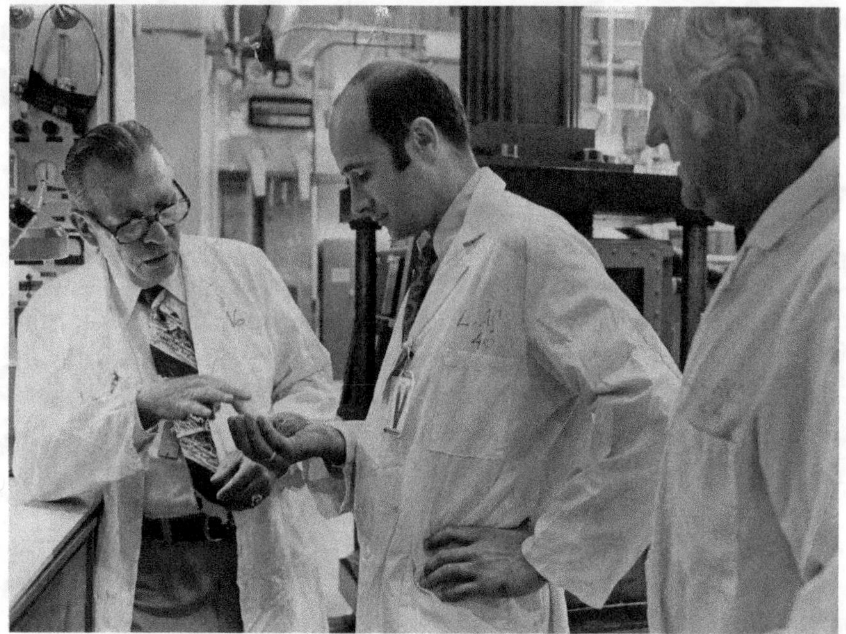

A whole kilogram of plutonium, with Director Harold Agnew, Los Alamos, 1977

Pakistan, India, and other hard cases

Perhaps the most important nuclear event of that year was one that did not reach the press at all. At the end of July 1977, I was in Paris for a major conference in the Kleber Conference Center to negotiate the framework for INFCE. After a hard day of negotiations, I asked to see the French undersecretary privately to discuss Pakistan. I had been authorized to show him classified information that proved Pakistan was developing implosion technology for a bomb rather than using the French plutonium processing plant for peaceful nuclear energy, as they professed. When my aide opened the locked briefcase and I showed the evidence to my counterpart, the poor man fainted. I worried I had killed him, and his aides rushed to his help. He was simply exhausted from chairing the meeting and I guess that when he then saw the basis of the French position cut out from under him, it was too much to process.

Fortunately, I was able to have a conversation with André Giraud. He was a tough, skeptical man devoted to the interests of France. He said that if the French confirmed the information, it could form the basis for a new political judgment, but that if we publicized it, nothing would change because they would not jeopardize their leading position as a reliable supplier. Remarkably, we were able to keep it out of the press, perhaps because earlier reports of a French change had proven to be false alarms. Instead, the French issued a series of announcements of delay caused by technical difficulties with the cutting machines for the front end of the plant. Finally, on November 7, we received a highly classified cable from our embassy in Paris that France would make no announcements but had decided it would not sell weapons-usable tools to Pakistan. This turned out to be a case of a major policy change caused by the soft power of quiet diplomacy, good intelligence, and information-sharing, rather than pressure or efforts at twisting arms. However, it slowed, but in the long run did not prevent, Pakistan from exploding a nuclear weapon in 1998. (They used fissile material obtained from centrifuge enrichment technology that the scientist A. Q. Khan stole from the URENCO consortium.)

From Paris, I flew to South Asia. In Islamabad, I was briefed by Ambassador Arthur Hummel in the secure intelligence bubble in the embassy. He warned me that although President Zulfikar Ali Bhutto had been overthrown, the new military government was unlikely to give up its weapons aspirations. When I met with Foreign Minister Agha Shahi and Atomic Energy Commission Director Munir Khan, and warned of the dangers of a nuclear arms race on the subcontinent, their response was polite, but they denied the danger and wanted to focus on India. I was impressed by their ability to lie to my face about the peaceful nature of their nuclear program. I do not know how much they knew of what I knew. I tried to convince them, but I wrote in my diary after I left that I thought the chances of success were one in ten.

Flying from Islamabad to New Delhi, I crossed the Indus River with its vast plains and villages under flood, marveling at the destructive forces of nature even without nuclear energy. Ambassador Robert Goheen, who had been president of Princeton University when I was a student, hosted me in the lovely lacy Delhi embassy designed by Philip Johnston. At meetings in the grand red sandstone imperial buildings that the British had built, I met with my friend Foreign Secretary Jagat Mehta and others for a long day of talks. Jagat wore his Harvard necktie, but that did not remove national differences over the discriminatory nature of the NPT and of IAEA safeguards, nor the impossibility of a South Asia weapons-free zone because it would not include China. I then called on Prime Minister Morarji Desai, a remarkably spry 81-year-old, who was very philosophical and when I mentioned a Comprehensive Test Ban (CTB), he promised there would be no more nuclear explosions while he was Prime Minister. Later, however, when he met with Carter in the White House, he turned down the idea of joining a CTB treaty even if the US did sign it.

From Delhi, I flew to Bombay (now Mumbai) with Foreign Minister Vellodi, and that provided an opportunity for private conversation. I explained INFCE and the importance of safeguards for our future supply of fuel for the Tarapur reactor. He said they were concerned about the Pakistan plant and China, but would not sign the NPT. India would not join the Nuclear Suppliers Group, but would restrain their exports and act as if they were members, and would consider the full scope of IAEA safeguards on all nuclear sales. A year later we learned that the Indians were as good as their word when they limited what would be transferred in a deal with Libya.

I then visited Tarapur with Homi Sethna, Chair of India's Atomic Energy Commission who had guided India's nuclear explosion. He was a sophisticated urbane scientist, and it was a fascinating trip. There was such a contrast between Indian achievements in mass spectography, hot cells, and remote handling of radioactive materials, on the one hand, and people washing, defecating, and living alongside roads marked by anarchic traffic. Twenty-four hours of plane travel later, I was home in Virginia. We might call it an American century, but there are an amazing number of different worlds on one planet.

Several other hard cases arose that year, regarding Taiwan, South Korea, and South Africa. Carter had promised during his campaign to withdraw American forces from Korea and that raised anxieties in Seoul. Eventually, Carter reversed his position, and in the interim we told the South Koreans that if they pursued a nuclear weapons program, it would weaken their American security guarantee. Similarly, Taiwan was concerned about the rapprochement between Washington and Beijing and began exploring the revival of a nuclear program, including laser isotope enrichment that the US had earlier persuaded them to halt. Again, we sent forceful and successful diplomatic messages warning against such steps. The message had to be repeated, but the American nuclear umbrella was an important non-proliferation instrument where it extended.

In contrast, our relations with South Africa were tense because of human rights issues as well as the question of the future of the white minority government in Rhodesia (now Zimbabwe), which South Africa supported, and questions about the UN over control of Namibia. During the summer, our overhead satellites discovered work in the Kalahari Desert that appeared to be a test site. The Soviets told us they expected an imminent explosion, but when we pressed the South Africans for an explanation, they assured us it was not a test site. At a White House meeting, I said that, unless we required dismantlement, we were vulnerable to sudden change by the South Africans, but Brzezinski felt that dismantlement was asking too much, given the other items on the agenda. Instead, we told them that we were closely monitoring any change in consistency with their assurances. A year later, we learned that South Africa had enriched its uranium by more than 60 per cent, approaching weapons grade. I argued that we should switch from moderation to sanctions to show that becoming an "nth country" was too expensive, but, again, the agenda was overburdened. As we learned years later, South Africa developed a handful of bombs from its locally enriched uranium. Fortunately, the post-Apartheid government eventually decided to give them up.

There was also worrisome intelligence from South America that the military junta in Argentina was exploring a major reprocessing program with an Italian company and, in November 1977, Vance made a trip to the region to raise issues of energy, proliferation, and human rights. In Buenos Aires, Patricia (Patt) Derian, the feisty Assistant Secretary of State for Human Rights and Humanitarian Affairs (who had bravely fought against racism in Mississippi) dominated the discussion. As she claimed, she "never traded off human rights," and the junta had an atrocious record. But they were also moving toward nuclear weapons. We wanted them to defer their reprocessing plant and join the Treaty of Tlatelolco, which established a nuclear weapons-free zone in Latin

America. As Admiral Castro Madero explained to me at a private breakfast, their program was a response to the fact that Germany had put Brazil in front of Argentina in the geopolitics of South America, and this was intolerable. Again, we played for delay and time, and fortunately, after the restoration of a civilian government in the following decade, both countries foreswore their incipient nuclear arms race.

After all these travels, Vance asked me to sum up our position. I wrote on November 25: "Our strategy was to isolate each country (e.g. Germany, Brazil) in its own club; avoid overt arm-twisting, and let internal criticisms and costs mount. A good result was a French message to the Germans to follow their example and not sell a plutonium power plant to Brazil." In December, intelligence reported that Brazil told Germany it wanted to cut back the enrichment plant to a test scale because of rising costs. And in January, we learned that Germany had refused to allow a company to offer heavy water to Venezuela. A article in the *New York Times* on January 16, 1978 quoted me as saying: "A long-term solution to the proliferation problem requires political consensus, not just confrontation." Max Weber once wrote that politics is often the "slow boring of hard boards." The same is true of diplomacy.

During the Latin American trip, I had a long frank talk with Patt about human rights. I believe human rights are an important component of our values and generate soft power for us, but a foreign policy has to balance a wide range of objectives. I told Patt she needed a strategy and a selection of targets if she were to avoid a crazy quilt pattern that would confuse the public and generate antagonism. She should set three targets and instruments to achieve them: basic human needs, civil liberties, and integrity of the person. She said she found this helpful, and she and Carter deserve great credit for raising the status of the issue in our foreign policy, but I fear they never articulated a strategy.

The highlight of my first year in the State Department came on October 19 and 20, 1977, when a large conference was held in Washington to establish INFCE. Building on my academic work on institutions and transnational relations, it was at the heart of my strategy to buy time, slow things down, and develop transnational webs of knowledge about the true costs and alternatives to what the nuclear mafia regarded as the immutable nature of the nuclear fuel cycle. Over the next two years, INFCE did much to advance these objectives. Carter spoke forcefully at the opening session in the State Department auditorium, followed by Vance. It was fascinating to hear the president launch my idea to a roomful of thirty-nine nations organizing a program that Bob Fri and I had sketched out in my office the previous February. And I was gratified at the end of the second day when my British counterpart, Patrick Moberly, passed me a note that said "Congratulations on a skillful job!"

The Second Year

I began the new year, 1978, with my unused muscles feeling stiff after a family cross-country ski trip to a cabin without electricity in the Adirondacks. Skiing for seven hours through the woods along Limekiln Creek was tiring, but watching my family in the sparkling sun on snow and green spruce was therapeutic. The past year had been exciting but narrowing. I had become a house plant in a building too far from home. Molly was amazing at holding the family together, feeding the boys four meals a day so that we could try to have family dinner when I got back from the State Department after 8 p.m. Although there were weekend bike rides along the Potomac, as well as visits to Civil War battlefields, there was never enough time. And the constant travel often left me tired or suffering from colds. After one trip, I returned with a fierce earache and went to the State Department doctor. He asked me why I had not come sooner and recommended I go home to bed. I said I had to chair an important meeting. He asked, "Why do you people think you have to kill yourselves?" I thought, "good question." There is more to life than work, sleep, power, and pride.

As I pondered the future, events precipitated a decision. Princeton called to offer me a professorship; Brookings asked if I would run their studies program; and in early April Patsy Mink decided to leave the State Department and Vance asked me to take her job as assistant secretary. Ironically, it was the job I had hoped for in December 1976. Warren Christopher urged me to take it. "Why write about science and diplomacy when you have a rare opportunity to do something about it?" On the other hand, my Harvard colleagues, Al Carnesale and Graham Allison, urged me to return with the question "Don't you want to write and think more broadly?"

On a Saturday afternoon in April, Molly and I rode our bikes along the Potomac to a point in the river where there is a bird sanctuary, sat on a log, and discussed the decision. She enjoyed living in DC and her work at the Corcoran Gallery of Art, but the boys wanted to return to Lexington and their friends. We decided that the overall quality of our family life would be better if we returned. In addition, I wanted to think and write more broadly about nuclear weapons and deeper values, but there was no time for that when my inbox was overflowing. The urgent drives out the important. When I eventually returned to Harvard, this led to my writing *Nuclear Ethics*, where I wrestled with issues for which I had no time to think on the job.

After much reflection, I informed the State Department that I would depart at the end of my two-year leave from Harvard. Ironically, the next person on the list for the job was Tom Pickering, then ambassador to Jordan, whose house in Hollin Hills we were renting; the contract required us to move if he was recalled to DC. So Molly and I moved to another house in Hollin Hills and Tom and I began to commute to work together, discussing the problems of the job. We also became close friends.

Any worry I had about becoming a lame duck was belied by the busyness of my schedule, with trips to Europe, India, Australia, and Japan, among others. An important milepost was Carter's signing of the Nuclear Non-Proliferation Act on March 10. After a year of tough negotiations, the bill passed both houses by overwhelming majorities. At various stages, industry had tried to kill or delay it; at other times, environmentalist and anti-nuclear groups tried to make it an instrument for rigid cut-offs. In each case, the State Department pleaded for flexibility for international diplomacy. As I wrote in my diary about Carter's signing ceremony in the White House: "I was right by the side of his chair and watched him read the notes that came out the way we wanted when he reaffirmed nuclear energy from light water reactors without reprocessing and with international safeguards. It is not the greatest bill, but it is good to have a firm base in place for policy."

I was often struck by how much power Congress wielded. After Christopher's morning staff meeting on May 4, I noted that we spent forty-five minutes on five issues (Turkey, the Middle East, arms sales, human rights, and the Export-Import Bank), but it was all about negotiating with Congress. I exaggerated only slightly when I wrote: "We spend more time negotiating with Congress than with other countries!" On a more trivial level, I had sent a perfunctory response letter to a freshman congressman about an export issue, and he told Vance he would not vote for the AID bill until I sent a fuller response. Needless to say, Vance called me, and I jumped through the hoop.

Not only did Congress sometimes make diplomacy difficult, but there was a network of congressional staffers, nonprofit advocacy groups, and the regulatory agencies, all of which did their best to steer us away from compromise. Some of the hawks, like the physicist Thomas Cochran of the Natural Resources Defense Council, were well informed and always worth listening to. Others were less so. But, informed or not, they had an effect on policy. An April cable from New Delhi complained that delays on exports by the Nuclear Regulatory Commission (NRC) had created "an emotional atmosphere in India that has seriously reduced our chances to achieve our non-proliferation goals." I called NRC Commissioner Victor Gilinsky, an intelligent non-proliferation hawk, and told him he was interposing his personal view over Congress's clear intent to give us a two-year period for diplomacy in the legislation. I laid it on hard because it was important.

President Carter had begun the new year in Teheran meeting with the Shah of Iran. In trying to smooth relations and reassure the Shah, Carter had promised him that we would give Iran treatment equal to other countries in our civil nuclear agreements. Unfortunately, he used the term "equal to the most favored nation [MFN]," commonly used in trade agreements, but MFN treatment does not fit well with non-proliferation, and raised problems in Congress. We were stuck with Carter's words to the Shah, but it was my job to fence off sensitive areas that would not be subject to such treatment in the nuclear cooperation agreement we were negotiating.

In October, we received intelligence that, a few years earlier, the Shah had approved a memo from a general who wanted to explore nuclear options at the Science and Technology University of the Armed Forces. We debated whether to continue with the civil nuclear agreement and decided that going forward with it would give us more insight and influence than if we cut them off. When Vance and I presented this case to Jim Schlesinger, whose approval was required, Schlesinger (and

Deutch) agreed, but at the price of merciless teasing about my having become a "nuclear pusher." Little did any of us know that in little over a year, the Shah would be overthrown in a revolution that would threaten Carter's re-election and delay Iran's nuclear program by more than a decade.

Another important issue at that time was the Comprehensive Test Ban. We had hoped that a CTB would help reinforce the promise of the NPT to reduce the role of nuclear weapons as well as provide an avenue for moderating the South Asia arms race. Unfortunately, as the year progressed and relations between the US and the USSR worsened, the CTB got whittled away. In March, I wrote that I worried that Soviet support for Cuban troops in the Horn of Africa would jeopardize negotiations. The Departments of Defense and Energy were seeking loopholes for "permitted experiments," and a five-year limit on the treaty.

When the Indian Prime Minister Morarji Desai met with President Carter in the Cabinet Room in the White House on June 13, I was asked to go over the nuclear agenda and I included SALT (Strategic Arms Limitations Talks) and CTB as steps toward a long-term goal of elimination. By July, however, Assistant Secretary of Defense David McGiffert told me the Joint Chiefs worried that even a three-year limit on tests might become a slippery slope and endanger our deterrent. In September, I went to a meeting on CTB with the operational deputies of the Joint Chiefs in their room in the Pentagon known as "the Tank." They were worried about the reliability of our deterrence of the Soviets and felt they would have to test again within three years. By the time Pickering and I went to India to discuss nuclear issues in November, we had little left to say about the prospects for a CTB.

The focus of that trip was our warning that the new legislation required full scope IAEA safeguards on all facilities within two years as a condition for continuing to fuel the Tarapur reactor. My lasting memory of the trip was an angry headline in an Indian newspaper: "MPs Protest the Role of Nye." Fortunately, not all press reactions were as hostile that year. After I gave a speech to the Uranium Institute in London in July, *Energy Daily*, which had previously been highly critical, wrote that I was "an elegant and urbane diplomat who did a superior job of improving relations." Win some, lose some, but don't count on living off good press!

As the end of my term approached, I thought about my values and how I had changed over the two years. On a weekend fishing trip with my friends Roy Hofheinz, Graham Allison, and John Sawhill, we sat around a campfire and I admitted that bureaucratic politics had become quite seductive, like winning in a game of poker. I had come to enjoy the power game. As I wrote: “It is hard to know the limits of work. If it is fun, who is to fault overwork? And political power and prestige are very corrupting because the excuse about the importance of your work is so good, and the ego kicks are so great. And thus, one becomes unidimensional. Ah life. Nothing like a fishing trip to get things in perspective.” Nonetheless, it was gratifying to end the two years on a high note, when Vance presented me with a medal, and Gerard Smith, who was the ambassador at large for non-proliferation, held a farewell luncheon at the Metropolitan Club at which he said that he “had never seen anyone accomplish so much in such a short time.” At least my pursuit of power had a purpose.

In my farewell call on Vance, I summarized our non-proliferation policy, and warned him of five possible problems: (1) overly restrictive policy on exports, in part because of the NRC; (2) phasing of important events in 1980, such as the completion of INFCE and the NPT Review Conference; (3) the withdrawal of troops from Korea; (4) the failure of the CTB and its effects on South Asia; and (5) managing the proliferation dimension of the complex diplomacy in South Africa. He asked me about the hard cases that we faced when I started. I said that I thought we had bought at least ten years on Brazil and Argentina but was worried that Pakistan would progress to a bomb by the centrifuge route that we had not been able to close off. Vance asked me to write him a private unclassified memo on my own letterhead after I returned to Harvard, evaluating whether we should use force to disrupt Pakistan’s nuclear weapons program. After wrestling with the pros and cons, I sent him a memo, which concluded there were too many uncertainties and possible unintended consequences. In 2004, I published a novel, *The Power Game*, which imagined how the opposite conclusion might have played out.

In January 1979, Secretary Vance presented me with the State Department’s Distinguished Service Award. He told me that, previously, the general view was that not much could be done about proliferation,

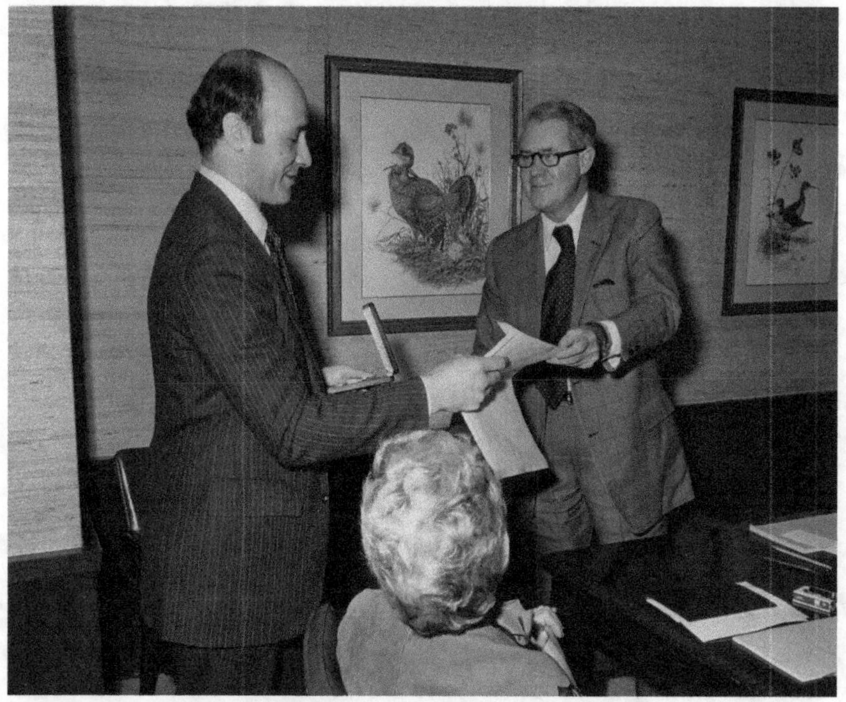

Receiving the State Department's Distinguished Service Award from Secretary Vance, 1979
Source: David M. Humphrey, Department of State

but that we now had a policy to slow it down. The French/Pakistan and German/Brazil sales had been scuttled and the US had set up an international study of the nuclear fuel cycle that decelerated the momentum toward reprocessing plutonium and the use of breeder reactors. Career Ambassador George Vest told me he was amazed I had learned diplomatic tactics so quickly to implement such a wide-ranging strategy. But, as my diary shows, it certainly had not felt that way in the beginning. I had started out by staring at a very steep learning curve.

Re-entry

My first reaction once I was back in Harvard was a sense of relief from the daily pressure and the tyranny of other people's calendars. But oddly, after a month or two, the sense of relief wore off and I found myself bored and disengaged at faculty meetings that dealt with the humdrum of daily academic life. I was suffering from adrenalin withdrawal, missing the daily doses that had driven my frenetic life. Fortunately, my friend Ted Marmor reminded me that the secret to daily happiness lies in small things and recommended that I get engaged with the details of Harvard life. I followed his advice.

I continued to go to Washington to consult for the State Department and the Department of Energy (DOE) and was struck by the magnitude of the problems caused by the Iranian revolution. Political instability was coupled with another dramatic increase in oil prices, and energy security became a top agenda item. At the beginning of the decade, the US was importing 3.5 million barrels of oil a day at a price around $2, and we were also the largest oil producer in the world. By the end of the decade, we were importing 8.5 million barrels per day – nearly half our needs – at fifteen times the earlier price, and our production was declining. Moreover, much of the oil in world markets came from the Persian Gulf, where it was vulnerable to war, revolution, and terrorism. After the Soviets invaded Afghanistan in December 1979, Carter announced his "doctrine" that we would use force to protect the oil of the Persian Gulf.

Many policy proposals, such as banning oil imports and government price controls, struck me as misguided and confused about the way the global oil market works. I convened a group of Harvard colleagues, including William Hogan, Frances Bator, Tom Schelling, Henry Lee, Alvin Alm, Al Carnesale, and David Deese, among others, with energy and foreign policy expertise. We met regularly to map issues and propose policies. In December 1980, Deese and I published the group's essays under the title *Energy and Security*. We warned that there were no quick fixes or single solutions, and it was important to consider different time dimensions. In the short term of one or two years, the problem was supply disruption and the solutions included stockpiles (public and private) and demand restraint. In the intermediate term inside a decade, the problem was reducing dependence on Persian Gulf oil and the solutions included conservation plus already available alternative fuels such as coal, gas, and non-OPEC oil. In the longer term of decades, the problem was how to adjust to higher price alternatives and the solutions included nuclear and solar power. The volume received favorable reviews in the press.

My Princeton roommate John Sawhill (who wrote a preface for *Energy and Security*) was Deputy Secretary of Energy and he asked me to come back to Washington as an Assistant Secretary of Energy for International Affairs to help implement some of these ideas. I was tempted, and Harvard granted permission, but I thought it better for family reasons to wait until after the election of 1980. Little did I realize that Carter would fail to be re-elected and it would be a dozen years before the Democrats won again and I would return to Washington. Politics is a lottery, and timing politics is as difficult as timing the stock market.

Summing up Carter

The Carter Administration ended under a cloud because of stagflation, the Soviet invasion of Afghanistan, and the hostage crisis in Iran. Part of this was bad luck. Imagine that he had coincided with Gorbachev rather than Brezhnev. But part of it was his own doing. My former Harvard boss Bob Bowie, who had worked for Eisenhower, had joined the Carter Administration as Deputy Director of the CIA. I noted his judgment after we rode home together from London in July. He was critical of Carter's process, believing he tried to do too much on paper rather than have his aides scope problems in front of him to see connections. Carter approached problems too much like a cadet cramming details for an exam, and Vance tended to focus on one big issue at a time and failed to push back enough when the NSC overruled him.

I had seen this for myself. It took a year of friction before I finally gave my conciliatory Uranium Institute speech in July 1978 (i.e. before I could get it cleared by the White House), even though friction with allies was what I had predicted at the Spring 1977 White House meeting. Carter regarded the friction between Vance and Brzezinski as providing him with options, and, despite my loyalty to Vance, I worked well with Brzezinski and often thought he was right. Unfortunately, Carter's failure to articulate his larger strategy gave an impression of inconsistency. At least an August article in *Science* magazine reported that "in the confusion of Carter's foreign policy, non-proliferation policy does not get bad marks."

Decades later when I published a book on presidents and foreign policy, I noted that, in the battles of partisan politics, it became fashionable to belittle Carter's foreign policy, but he nevertheless accomplished a great deal despite some bad luck. People often say that Jimmy Carter was a better ex-president than president, and that might be true. But: "If Carter's foreign policy were a stock, we might predict its price among historians to rise over time."[5]

[5] Joseph S. Nye, Jr., *Do Morals Matter? Presidents and Foreign Policy from FDR to Trump* (New York: Oxford University Press, 2020), p. 112.

4

The 1980s: Reagan, Bush, and the End of the Cold War

The 1980s, like the 1960s, was a schizophrenic decade in terms of the contrast between its beginning and its end. In the early years, there were deep fears about the risk of nuclear war with the Soviet Union. By the end of the decade, the Cold War was over, the Soviet Union was about to collapse, leaving America as the sole superpower. Ronald Reagan is sometimes credited with ending the Cold War, but the causes of the momentous changes that led to America's "unipolar moment" were far more complex, particularly the accession of Mikhail Gorbachev to power in Moscow in 1985. Moreover, Reagan's successor, George H. W. Bush, gets the credit for skillfully managing the negotiations that ended the global conflict without a conflagration.

In the meantime, however, we had to live through an intensification of the nuclear threat. In the early 1980s, Soviet aggressiveness following their invasion of Afghanistan in December 1979, combined with Reagan's bellicose rhetoric, heightened fears of nuclear war and led to the Nuclear Freeze Movement, which brought millions of people onto the streets in the US, as well as strong anti-nuclear protests in Europe. The era of bipartisan agreement on détente and arms control was over. Serious experts estimated that the probability of nuclear war was increasing. In August 1983, 61 percent of participants in the Aspen Arms Control Consortium estimated the odds of a US–Soviet nuclear war by the end of century as one in fifty. In a discussion on March 1, 1982, my colleague Thomas Schelling, a Nobel Laureate economist and one of the great figures of game theory and nuclear strategy, told me that he thought the odds were one in thirty. I wrote in my diary that my estimate was more like one in ten thousand, but in either case the odds were uncomfortably high. And this wasn't just hysteria. In November 1983, for example, fearful that the Able Archer 83 exercise was a cover for a NATO nuclear strike, the USSR readied its weapons for launch.

Avoiding nuclear war

When I left government, I worried about whether the world could avoid nuclear war, and I started teaching a seminar in the Kennedy School on the subject. Jonathan Schell had just published a powerful book, *The Fate of the Earth*, calling for the abolition of nuclear weapons. Harvard president Derek Bok asked me to join four other professors (Al Carnesale, Paul Doty, Stanley Hoffmann, and Sam Huntington) to assess the nuclear threat and what to do about it. (We were aided by an able graduate student, Scott Sagan.) We met regularly for a year and, in 1983, Harvard University Press published the result under the title *Living with Nuclear Weapons*. We concluded that abolition was not possible in our lifetimes, but steps could be taken to reduce risks. The volume received major press attention and led to debates and discussions with major leaders in the Freeze movement, like Randall Forsberg, John Mack, and Jonathan Schell. Ironically, it also caused a significant Harvard alumnus in the New York cultural world to write to Bok and vow never again to contribute to Harvard!

Subsequently, at the behest of David Hamburg of the Carnegie Corporation, Allison, Carnesale, and I launched an "Avoiding Nuclear War" (ANW) project at the Kennedy School. We held regular meetings and an annual conference that attracted other faculty and, even more important, a young cohort of bright predoctoral and postdoctoral fellows, many of whom later went on to become leading figures in the field. In Spring 1985, we published *Hawks, Doves, and Owls: An Agenda for Avoiding Nuclear War*. We argued that neither the hawk's position of peace through strength and military build-up nor the dove's position of peace through disarmament was sufficiently stable, and both involved great risks. We outlined a middle position that focused on risk reduction rather than the number of armaments or weapons, labeled this the "owl's" position, and suggested a practical list of "do's and don'ts". Our hope was that careful academic analysis could help move the national debate in a more productive direction, and we made major efforts to promote the message. For example, on one day we held a press breakfast in Washington, testified before the House Armed Services Committee, and appeared on ABC-TV. What effect all this had is hard to determine. Launching policy ideas from outside government is like dropping pennies into a deep well. Sometimes you hear a splash; sometimes you think you hear it but are just fooling yourself.

In any event we were not satisfied intellectually. We joked with David Hamburg that Carnegie should renew our research grant as long as we avoided nuclear war, with the understanding that if we ever failed, we would not reapply. More seriously, we felt that risk reduction was not enough, and we still needed to address the long-term question of "How does this all end?" We held a series of meetings and conferences around this question and in 1988 edited a volume *Fateful Visions*, which described various possible outcomes that included zero nuclear weapons, ballistic missile defense dominance, civilian-based defense, as well as prospects for transforming the US–Soviet relationship from confrontation to cooperation. Kurt Campbell wrote an essay with the title "Prospects and Consequences of Soviet Decline." Little did we know that the Berlin Wall would be pierced a year later. I certainly did not predict it.

Behind the Iron Curtain

Reducing nuclear risk had to include improving relations with Moscow. France had nuclear weapons, but they did not cause us to lose sleep. Moscow and Washington had to develop a better understanding of each other. Robert Legvold, a distinguished scholar of Russia at Tufts (and later Columbia University), told me in the early 1980s that there were interesting changes occurring below the visible surface of events in the Soviet Union. He persuaded me to lead a project and edit a volume on *The Making of America's Soviet Policy* for the Council on Foreign Relations. I convened a series of meetings and Yale published the essays in 1984, with authors, including Strobe Talbott, Ernest May, Marshall Goldman, and Dimitri Simes, exploring six decades of tense relations, some successes, and missed opportunities.

I also began a series of week-long visits over a number of years to Georgi Arbatov's Institute for US and Canadian Studies in Moscow (ISKRAN). I had not been back to the Soviet Union since my student tour in 1959 and was surprised to see that conversations were even more tightly constrained in the early 1980s. The Cold War had become chillier. Some of the frankest conversations I had inside people's offices were with ISKRAN's Deputy Director Bogdanov, who was reputed to be a member of the KGB and could speak more freely. Other frank conversations were possible with researchers like Henry Trofimenko, but only when we were walking outside along promenades like the Arbat. I was struck by the warmth of my counterparts when they felt they were not being surveilled. Sometimes, Russians would pass on hints that were highly elliptical. In 1984 when I asked about the new leader Yuri Andropov, the reply was he was "very plugged in." That meant he was on a kidney dialysis machine. Russians have a wonderful sense of humor even when running scared.

All told, over the course of the decade, I made eight trips to Moscow. On the first trip, in May 1980, they put me up in the Academy of Sciences Hotel, a decrepit relic of the 1930s. On a later visit, I was promoted to the Ukraine Hotel in one of the seven giant stone buildings with a sweeping crown known as Stalin wedding cakes. Unfortunately, when I returned from my morning run along the Moscow River, I was informed that there would be no hot water for three weeks while they worked on the pipes. On a later visit, I was accommodated in the Rossiya, a more modern skyscraper just off Red Square, but even there the service was limited. It was not until 1993, when I accompanied Secretary of the Treasury Lloyd Bentsen on a visit to Boris Yeltsin, that I stayed in a fancy hotel, the Metropole, where a harpist played during breakfast in the dining room. Seen through its hotels, Russia appeared less formidable than when seen through its missiles. Perhaps it was not surprising that, on the return flight to Frankfurt, the mostly Western passengers burst into spontaneous applause when their plane lifted off from Sheremetyevo airport.

In May 1981, the ISKRAN experts on America were puzzled and angry about American policy and did not understand what Reagan intended. Was he willing to risk nuclear war? On my third visit, in January 1983, I described the Harvard project on avoiding nuclear war and discussed approaches to international relations. Many of my counterparts, such as Vitaly Zhurkin, Andrei Kokoshin (later Defense Minister), Sergei Karaganov (later Vladimir Putin's advisor) and others focused on traditional balance-of-power concerns, and said they regarded Marxism as more important for political legitimacy than for analysis. Georgy Shakhnazarov even surprised me by praising George Orwell.

Molly accompanied me when I returned to Moscow in January 1984, and we were treated to wonderful cultural events, including the Bolshoi Ballet. We took a sleeper train to Leningrad (now St. Petersburg) where we enjoyed such Russian splendors as the Hermitage Art Museum, the Kirov Ballet, and Catherine the Great's palace at Pushkin. But the political climate was not good. We were briefed by Ambassador Arthur Hartman in Spaso House, the residence that had belonged to a Russian sugar merchant before the revolution. He told us that official US–Soviet dialogue was minimal.

In February 1985, temperatures in Moscow fell well below zero, but there was a slight improvement in the political climate. After briefings by Hartman, I had serious conversations at ISKRAN about deterrence, crisis stability, and measures to deal with accidents. I enjoyed a good discussion of the controversial Strategic Defense Initiative with Alexei Arbatov (who went on to become a liberal member of parliament). That year, 1985, was a turning point in US–Soviet relations. Gorbachev came to power in March and the first summit with Reagan in Geneva was in December.

By the following summer, things were somewhat different. Bob Legvold had arranged for a meeting of American and Soviet international relations theorists, and included scholars like Bob Keohane and Richard Ullman. The conversations were interesting, but limited by a heavy admixture of propaganda. Georgy Arbatov and Bogdanov told me they were advising Gorbachev against attending another summit, but it did ultimately occur in Reykjavik in October, without reaching an agreement.

The politics were still cloudy but had improved by June 1987 when Allison, Carnesale, and I went to brief the Russians on our ANW project. We were told that Gorbachev's "new thinking" was pragmatic and important. We also expressed an interest in seeing the Russian Far East and our hosts promised a trip to Khabarovsk and Vladivostok. We flew to Khabarovsk in a military transport in which the passenger seats were canvas slings, and we were treated to a boat trip on the Amur River, but while we were there Moscow denied us permission to visit Vladivostok. New thinking apparently had geographical limits. On the other hand, we were taken to a showing of the film *Repentance*, a then daring and powerful exposé of past dictatorship.

Our trip in January 1989 illustrated the extent to which the political climate had changed since the beginning of the decade. The purpose of the trip was to discuss the lessons of the Cuban Missile Crisis (outlined more fully in the next section). We arrived early and met with Roald Sagdeev at the Space Institute and attended a meeting on confidence-building measures at the Peace Academy with four Soviet generals. We met with Vladimir Lukyn at the foreign ministry who (along with other old acquaintances) told us that Gorbachev's reform was real, though Yevgeny Primakov (later Prime Minister) admitted they were having a problem in handling price reforms.

The discussions of Cuba were fascinating because the delegations included McGeorge Bundy and Robert McNamara on the American side, and Andrei Gromyko for the Soviets. (Jorge Risquet attended from Cuba.) Fyodor Burlatsky told me that Shakhnazarov, a close advisor, would brief Gorbachev about how close we had come to disaster. But perhaps most touching was a side trip after the meeting in which Sergei

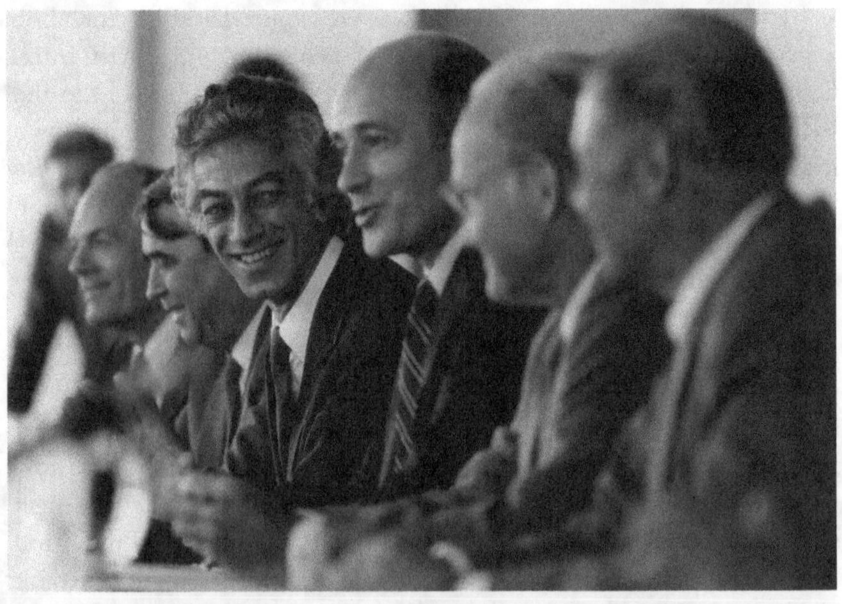

Discussing the Cuban Missile Crisis with Fyodor Burlatsky, Sergo Mikoyan, McGeorge Bundy, and Robert McNamara, Harvard Kennedy School, 1987
Source: Joseph S. Nye Personal Archives, Harvard University Archives

Khrushchev and Sergo Mikoyan escorted us to the grave sites of their fathers who had been key actors on the Soviet side.

Cuban Missile Crisis

One of the studies in the ANW project was a series of meetings to construct an oral history of the 1962 Cuban Missile Crisis, when the risks of nuclear war had been at their highest. Kennedy had put the risk of war as high as one in three. James Blight, a psychologist at the Kennedy School, worked out a process of "living oral history," in which former participants would not just be interrogated for the archives, but would have a chance to question each other and check their memories. He was ably assisted by graduate students like David Welch, Bruce Allyn, and others. At various times, these meetings in the US and Moscow included people like Bundy, McNamara, Ted Sorensen, and Douglas Dillon on the American side, and Anatoly Dobrynin and Andrei Gromyko on the Soviet side.

Our first session was October 11, 1987, on the twenty-fifth anniversary of the crisis. Our Russian participants were Burlatsky, Mikoyan, and Shakhnazarov, and we spent the first evening viewing tapes from 1962. The next day, I chaired sessions at which we walked through the history, and Blight's process worked. When McNamara assured the Soviets that we had no intention of invading Cuba in 1962 (having failed in 1961), Sorensen reminded him that the CIA was then implementing a covert action plan to destabilize Cuba. McNamara said that operation "Mongoose" was not effective but admitted that it may not have looked that way to the Cubans or the Soviets. On their side, Mikoyan criticized the Soviet actions as "adventurist." Subsequent sessions were equally frank, and over time Blight and Welch published various books and articles making the content more broadly available.[6]

[6] James G. Bright and David A. Welch, *On the Brink* (New York: Hill and Wang, 1989). Bruce Allyn, James Blight, and David A. Welch, eds., *Back to the Brink: Proceedings of the Moscow Conference on the Cuban Missile Crisis, January 27–28, 1989*. Harvard CSIA Occasional Paper Series, #9 (London: University Press of America, 1992).

A new frontier: China

In 1982, I made the first of what would become many visits to China. I was invited as a guest of the government, but that was not unusual – Japan and Israel had treated me similarly. But it was unexpected because China had long been closed. Behind the invitation was Ni Xi Xiong, who had shown up at my office in 1980 and explained that he had been a professor at Fudan University in Shanghai but had been sent to the countryside for ten years during the Cultural Revolution. Now the Chinese government was sending him to Harvard for a year to catch up. As he said: "I have lost a decade of my intellectual life. Can you help me recover a decade in a year?" I became his informal tutor, invited him to our home, and we became friends.

I flew to Shanghai in July and stayed in an old hotel from the European era. When I went for my run at 6 a.m., I was amazed to find the streets full of people doing exercises. I was driven to Fudan University for a formal greeting and talk and was pleased by the quality of the questions. I then lectured on nuclear issues to the Shanghai Institute of International Relations, where I encountered a strange mix of rhetoric and realism. I was also treated to sumptuous banquets and a river cruise. At that time, the district of Pudong across the river was largely empty. When I returned as an official of the US government in 1993, Pudong was full of skyscrapers.

After touring the sights of Shanghai, I was flown to Beijing, where the open spaces of Tiananmen Square were in sharp contrast to the crowded streets of Shanghai. After visiting the Great Wall and the Ming Tombs, I went to Peking University and spoke with a variety of faculty members; I also spoke at the Institute of International Studies. Many Chinese were critical of Reagan, but the discourse was somewhat franker than I had found in Moscow. On the other hand, although Ni and I were accommodated in an old-fashioned hotel in Beijing, we were not allowed to eat in the same dining-room. Foreigners ate separately. When I returned a decade later, there was no such distinction in the modern hotel.

Influence from outside

I continued to teach, write, speak, and testify on nuclear issues during the Reagan years, often appearing on television, in the *New York Times*,

TIME magazine, and others. Although I did minor consulting for the State Department and the Lawrence Livermore Laboratory, and testified before House and Senate committees, I no longer had the type of hands-on policy influence that I had experienced while I was in the government.

In 1984, I played a secondary role in efforts to help the Walter Mondale presidential campaign. I attended some meetings, working with Madeleine Albright, Barry Carter, Richard Betts, and others. I met with Mondale (whom I admired as a human being), wrote some position papers on nuclear issues, and voted, but all to no avail. Despite some encouraging polls early on, Reagan won by a landslide.

My influence on policy had to be indirect. It could come from my students who went on to become leaders; the "trickle-down" effect of my academic writings; opinion pieces written for a variety of journals and papers; participating in nongovernmental organizations; and various television commentaries, such as helping to anchor CBS live coverage of the 1987 Reagan–Gorbachev summit from a tent on the Ellipse behind the White House. One never knows what influence such actions have, but I was particularly amused when an op-ed piece I published in the *New York Times* in January 1982 was reported on the front page of *Pravda* in Moscow. At the same time, I tried to keep a balance between influencing debates on policy and maintaining my academic work, including reading and publishing in academic refereed journals.

Of course, academic life had its compensations. Government differs from academia in its enormous pressure on time and the power of being able to make decisions. It is intense but narrow. University life is less directly concerned with time and power, and that allows one's curiosity to range more broadly and provides a chance to ask deeper questions. I benefited from this in teaching my course on nuclear ethics. There were many times in the State Department, as I was in the thick of trying to persuade foreign governments not to develop nuclear weapons, when I would wonder about how I justified our own arsenal. There is nothing like a seminar of bright students (including foreigners) to force one to clear up one's thinking, and academic life allowed me the time to read and think about how to do that.

Another benefit of academic life is that you are often invited to visit beautiful conference sites that were once reserved for the aristocracy in earlier centuries. A good example is Ditchley Park, a lovely eighteenth-century country house outside Oxford, where I attended many conferences and eventually joined the board of the American Ditchley Foundation. In February 1985, I spent a month at the Rockefeller Foundation's beautiful Villa Serbelloni located in Bellagio on the shores of Lake Como. In such a setting not only did Molly and I enjoy ourselves, but I was able to finish the first draft of *Nuclear Ethics* in under a month. I explored various moral philosophy approaches to war and applied them to nuclear weapons, concluding that abolition was a worthy long-term goal, but not practical in the foreseeable future. Moral justification had to focus on reducing risk, and I examined the various means to do so. Fortunately, when the book was published, it received very favorable reviews in the *New York Times* and elsewhere. Among my various books over the years, it remains one of my favorites because it allowed me to dig deeply into values.

Using and creating networks

I was also able to advance policy ideas through participation and/or by serving on the boards of organizations like the Council on Foreign Relations, the Trilateral Commission, the World Economic Forum (WEF) in Davos, the Ditchley Foundation, the International Institute for Strategic Studies (IISS) in London, the Carnegie Endowment for International Peace, the Center for Strategic and International Studies, the Institute for East–West Security Studies, the United Nations Association, and others. I should also include the founding editorial board of *Foreign Policy.*

Such organizations allowed me to meet with American and foreign leaders as well as broaden my understanding of issues. I tried to promote ideas, but these organizations were also part of my education. For example, at Davos, I learned a lot about Europe from chairing a meeting between Raymond Barre, former French Prime Minister, and Denis Healey, former British Defence Minister, and, in the early 1990s, attending a small dinner discussion on Russia that included Dmitri Medvedev, a future Prime Minister and President of Russia. (He impressed me then as relatively open and a reformer, but his subsequent record was disappointing.) Among the memorable side events were an audience with the Pope when the Trilateral Commission met in Rome; a visit to North Korean tunnels in the Korean demilitarized zone organized by the IISS; and a trip through Checkpoint Charlie into East Berlin arranged by Aspen Berlin during the Cold War.

Aspen Strategy Group

The most important nongovernmental group for me was the Aspen Strategy Group (ASG), which I helped create in 1983. In the early 1980s, American attitudes on foreign policy and strategy were sharply polarized. In those circumstances, the Ford and Rockefeller foundations announced they would no longer finance the inter-university consortium on arms control that had been established in the 1970s by my colleague Paul Doty, a distinguished Harvard biochemist and long-time participant at the Pugwash Conferences on Science and World Affairs. On August 12, 1983, Doty and Joseph Slater, president of the Aspen Institute, asked me to try to rescue the program. Ford said it was not interested in continuing support, but Edwin Deagle, the program officer for Rockefeller, indicated that they might consider support if the group became less academic, more bipartisan, and more policy oriented. He cited the Group of 30 in international finance as an example.

Deagle and I discussed how to construct such a group and agreed that a key to success would be to select co-chairs with partisan identities, but who were highly respected "across" the aisle. We were fortunate that Brent Scowcroft, former National Security Advisor in the Ford Administration, and William Perry, former Undersecretary of Defense in the Carter Administration, agreed to serve. It was also important to pick congressional members who had similar reputations and to avoid the partisan "bomb-throwers" of Washington politics, such as Newt Gingrich. Our first congressional members were Les Aspin and Dick Cheney from the House and John Warner from the Senate. Over the years, they have had many good successors, including Jane Harman, Dianne Feinstein, Jack Reed, Dan Sullivan, Chris Coons, and others.

The ASG first met in August 1984 with a bipartisan group of participants selected from think-tanks, universities, companies, and former officials. Many went on to serve in high policy positions such as Secretary of State, Secretary of Defense, and National Security Advisor in both

With Scowcroft and Perry at the Aspen Strategy Group, mid-1980s

Republican and Democratic administrations. (Robert Gates served in both.) One early participant, Condoleezza Rice, became Secretary of State and later my Republican co-chair of the Group. I initially served as Executive Director. I gave up that position when I entered the Clinton Administration in 1993, but eventually returned as co-chair.

The initial agenda was dominated by questions of nuclear stability, including the vulnerability of Minuteman missile silos, whether to build the MX missile, and the prospects for a Strategic Defense Initiative that Reagan hoped could be built in seven years. Many members from both parties were skeptical. The following year, the Group focused on space, anti-satellite weapons, and the future of deterrence, and in 1986 we included chemical warfare. Over the years, the agenda broadened further to include the Middle East, the Gulf War, Japan, China, South Asia, the future of NATO, cyber threats, and many other topics of strategic significance.

On many of these topics, members differed sharply over both facts and policy, particularly the Iraq War, but we worked to develop a culture of civility and listening. In some cases, members announced that they had changed their mind, and I regarded that as a hallmark of success. We published an annual report or book about our meetings and held press briefings (sometimes in Senate office rooms). But in my view, our most important product was persuading key policy people to listen and take each other's arguments seriously without the hub-bub and thirty-second sound bites of Washington.

We contributed to this atmosphere by keeping meetings informal, allowing ample down time. Scowcroft often led hikes to Independence Lake (12,000 feet) or Thomas Lake (in the bowl of Mount Sopris), which were affectionately known as "Brent's death marches." I tagged along with my fly rod and occasionally offered fly-fishing sessions for those inclined, including Walter Mondale and John Warner. We organized raft trips on the Roaring Fork and Colorado rivers. You can't appreciate the West unless you have seen Cheney and Warner each captaining a raft full of ASG members through the rapids of the Colorado. More seriously, it is hard to hate the other party when you have such shared experiences.

Over its four decades, the ASG broadened the age composition of its membership, the diversity of topics, and the length of meetings, and included more members of the press, who followed the Chatham House rule of using information but not naming the source without permission. This helped with direct outreach to a broader audience, but, most important, the Group managed to maintain an all-too-rare culture of civil bipartisan listening.

The perils of public intellectuals

I enjoyed teaching graduate seminars and writing about international relations theory for refereed academic journals, and regularly participated in panels at professional organizations like the American Political Science Association (APSA) and the International Studies Association (ISA), but I did not aspire to lead such organizations. I found that more of my time was taken up by the role of a so-called "public intellectual," speaking and writing for a non-academic audience. That did not seem to diminish my ranking as one of the top contributors to academic theory in my field. After publication of my book *The Future of Power*, I was pleased that a 2012 poll ranked me #2 as "the scholar who had done the most interesting work over the past five years." At the same time, I was ranked as the most influential scholar on foreign policy. But it would be misleading to imply that there were not a number of ethical questions about balancing roles as an academic and someone trying to directly influence policy debate. There was a trade-off between time spent on academic and public audiences.

One problem was travel. I went to an extraordinary number of meetings both at home and overseas. Looking at my diary for 1981, I was out of town on business for eighty-six days domestically and thirty-one days overseas. I kept my vow never to miss a scheduled class, and that required short trips and careful planning. Friends joked that I was the frequent flier professor, and Molly replied that airline frequent flier miles (an innovation of the 1980s) saved our marriage, because I could often take her along. While she saw some interesting places and people, nonetheless I placed a heavy burden on her patience and understanding, and I am grateful.

Another issue was intellectual integrity. Policy involves power to implement ideas, but academia must privilege truth over power. When playing the power game, there is always a temptation to tailor ideas for the sake of power and this must be resisted as much as possible. Other temptations involve consulting for businesses that offer lucrative fees. While I often consulted, I also tried to limit its effect on my ideas. I remember one case in which a company offered a fat fee if I would publish an article advocating access for Mexican oil. I actually agreed with that position, but turned it down when they said that the conclusion was a premise of the contract.

A different type of challenge arose in 1985 when Bob Gates, a person I admired, asked me to consult for the CIA. Harvard, properly, has a policy of no classified research on campus, but it is also important for universities to take intelligence seriously as a significant part of foreign policy. I passed the required polygraph test, but balked when the CIA wanted me to sign a contract giving them the right of prior clearance of all I published. I thought this was inconsistent with my role as an academic. During the Clinton Administration, when I chaired the National Intelligence Council, I had to sign such a document, but people would know that I represented a public government position. It is possible to combine the roles of an academic and a public intellectual, but one has to be cognizant of the boundaries.

1988 presidential campaign

Massachusetts Governor Michael Dukakis declared his candidacy for the president in 1987. As someone who was listed in a February issue of *US News* as one of the thirty-five members of "the foreign policy establishment," it was inevitable that I would be drawn to that flame. At first, the role of an outside advisor took a leisurely pace that was easy to fit in with my academic life, involving phone calls and planning sessions with Christopher Edley and Madeleine Albright among others, and occasional memos. But after Dukakis won the New York primary in April 1988 and Senator Gary Hart dropped out of the race, it was clear that the former would win the Democratic Party nomination.

I was asked to brief Dukakis on nuclear issues and on the Soviet Union. On one occasion, he asked Senator Bill Bradley to join us in the big corner office of the State House on Beacon Hill, hung with portraits of former leaders like John Adams. Bradley and Dukakis both had very clear minds and the discussion was fruitful. At other times, I would send Dukakis memos or speech drafts through Chris Edley, and it was always satisfying to learn that he had read them and sometimes to hear my own words being used.

As the pace quickened, the press wanted to know more about Dukakis's advisors. On April 25, *TIME* magazine ran my picture speculating that I might become National Security Advisor. Leslie Stahl of CBS news came to interview me in my office, and William Safire mentioned me in his column in the *New York Times.* Such attention then attracted others. The American Israel Public Affairs Committee (AIPAC) requested to see me to check my views on Israel. When I visited Paris for a speech, the Elysée Palace sent a car to drive me at a frenetic pace to meet with Jacques Attali, the president's advisor, who wanted to know more about Dukakis. By early June, polls showed Dukakis in the lead five points ahead of Bush.

In July, I was invited to the Democratic Convention in hot Atlanta. After getting credentials, I attended a staff meeting in the Hyatt Hotel, went to a symposium at the Carter Center, did press interviews, briefed financial types on security issues, spoke to a DNC panel, and attended numerous events. I had a ringside seat when Governor Ann Richards of Texas, a witty Democrat, told the assembled delegates that Bush was born on third base and always thought he had hit a home run when he crossed the plate. While I had never considered myself to be strongly partisan, it was difficult not to get caught up in the enthusiasm of a large partisan crowd. And experts on politics like Norman Ornstein and William Schneider were predicting a Dukakis victory in November.

That was still the mood in September when I sat in the front row as Dukakis gave a speech on defense policy at Georgetown University using some of my words. I was asked to brief the press afterwards and then accompanied him to a political rally in Annapolis. He asked me to ride on his campaign plane back to Boston, and I experienced a certain frisson when beckoned from the back to sit in the empty seat next to him. Power does odd things – like transforming the significance of an empty seat. But as we chatted, he did not ask for a briefing but instead mused philosophically about how different national politics was from state politics.

By this time, the polls were shifting in Bush's favor and the presidential debates did not reverse the decline. I was invited to join the campaign flight to the debate in Winston-Salem in September 1987, where I thought Dukakis did well on substance, but Bush succeeded in painting him as being too liberal. Of course, I did not say that when I went to the press room to help spin the results after the debate. On September 26, the *New York Times* published my picture and the *Wall Street Journal* called me an important centrist, but I began to realize that I was unlikely to be returning to government the following year. On November 8, the voters confirmed that.

Defeat and recovery

Writing has always helped me to recover from defeats. I began to ponder the book that eventually became *Bound to Lead: The Changing Nature of American Power*, published as we entered the twentieth century's final decade. Americans go through cycles of belief in our national decline, and in the 1980s there was a prevalent belief that the United States was weakening. The great British historian Paul Kennedy's *The Rise and Fall of the Great Powers* put the US in the category of states like Phillip II's Spain or Edwardian Britain because of "imperial overstretch." His book was a best-seller. I doubted this view and decided to spend my sabbatical in the Spring of 1989 writing in the welcoming surroundings of St Antony's College in Oxford, where Ralf Dahrendorf, Warden of the college, had invited me to be a visiting fellow.

It is curious how widespread the belief in American decline had become by the beginning of 1989 because, by the end of the year, the Berlin Wall had been pierced and, by 1991, the Soviet Union was dissolved, and the US became the sole global superpower. I certainly did not foresee the timing, but I was correct about the direction of Soviet decline. With more than 16 percent of its GDP going to defense and foreign affairs (compared to 6 percent for the US), it was the USSR that was suffering from "imperial overstretch."

Nor was I convinced by the view that Japan, with its impressive economic growth, would overtake the US. The press liked to point out that Japan had the largest banks, and the price of real estate in Tokyo meant that the imperial palace alone was worth more than all of Manhattan. I was skeptical of the raft of books with titles like *Japan as Number One* and *The Coming War with Japan.* I was more impressed by the analysis of my friend (and later editor of *The Economist*) Bill Emmott, whose book title was *The Sun Also Sets.*

When I compared American economic and military power with those of the Soviet Union, Japan, Europe, and China, I found the US well ahead in both respects, but I felt that something else was missing. I had read extensively in the academic literature on power and concluded that if power is defined as the capacity to affect others to get what you want, that can be accomplished in three ways: coercion, payment, and attraction. Given its culture, the US was uniquely placed to persuade others (though not everyone) to want the same things it wanted. And when others want what you want, you can exercise power. That is why a Norwegian analyst described postwar Europe as divided by the two empires, but, in contrast to the Soviets, the American one was "an empire by invitation."

In *Bound to Lead*, I developed the concept of soft power – the ability to affect others through attraction rather than coercion or payment. If you can get others to want what you want, you can economize on sticks and carrots. I developed it as an analytic concept to round out my description of American power and add to my reasons for why the American century was not over. Little did I imagine that, two decades later, the President of

China would urge his compatriots to invest in "soft power." The concept also became used by European leaders and in the press. But although it crossed over from academic to public discourse, the result was at a cost to analysis. Some people used it to mean anything non-military, while others exaggerated attraction compared to hard powers of coercion or payment. As I wrote in 2021: "With time, I have come to realize that concepts such as soft power are like children. As an academic or a public intellectual, you can love and discipline them when they are young, but as they grow, they wander off and make new company, both good and bad. There is not much you can do about it, even if you were present at the creation."[7]

Gorbachev and the fall of the Wall

In the 1950s, George Orwell's dystopia about 1984 had great influence and we were not sure what the decade would bring. As it turned out, the second half of the decade began when Gorbachev came to power with his new thinking of *perestroika* (restructuring) and *glasnost* (openness). In December 1985, Reagan met Gorbachev in Geneva, the first of five such meetings. Reagan had the personal savvy to understand (well ahead of some advisors) that he could deal with Gorbachev.

For nearly everyone, the end of the Cold War came as a surprise. I was in Tokyo on November 10, 1989 (their time) speaking at a Yomiuri Shimbun conference and debating with Paul Kennedy on American decline. I turned on CNN in my hotel room and learned that the Berlin Wall, a defining icon of the Cold War since 1962, was now open. Within a few weeks, people were speculating on the reunification of Germany, whose partition had been a defining feature of the settlement of World War II. At a Kennedy School Forum, MIT political scientist William Griffith speculated that Germany might be reunited within five years, but British politician Shirley Williams thought it would take longer. Given the opposition of Prime Minister Thatcher and French President Mitterrand, I sided with Shirley (and was wrong!). Of course, it actually took less than one year (October 1990) and George H. W. Bush deserves

[7] Joseph S. Nye, "Soft Power: The Evolution of a Concept," *Journal of Political Power*. https://doi.org/10.1080/2158379X.2021.1879572.

great credit for the skill with which he handled the diplomacy that made that possible without bloodshed.

We now know through the work of Mary Sarotte and other historians that the original opening of the Wall was a mistake, and many experts believe that the USSR could have lasted another decade if Yuri Andropov, former head of the KGB, had lived and not been succeeded by a reformer like Gorbachev.[8] Gorbachev's reforms were designed to save the Soviet Union, but wound up speeding its demise. He was like a man pulling on a loose thread in a sweater who winds up unraveling the whole thing. I was not surprised, however, by the longevity of American power along the lines described in my 1990 book, and how we used (and misused) that power was a theme that would continue to intrigue me for the next two decades.

1990 Gulf War

The fall of the Wall was not the only major geopolitical event around that time. On August 2, 1990, Saddam Hussein invaded and occupied his neighbor Kuwait, seizing its oil fields. The Aspen Institute was celebrating its fortieth anniversary with speeches by President Bush and Prime Minister Margaret Thatcher. I remember sitting in the audience listening to Bush, looking at Scowcroft, and wondering how they would respond. The presence of the two Western leaders in the same place helped them coordinate a tough response of sending troops to Saudi Arabia and demanding that Iraq withdraw from Kuwait. As an amusing aside, the Aspen Institute asked me to brief Thatcher on North–South relations. In my experience, most briefings of political leaders consisted of my providing information and the principal asking questions. With Thatcher it turned out that I did a lot of listening.

I agreed with the tough position on Iraq and said so, but over the next few months there was considerable debate about the use of force. Saddam's army looked formidable, and I remember Les Aspin, then chair of the House Armed Services Committee, telling me in December that some of his briefings suggested there might be as many as 15,000

[8] Mary Sarotte, *1989: The Struggle to Create Post-Cold War Europe* (Princeton, NJ: Princeton University Press, 2009).

With British Prime Minister Margaret Thatcher, Aspen 1990

American casualties. Bush handled the crisis with skill, first trying negotiation, seeking a supportive resolution from Congress, getting a UN Security Council resolution authorizing the use of force, and including in his coalition troops from the Arab League, though he did not need them militarily. In my terms, Bush ably combined the soft power of legitimacy with hard military power. I later came to call such successful combinations "smart power."

On January 15, 1991, I had flown from Perth, Australia to Taiwan, where I met with Ma Ying-jeou, the future president. I was traveling between meetings in Taipei when I learned from the car radio that war had begun. Some experts worried that the conflict could continue into the summer, but Bush had the sense to settle for the expulsion of Iraq from Kuwait in February rather than pursue maximalist goals. It was another success, and when I went to Davos later that month, I found broad European support. It also occurred to me that it was ironic that I had spent much of 1988 trying to prevent Bush from becoming president. Such bipartisan inclinations did not prevent me from attending a Congressional Democratic Caucus retreat in Leesburg on March 8, 1991, where I had lunch with Richard Gebhardt and dinner with Nancy Pelosi. My talk to the panel warned against turning inward.

Personal life

For years, I had turned down offers to chair the government department at Harvard on the grounds that teaching and writing were what attracted me to academic life, not administration. I had also turned aside inquiries about being a provost or president of a number of major and minor colleges and universities. I had briefly been tempted by an offer to run the studies program of the Brookings Institution as I left the Carter Administration, and in November 1985 I went to New York to meet with David Rockefeller, Cyrus Vance and Peter Peterson about becoming president of the Council on Foreign Relations, but I did not want to live in New York and disrupt our family, including Molly's new art gallery.

But after hitting 50, I felt an itch to run things. My teaching was going well, with the fourth largest course in the university. A poll found that more than a fifth of the students who decided to major in government did so because of my course. More amusingly, the student *Confidential Guide* assigned me to a "pantheon of faculty" as "the god of war." I did not feel that I had written all that I wanted to say, but when the dean of Arts and Sciences Mike Spence asked me to become an associate dean for International Affairs, as well as direct two research centers, I succumbed to the temptation. I was glad that I did it even though, at times, I felt I had bitten off too much. As I wrote wryly at one point: "I need a vacation so I can catch up on work."

Along with four other women, Molly had started Gallery on the Green in Lexington, and it was a success. I tried to be supportive. I learned that the role of a gallery husband was to shift partitions, help hang large pictures, and politely sip white wine at openings while waiting for customers to put red purchase dots next to pictures – and to offer moral support.

The boys were flourishing. Early in the decade I learned to stop arm-wrestling with them because, even if I won, my elbow was too sore to use the next day! And I also learned that in skiing they soon outpaced me. At the end of the decade, when Ben graduated from Harvard in 1987 and John and Dan from Hamilton in 1988, I remember pride being followed by a deep hollow sadness as I realized that the nesting years were over, and they had flown away. But I cherished memories of many fishing, hunting, and camping trips to the Adirondacks, Maine, and Alaska. I particularly remember one trip to Alaska when we were charged by a grizzly bear with cubs. The boys had worked as guides in a fishing camp in Alaska, and we decided to do a self-guided float trip on the Koktuli River in the Bristol Bay watershed. After being dropped off on a remote lake by a float plane, we blew up two rafts and set off downstream. As we rounded a bend in the shallow river, we saw a nine-foot grizzly standing up on the bank with four cubs. I jumped out to try to hold the raft before we floated into her, but she got down on all fours and charged us. Fortunately, she broke off the charge about fifteen yards from us and ran off into the tundra with her cubs. Otherwise, I might not be writing this! The sequel is quite funny. In the haste of packing the rafts we had put our shotgun in the second one. When it arrived, we fired several shots in the air, ostensibly to frighten the bear from coming back, but really for our own psychological benefit. We have fished in Alaska many times since then and seen hundreds of grizzlies, but never again that close.

Fishing in Alaska with sons John, Dan, and Ben, 1988

Another satisfaction of the late 1980s was my turn to fiction. I had always dreamed of writing a novel since my time at Oxford, but I had learned that it is not as simple as it seems. In 1989 and '90, I attended the Stonecoast Writers' Conference in Gorham, Maine, where I learned greatly from Stephen Dobyns and others. At Harvard, I joined a fiction workshop taught by Anatole Broyard, a onetime critic for the *New York Times*, and was also helped by my colleague Richard Marius, who taught expository writing. I found that in my academic writing I would try to generalize and incorporate as wide a view as possible. Fiction is almost the opposite. One particularizes in order to illuminate the general, almost like looking through the telescope backwards. In prose, I would use the glass to survey the whole meadow; in fiction, I might convey the meadow by focusing on a sunlit dewdrop on a single blade of grass.

I did not participate much in the Clinton campaign beyond writing a few memos in 1992, and many people expected Bush to be re-elected. Clinton had the guts to challenge the conventional wisdom, but I planned to spend my sabbatical year writing a book on the national interest at the Woodrow Wilson Center for Scholars where I was given an office in the wonderful old Smithsonian building with a view out over the Mall. But that was soon interrupted by Clinton's surprise election.

5

The Clinton Years: The National Intelligence Council

Like Jimmy Carter, Bill Clinton was a southern governor with little experience of Washington or world politics, but he was a much more adept politician. He inherited a world without a Soviet Union, and thus no country could balance American power. Commentators called it a "unipolar world" or the peak of the American century. But the absence of constraints made it difficult to formulate a strategy. With the demise of the Soviet Union, the US lost the North Star that had oriented its foreign policy for better and worse. National Security Advisor Tony Lake's "enlargement and engagement" strategy did not provide very specific guidance. I remember sitting in White House meetings in 1993 where we were clearly fumbling with principles that would guide our actions on issues like intervention in Bosnia or dealing with Japan or the North Korean nuclear threat. But Clinton was smart, and he practiced "on the job learning."

I was happy at Harvard in 1992 as an associate dean for International Affairs and Director of the Center for International Affairs, where I had started as a research assistant thirty years earlier. But I welcomed the opportunity to return to government. On January 3, 1993, James Woolsey, the incoming Director of the CIA, called to invite me to chair the National Intelligence Council (NIC), which prepares intelligence estimates for the president. While I was pondering this, Les Aspin, the incoming Secretary of Defense, asked if I would become an Assistant Secretary of Defense. I had known both men from the Aspen Strategy Group, and while Les was a friend and a great defense intellectual, I was concerned about the way he was organizing the department. As chair of the NIC, I would have much more autonomy, and I would sit on the Executive Committee of the Intelligence Community where the heads of the (then) sixteen intelligence agencies met every other week. I sometimes joked that the choice between defense and intelligence was like choosing between the temptations of omnipotence and omniscience. In policy, you have your hands on the levers but lack the time to see the broad perspective; in intelligence, you can see everything but are not supposed to touch the policy levers.

Look but don't touch

Chairing the NIC was fascinating work. All jobs have a certain amount of tedious bureaucratic and representational duties, but this one had a higher ratio of substance to scutwork than most. The NIC had a staff of more than one hundred, including twelve National Intelligence Officers (NIOs) who were responsible for coordinating intelligence for various regions and functions. It was housed on the executive seventh floor of the CIA headquarters in Langley, and I had a glassy corner office with a splendid view of the surrounding wooded park, as well as Washington in the distance. Although the NIC reported to the Director of Central Intelligence, only about half the staff came from the CIA, while the rest came from other government agencies or were recruited for limited periods from outside. Each year, the NIOs coordinated and produced about forty formal National Intelligence Estimates (NIEs), which had to be approved by the heads of all agencies meeting as the National Foreign Intelligence Board.

We produced estimates on topics as varied as North Korea's nuclear program, transnational drug cartels, AIDS in Africa, and economic conditions in Russia. The job also involved meeting with officials, briefing Congress, attending meetings in the White House, as well as interesting travel such as joining Secretary of the Treasury Lloyd Bentsen on a visit to Boris Yeltsin, or accompanying Senator William Cohen's congressional delegation to Southeast Asia. Other trips involved sitting in on Britain's Joint Intelligence Committee in London; and being escorted by the son of the president of Croatia to a bunker in Mostar, Bosnia where a battle was going on. And there was the fascination of learning about secret programs and visiting special sites.

But that came later. First, I had to get a temporary badge, pass a polygraph test again, and be sworn in. I had two deputies, Sam Hoskinson, a veteran intelligence official, and Gregory Treverton, a friend from Harvard who later went on to himself become chair of the

NIC. Though I inherited my deputies, I was fortunate in the inheritance. I was also lucky to hire Barbara Acosta, a career intelligence service secretary. And one day, a mid-career student whom I thought was from the State Department when I had tutored her at the Kennedy School, walked into my office. When I saw the CIA blue badge dangling from her neck, I knew Gayle von Eckartsberg was so good that I hired her as a special assistant. These people and others helped familiarize me with the extraordinary number of classifications and clearances I would need, as well as many intricate organizational and procedural issues. As with my experience at the State Department in 1977, I felt I had been thrown into a pool and told to swim or drown, but fortunately the second time round was easier.

Many issues were already on the boil. North Korea announced it was withdrawing from the NPT; the odds of Yeltsin prevailing in Russia were assessed at less than even; and civil war was raging in Bosnia despite the presence of outnumbered UN peacekeeping troops. I was behind all the professionals in my reading, and because I could not take classified papers home, I had to stay late in the office at night. It was probably a good thing that I was living alone in an apartment near Rock Creek Park and that Molly had remained in Lexington until the boys finished the school year.

I soon felt comfortable enough to set out my goals for the NIC. I wanted to improve the quality of the way NIEs dealt with uncertainty. I insisted that after the analysts had examined different scenarios and assessed the probabilities that they thought might unfold, the estimate should include a box outlining possible conditions that might make the analysis wrong. The analysts did not like this, because, as they said, the probabilities they assigned to the scenarios were the results of a lifetime of expertise as well as hours of interagency meetings spent hammering out the draft. But I pointed out that a short readable box would alert policymakers to the possibility of low-probability events as well as reveal the assumptions built into the NIE, which would be important knowledge for them as they weighed up their decisions.

I also wanted to provide short summaries to accompany the long NIEs to make the conclusions more accessible to policymakers rather than just their staffs. Finally, I sought to improve the quality of basic economic reasoning in the process. For example, when a draft NIE proclaimed the war on drugs a success based on the rising number of confiscations of drugs on the border, I sent it back insisting that it also include information on what was happening to drug prices in central cities. Without that information, all the beautiful charts we had were just measures of efforts, not outcomes.

A second goal was to get better procedures for warning and planning into the intelligence and policy process, and to that end I worked with the NIO for Warning, a savvy professional named Charles Allen. I also worked with Samuel Lewis and James Steinberg at Policy Planning in the State Department to arrange special briefings for Tony Lake; the NIC would lay out a problem, State Department planners would suggest options, and we would together assess possible consequences of different policy responses. All this took place without our crossing the red line between intelligence information and policy values.

A third goal was to open the process to take better advantage of sources outside the Intelligence Community. Every day I read a copy of the President's Daily Brief (PDB) prepared by the CIA's Directorate of Intelligence, and I was surprised how much of it I could have learned by reading *The Economist*, the *Financial Times*, or the *Washington Post*. Even before the age of the Internet, public or open-source intelligence was an important but undervalued resource. Understandably, there was an institutional bias toward things marked "secret." This did not mean that the nuggets of classified secrets were not important, but public sources helped to explain things by providing crucial context. I used to tell the analysts that open-source intelligence was like the picture on the cover of the box of a jigsaw puzzle. It often helped one figure out where a secret piece fit. And the secret pieces often solved an unfinished puzzle.

That is also why I wanted to balance the mix of NIOs between intelligence professionals and outsiders and wanted them all to participate in outside events and conferences. And finally, I endeavored to broaden the scope of our coverage to include a wide range of emerging global issues such as climate change and pandemics. I was also committed to having more women on board, and I hired Enid Schoettle from the Ford Foundation to fill a new role as NIO for Global Issues. I was pleased when the *Washington Post* published a story on August 2 that reported that the NIC had become "a powerhouse of heavyweights."

Japan and China

The NIC provided an unparalleled vantage point for some issues, but it was frustrating to go to meetings in the Situation Room at the White House and have to refrain from commenting on poorly thought through policies because intelligence officials are supposed to behave like good Victorian children, seen but not heard unless asked. I was particularly distressed by discussions of Japan as different agencies echoed campaign slogans in an effort to devise economic punishments without considering security issues like the threat from North Korea or the challenge of the rise of China. I had co-chaired a faculty study group at Harvard that concluded Japan was not a threat, and I invited my colleague Ezra Vogel to become NIO for East Asia and to prepare scenarios about possible future paths for China and Japan and the Asian balance of power.

The 1992 Clinton campaign had fought the election with the slogan "It's the economy, stupid," and Japan was cast as the largest threat. In April, Winston Lord, a friend and moderate who was Assistant Secretary of State for East Asia, chaired an interagency Deputies Committee to hammer out a policy. The small Situation Room was jam-packed, with twelve people at the table and fourteen others crowded along the walls. The economic agencies vied to show how tough they would be with Japan. The atmosphere was the same when I briefed the deputies again on April 21, except that the meeting had been moved to the larger Cordell Hull Room to accommodate the crowd. My Harvard friend Larry Summers, who was then Undersecretary of the Treasury, tried to set a reasonable general goal like asking Japan to cut its surplus to 1.5 percent of GDP and increase its imports by 8 per cent a year, but Commerce and the Special Trade Representative's (STR) office had the wind in their sails and focused on a variety of specific punitive measures. The mood was similar a month later when I briefed the principals, though we did at least graduate to the Roosevelt Room. As Michael Morrell, then a young analyst but later to become acting Director of the CIA, explained to me, this administration is "much more united on Japan than the previous one was." I thought that was too true and too bad.

In contrast, there was remarkably little attention being paid to China at that time. It was still recovering from the Tiananmen Square uprising and seen largely as a human rights problem. At a June meeting with

State Department's Policy Planning in Tony Lake's White House office, I described four possible futures for the East Asian balance of power in 2000: Chinese hegemony; China–Japan economic cooperation to the exclusion of the US; a conflictual local balance without the US; and the US maintaining the balance (which I estimated to be most likely). I wrote in my diary on June 19: "China will be much larger after 2010, but we can still have leverage if we join with Japan." But our Japan policy seemed to be on a track that would make that unlikely. From the NIC, I could point that out but I could not do much about it.

Russia

At first glance, relations with Russia seemed to be going well, though I remember feeling bemused when I joined CIA Director Woolsey for lunch with Yevgeny Primakov, head of Russian foreign intelligence (and later Prime Minister), in the CIA Headquarters. That could not have happened five years earlier. Strobe Talbott in the State Department and Nick Burns at the White House were both deeply knowledgeable about Russia and committed to a conciliatory policy. The US was providing aid and advisors to Russia. But the situation inside Russia was far from clear. We were receiving reports that Yeltsin was becoming unpopular and was succumbing to binge drinking. George Kolt, the NIO for Russia, told me he saw four possible Russian futures: pluralism, stagnation, disintegration, or dictatorship. He said the odds favored the first, but only if Yeltsin acted boldly. It took a while, but as we now know, we wound up with the fourth scenario.

I had a chance to judge the situation for myself when I was invited to accompany Summers and Bentsen on a Treasury trip to Moscow. My old friend from the Carter Administration, Tom Pickering, now ambassador to Russia, met us at the airport. He said that Yeltsin did not look so bad, but the economic situation was uncertain. At lunch at Spaso House the next day, the invited Russian dignitaries disagreed with each other on the economy and the success of privatization.

We met with Yeltsin in the Kremlin office where Gorbachev had recently reigned, with its green brocade walls, white panels, golden French-style furniture, and eight seats at a small table with red roses in the center. Yeltsin told Bentsen he needed a financial shot in the arm at a time of difficult politics and praised "his friend Bill" for providing more assistance than Bush. I was particularly focused on Yeltsin's face, tan but slightly puffy, and hands, which had no tremble as he jotted down notes. He did not appear debilitated, and that's how I reported it when I returned home. An interesting coda to the trip was a stop in Stockholm, where Carl Bildt, the wise and perceptive Swedish Prime Minister, talked about Russia's problems and its difficulties with Ukraine as he entertained us at a pleasant luncheon on a boat trip along a lake.

As we later learned, the Russian economy grew worse, suffering high inflation and corruption in the privatization process. When the Aspen Strategy Group met that summer, former Reagan official Harry Rowen speculated that China might swamp Russia in size in twenty years. Ambassador Vladimir Lukin said that ratification of the constitution was not going well, and the group around Yeltsin would only get 30 percent of any vote. Yeltsin was fighting with the Parliament, and on October 4 he settled it by shelling the parliament building. I remember a sense of shock when I visited Moscow a few months later and looked at the black smudges on the white parliament tower where the tank shells had penetrated the building.

Bosnia

Of all the issues on the agenda during that first year, 1993, none took up more time of high officials than the war in the former Yugoslavia. NIEs written in 1992 had predicted it, but the Bush Administration's attitude had been that "we have no dog in this fight." But the US *was* involved because our European allies had peacekeeping troops there under a UN flag; and televised pictures of Bosnian Serb atrocities against Muslims in Sarajevo put it squarely in the public eye every day. Even before Clinton, an August 1992 panel on Bosnia at the Aspen Institute had divided between Strobe Talbott and Daniel Schorr, who urged US intervention, and William Hyland, who opposed it. This was far from hubristic unilateralism.

The Clinton Administration did not want to put US troops on the ground, but did want to lift the UN arms embargo that prevented giving weapons to the Bosnian Muslims and to use NATO air power to strike the Bosnian Serb positions that were shelling Sarajevo. The

Europeans objected to a "lift and strike" strategy, however, because they feared the Serbs would then use European peacekeepers as hostages. I remember sitting in an intelligence meeting in April with Clinton in the Old Executive Office Building when the conversation went round and round. I was not altogether surprised when Matthew Nimetz, Counselor to the State Department, told me that he had "a two-foot file on Bosnia while most of the others are a few inches." As I noted in April: "Today a Situation Room meeting on North Korea was pre-empted by another meeting on Bosnia. And our NIEs were pessimistic about the situation improving."

In late May, I was invited to Zagreb to meet with Miroslav Tudjman, son of the president of Croatia and head of Croatian intelligence, whom I had met when he visited Langley. After consultations in Zagreb, we flew to Split on the lovely Croatian coast and visited towns and villages that had been damaged by Serbian forces. He asked me if I would like to continue to Mostar in Bosnia, and we flew in an old Russian helicopter before transferring to a car driven by Bosnian Croats without ever stopping for the border. No passports necessary.

Mostar, known for its graceful bridge that was toppled in the war, lies in the deep green valley of the Neretva River. As we approached it from a road in the mountains, I could see that the high-rise buildings had been devastated in the previous year's battle with Serbs. Now, Croats and Muslims were fighting for control. We stopped at a bend in a pass overlooking the city but were warned not to linger for fear of snipers. When we arrived at the Bosnian Croat headquarters, housed in a bunker in an old bank lined with sloped timbers and sandbags, I was greeted by a General Petković. He said he had just called his Muslim counterpart (whom he had known before they all began fighting) and they shared the information that each had just lost three soldiers in the latest skirmish. Sounds of rifle shots, machine guns, and the occasional low thump of rocket-propelled grenades could still be heard.

I was then driven to a lunch on the terrace of an inn next to a trout stream in a peaceful village. The contrast was overwhelming. I asked my escort, Colonel Lucić, what the fighting was all about. His reply: "land and control." I then asked him how he could tell his Muslim and Serb enemies from fellow Croats when they were in the city. His reply: "It used to be difficult if you did not know their names, but now it is easy because of the insignia," and he smiled as he pointed to the badge on the shoulder of his uniform. I marveled about this as we drove back over the mountains to Split and flew back to Zagreb. There, I discovered that the American headlines were dominated that day by the cost of Clinton's haircuts and problems of the White House travel agency. (I did not include that contrast in the trip report I wrote later upon return to Washington.)

Southeast Asia

In August, Senator William Cohen, the genial Republican from Maine who later became Secretary of Defense, asked me to accompany him and Senate colleagues on a congressional delegation to Southeast Asia. Our first stop was Kuala Lumpur, where I was impressed by the modern skyscrapers. Ambassador Wolfe met us and stressed three points: high economic growth, successful management of ethnic conflict, and modernization of Islam. But he worried about the spread of corruption. In meetings with the smart young Minister of Finance Ibrahim Anwar, we were impressed that he was not worried about Chinese military expansion, and felt the best response was economic integration. Malaysia clearly did not want to isolate China, and a Cold War policy of containment would not work. On Bosnia, he complained that we were not doing enough for the Muslims. We heard similar themes during our call on Prime Minister Mohamed Mahathir, where I was struck by the number of model planes he kept in his office and his equal number of complaints about the Western press.

After touring microchip factories, we flew from Kuala Lumpur to Singapore, where the US had a few hundred military personnel on regular visits consistent with a policy of "places, not bases." Singapore was attractive, clean, orderly, and prosperous. George Yeo, the Minister of Information, defended their apolitical elections and strict limits on the opposition and the press. I told my friend Kishore Mahbubani (later their ambassador to the UN) that Singapore reminded me of Plato's Republic ruled by guardians who limited political freedom but produced safety, relatively honest government, and prosperous conditions. I said I worried that in the long term they might also be limiting creativity.

I once mentioned this Platonic analogy to the founding father Lee Kuan Yew, whom I knew over the course of many years, but he called it an exaggeration. I suggested that he allow more freedom of speech by establishing the equivalent of a Hyde Park Corner where all voices could be heard. He did eventually, but in a very controlled Singaporean fashion and without loosening the extremely restrictive libel laws. When our delegation called on him in the Astana Palace (the former British governor's residence), Lee gave us a fascinating discourse on the rights of the individual versus the rights of society, and the relative decline of the US and the prospects for our recovery. He wanted a US presence to balance China, but worried about whether Congress and public opinion would sustain it. He wanted an American century that included rather than excluded China. People who later criticized Clinton for not isolating China seem to forget that we would have had few allies in the effort.

Our last stop was Hong Kong with its spectacular towers and harbor views, where we called on the British governor. We also met with Martin Lee, a heroic voice for democracy, but it seemed that most of his fellow citizens cared more about money and not alienating China. We discussed how long Hong Kong's relative freedom would last after it passed from a British colony to Chinese sovereignty in July 1997. We now know that the Chinese formula "one country, two systems" was only good for about two decades.

Europe and NATO

In September, I flew to London and Brussels. In London, Sir Rodric Braithwaite invited me to sit in on a meeting of the Joint Intelligence Committee, the British counterpart to the NIC. There were eighteen people at the table and they discussed three estimates that were only three pages each, reinforcing my view that ours were too long. On the other hand, Sir Robert Wade-Gery told me that British intelligence involved too much "seat of the pants" and lacks the American analysis. Since we regularly read their products and they read ours, there were benefits in complementarity. One of the things that struck me was how close British and American intelligence agencies were. I remember a dinner at the British embassy in Washington a few months later where some guests were bemoaning the decline of "the special relationship" between the two countries. I said that it did not look that way from inside the Intelligence Community.

After the meeting, Braithwaite took me to lunch at the Reform Club, one of the grand London clubs. On Bosnia, he said British public opinion would not support more intervention. He felt that air strikes would not do much good and lifting the arms embargo would simply mean more deaths. He advocated containment, humanitarian relief, and avoiding a quagmire. As for the future of Europe, he thought Germany was too weak rather than too strong, and hoped for better Franco-British security cooperation that understood the relationship of force to diplomacy. On NATO, he favored expanding membership to include Poland, Hungary, and Czechoslovakia.

In Brussels, by contrast, the French official Jean-Marie Guéhenno (who later became a high UN official) said that France was skeptical of NATO expansion, and François Heisbourg, the distinguished French analyst, told me he did not expect NATO to even exist at the end of the decade. At an all-day meeting in the residence of American Ambassador Robert Hunter, there was a wide range of opinions. Manfred Wörner, the Secretary General, felt NATO should go ahead on Bosnia or it would lose credibility. There was a general feeling that UN peacekeeping had failed, but many wondered whether NATO would do any better. After all, in the Bosnian ethnic civil war, the combatants were mixed like a marble cake rather than an easily divisible layer cake. As for NATO expansion, former ambassador and general John Galvin thought NATO should admit three new members, but Hunter and Chairman of the Joint Chiefs of Staff John Shalikashvili thought it was premature. They preferred a more open structure called Partnership for Peace (PFP), which allowed defense coordination without membership. This was also my view, but I could not advocate it. Informed opinion was in disarray. In other words, all was not quiet on the Western front.

The Somalia debacle

Nor on the Southern front. In Mogadishu, Somali warlords had been attacking the UN peacekeepers distributing humanitarian aid, and the US forces were becoming increasingly involved in support of the UN. An intelligence assessment in late September 1993 warned against personalizing the struggle with the warlord Mohamed Aidid, but on October 4, a Blackhawk helicopter was shot down in Mogadishu; nineteen American soldiers were killed, and a dead American sergeant was dragged through the streets before cheering crowds – all repeatedly played on American cable television. In December 1992, when President Bush had sent US forces to support UN peacekeepers feeding starving Somalis, the humanitarian mission was very popular, but after "Black Hawk Down" American public opinion in support of humanitarian missions turned out to be a mile wide and an inch deep. Clinton resisted congressional calls for immediate withdrawal, but announced they would occur within six months.

Some in the press called Somalia an intelligence failure, but it was not. Scowcroft later told me that Bush had read the intelligence warnings but planned to get out and turn it over to the UN. When this turned out to be impossible, American forces became more deeply involved. I remember participating in an early December postmortem by the President's Foreign Intelligence Advisory Board, which concluded that the intelligence warnings were correct but unheeded. Les Aspin became the scapegoat and, on December 15, resigned from his dream job. He died a year and a half later. He deserved better.

One spillover from the battle of Mogadishu came a week later when the US ship *Harlan County*, bringing humanitarian assistance to Haiti, turned around rather than docking after rioting in the streets of Port au Prince. The military leader Raoul Cédras, who had agreed at an August meeting in New York to allow the elected leader Jean-Bertrand Aristide to return, had decided that he no longer needed to do so. This led to sanctions that many felt would lead to greater emigration, and the situation was complicated by intelligence analyses that questioned Aristide's mental stability.

Nuclear North Korea

By November 1993, my attention was absorbed by a different crisis. Our analysts had concluded that North Korea had misled IAEA inspectors and was proceeding with their nuclear weapons program. In mid-November, the analysts estimated that there was a 50:50 chance that North Korea had extracted enough plutonium for two bombs. I was summoned to the White House for a meeting with Deputy National Security Advisor Sandy Berger and the Vice President's advisor Leon Fuerth, who were worried that potential leaks of the estimate would put another crisis on their already crowded plate. They complained that "a 50:50 estimate in your world will have big consequences in ours." I said we could not change the estimate but that they could point to the dissent from the State Department's Bureau of Intelligence and Research. I reported the conversation to Woolsey, who backed me up on not changing the estimate but said we could limit its distribution. However, with multiple copies already distributed to Congress, other agencies, and liaison representatives, the situation was not promising. By December 3, the *Washington Post* ran a story about the estimate. I then spent two and a half hours testifying in a closed session of the House Intelligence Committee about what the evidence was behind the differences within the Intelligence Community.

On the policy front, the State Department had hopes for diplomacy, but my friend Ash Carter, Assistant Secretary of Defense, thought that, even though it was worth trying to negotiate, there was only a 15–20 percent chance that North Korea would give up its program. The policy result was that Robert Gallucci, an able diplomat, was appointed special coordinator for North Korea. In the intelligence world, the events launched discussions of how broadly to distribute estimates and trade-offs between secret intelligence and political information in a democracy.

We also began a study of nuclear terrorism, an issue of concern since earlier in the year, when terrorists had tried to topple the World Trade Center in New York and shot and killed two CIA employees outside headquarters in Virginia. In December, I went with a team to the Department of Energy's amazing Pantex plant in Amarillo, Texas to see how nuclear weapons were dismantled and fissile material is stored. I have never seen such tight security!

Moving from truth to power

I began 1994 in Intelligence but ended it in the Pentagon. The year started in Hilton Head, South Carolina, where Molly and I attended a weekend event organized by Philip and Linda Lader. Bill and Hillary Clinton also attended, and, despite the tight Secret Service security, I chatted with Bill on the beach. He told me he had shot an 84 in his golf game, and I told him I would keep it secret (until now).

I was soon back in the whirlwind of air travel, setting off on a round-the-world trip with Lloyd Bentsen in a Boeing 707 that used to be Air Force One. Our first stop was Moscow, where Clinton was attending a summit with Yeltsin. I talked to Clinton at a Spaso House reception and went to his press conference in the Kremlin, but Bentsen's focus was on the economy and its political effects. Anatoly Chubais told us that he was pleased with the progress in privatization. I wrote in my diary that the odds seemed at best 5:4 that reform would work, but much would depend on personalities and accidents of history. Some close observers in Moscow told me I was too optimistic, and they doubted the Russians could dismantle so many big state industries. They also worried that reform could be driven off course by a crisis brewing over Crimea or Ukrainian nuclear weapons. Later, I toured the new American embassy, where whole floors were being torn apart and reconstructed because of listening devices Russia had implanted during its construction. When I left Moscow, I noted "that I was more optimistic than I was a year ago. They seem to have survived more crises than I expected, but much will depend on time horizons and path dependency."

From Moscow, we flew to Indonesia. In Jakarta, General Sumitro told us that stability was the key to opening up political discourse. He said that Korea and Taiwan became more open when their per capita incomes rose above $6,000. AlthoughIndonesia's was only $750, he expected this to improve given modern communications and no external threat. He did not see a Chinese military threat, but was concerned about their growing influence, which he said "only the US can counter." On our next stop in Thailand, Prime Minister Chuan also seemed relatively unconcerned about China.

From Bangkok we flew to Beijing. The Joint US–China Economic Commission was pretty much scripted in advance, but our meeting with President Jiang Zemin turned out much better. He was sophisticated and engaged in a more interesting discussion of human rights than I had expected. Ambassador Stapleton Roy, a great China expert, later described the collective leadership as divided, but hoped that, as prosperity increased, they would be likely to manage conflicts in our relationship without too much chauvinism. He foresaw a period of fast growth, decentralization, corruption, and a moderate foreign policy, but doubted that China could follow the Taiwan or Korea model because of the difference in scale and the difficulty of governing such a large country with many backward peasant areas. A Chinese professor whom I saw at the Academy of Social Sciences confirmed that political conditions were improving. The economic transformation was also impressive, and, when we visited Shanghai, I was amazed at the amount of construction since my visit a decade earlier – and also the heavy smog that accompanied the progress.

Visit to Shanghai with Secretary of the Treasury Lloyd Bentsen, 1994

On our last stop in Tokyo, I saw my former students David and Cheryl Sanger, as well as Tom Friedman, who were all there for the *New York Times*. They described Japanese politics as unsettled, with multiple challengers to Prime Minister Hosokawa. I also saw Ambassador Fritz Mondale at the Okura Hotel where I was staying, and he complained about the heavy-handed approach of American trade lawyers. I agreed. An STR lawyer once said to me: "There is no such thing as too much pressure on Japan."

After flying from Yokota to Elmendorf in Alaska and finally arriving at Andrews Air Force Base, I realized that I had been around the world in twelve days. That beats eighty, but still seemed too long. Nonetheless, a few days later, I departed for the WEF in Davos, where my status as a government official gave me access to an inner circle that included leaders like Russian Prime Minister Viktor Chernomyrdin, Yasser Arafat (who told me "we will need you"), and Aleksander Kwaśniewski of Poland, who told me that NATO's Partnership for Peace proposal could be "an acceptable compromise." This trip only lasted four days, but when I reached Dulles Airport, the car did not take me home but whisked me to the office, where the piles of paper on my desk were neatly arranged but all gloomy, particularly on North Korea.

Estimating the future

The next two months were marked by less travel, but more time analyzing and planning about major long-term problems. On China, we worked with the State Department to estimate what it might look like in 2000 and discussed the results at a White House meeting with National Security Advisor Tony Lake. The experts were surprisingly optimistic, predicting a 95 percent chance of high economic growth, a 10 percent chance of fragmentation, a 20 percent chance of increased authoritarianism, and a 90 percent chance of a non-aggressive foreign policy. This was at a time when China was rebuffing Secretary of State Christopher's efforts to discuss human rights during his visit to Beijing.

The other major concern was nuclear weapons and proliferation, because of the worry about North Korea and about "loose nukes" after the breakup of the Soviet Union. George Kolt described Crimea as a potential tinderbox, and many people said Moscow would not allow Ukraine to keep its nuclear weapons. An NPT Review Conference was scheduled for 1995 and visits to Sandia and Los Alamos Laboratories confirmed that verification of a CTB would be difficult for low-yield explosions. I was also briefed on safeguards, satellite detectors, and different dimensions of biological warfare. My guess was that there would be about ten nuclear weapons states in 2000 (which turned out to be close to the actual number: nine).

I also decided and got permission to write an article – eventually published in *Foreign Affairs* with the title "Peering into the Future." I described the work of the NIC and, more broadly, the importance, limits, and prospects for estimative (rather than current reporting) intelligence. I argued that we did not have a crystal ball and there was no single future, but multiple potential futures. Our job was not to predict the future, but to describe for policymakers the relative likelihoods of alternative futures, explaining our assumptions and internal differences in the text (not a footnote) in a way that sensitized policymakers to low-probability events and unexpected outcomes.

Changing my future

At the beginning of April, my personal plans were disrupted by a call from John Deutch, now Deputy Secretary of Defense, telling me that Secretary of Defense William Perry wanted me to become Assistant Secretary for International Security Affairs. That bureau, once headed by the legendary Paul Nitze, was known as the "Pentagon's little State Department" responsible for defense relations with all countries except the former Soviet Union. I discussed it with Molly and was torn. On the one hand, I loved my job chairing the NIC, but, on the other, this would give me a chance to change policy. The gnawing question was why write about the future of Asia when I could actually do something about it, particularly what I viewed as our misguided policy toward Japan. Within a week, I told Deutch that I was leaning to yes, and he warned that vetting and Senate confirmation could take months (which was a correct prediction). I explained my decision to Woolsey, who was understanding and later presented me with the Intelligence Community's highest award. Barbara Acosta wisely warned me to tell the NIOs before it leaked to the press. We had a good team, and that morning staff meeting was one of my most difficult. Barbara was right: the *Washington Post* carried the story in May. Ironically, at about the same time, Neil Rudenstine, president of Harvard, told me the Kennedy School deanship was coming open and asked if I would take it on. I said no.

In the meantime, my life at the NIC remained full. After a NATO airstrike on their artillery at Goražde, Bosnian Serb forces took UN peacekeepers as hostages, as had been feared. My European friends had mixed reactions: from Germany, Uwe Nerlich said escalate to a full air response but, from France, Thierry de Montbrial said stay out of a mess. I spoke with Robert McNamara, who was writing a book on mistakes in

Receiving the Distinguished Service Medal for NIC performance from James Woolsey, CIA, 1994

Vietnam, and he said the problem looked familiar; and he warned that once you carry out major strikes "you own the problem."

Somalia and Bosnia had a spillover effect on the Clinton Administration, which reversed its early enthusiasm for UN peacekeeping and, on May 6, issued a restrictive Presidential Decision 25. A month later, I wrote in my diary that I thought the pendulum had swung too far against peacekeeping and that we could do more to help the UN limit the genocide in Rwanda. But "twice burnt, twice shy!" A friend in the White House later told me that the decision-making on Rwanda was excessively timid and he did not remember there having been any principals' meetings in the Situation Room on the subject. Unipolarity was still uncomfortable at that point. Years later, Clinton confessed that Rwanda was one of his failures, but there was little public or congressional support for action.

In early June, I flew to Europe to make a presentation at a European-American Bilderberg meeting in Helsinki. En route, I stopped in Tallinn, which then looked like a Soviet provincial capital with spots of bright Scandinavia thrown in. Our embassy was so small that we shared a building with the British. The Estonians said that they hoped the last 3,000 Russian troops would be gone by August. At the meeting in Helsinki, Kissinger criticized the timidity of the PFP program, while Hunter and I defended it. Pickering told me that he thought Russia was muddling through and that Chernomyrdin was doing better as Prime Minister than expected. At dinner I was seated with Finnish Prime Minister Esko Aho and Lord Carrington, both of whom were concerned about Russia–Ukraine relations, but not alarmed.

When I returned to DC, the focus was again on North Korea. A visit by Jimmy Carter had forestalled planning for sanctions or an airstrike, but in July Kim Il Sung suddenly died and was succeeded by his son Kim Jung Il – an oxymoronic "Communist monarchy" later continued by grandson Kim Jung Un. There was talk of negotiated solutions such as trading heavy fuel oil for a freeze in their program. I had never been optimistic about the Kims giving up their nuclear program, though I had hopes that delays and limits might be possible.

I used the fourth of July to take another vacation camping and fishing in the Alaskan wilderness. Again, a float plane dropped us off at a remote lake, and we inflated two rafts that would be our only transport for 100 miles down a river with no other humans. The first day we covered twenty miles, passing caribou, moose, bears, and eagles, and avoiding fallen trees or "sweepers" that threatened to sink our rafts. We camped on a gravel bar, but the driftwood was wet, and I struggled to start a fire while the boys set up the tents. I finally split enough sticks with my knife to get dry tinder and then a large enough fire to warm ourselves and grill steaks. It's funny how simple things like a camp fire suddenly loom larger than Bosnia or North Korea. Camping in Alaska gives a totally different perspective on what matters in life: survival, warmth, a dry tent, fish, etc. A refreshing change and a good reminder that the power of nature is greater than the power of Washington!

6

The Clinton Years: The Pentagon

Back in Washington, I continued to manage the work of the NIC and help my successor Christine Williams get established. I also had to prepare for my new position in the Pentagon. I met with the two colonels who would be my military assistants and with Fred Smith, the able career principal deputy who oversaw the six deputy assistant secretaries responsible for various regions. In addition, I wanted to establish a new Policy and Analysis Group for planning and recruited Kurt Campbell to fill the job. I also had to learn a new bureaucratic jargon and try to understand a vast organization that made the State Department and Intelligence bureaucracies look simple in comparison. Richard Armitage, who held my job in Republican administrations, offered invaluable guidance at the time, for which I was incredibly grateful.

First, I had to get confirmed by the Senate, and that involved office calls on key senators. They could not have been more different. Most courtesy calls are pro forma, but John McCain was a sheer delight as we became involved in a substantive conversation about Korea and about the defense budget. When an aide opened the door and poked his head in after twenty minutes, McCain waved him off and continued the discussion for nearly an hour. My call on Strom Thurmond, the Republican from South Carolina who was in his 90s (a year older than my father), was totally different, as he read some questions from a card prepared by his staff. My hearings before the Senate Armed Services Committee, presided over by Sam Nunn, were uneventful, but Senator Kempthorne put a hold on all Pentagon nominees until the administration accepted his position on an extraneous environmental dispute in Idaho. Then the Senate adjourned for its August recess. Finally, I was unanimously confirmed on September 15, 1994, and sworn in the following day. What an odd system we have!

My second day on the job was memorable for a scene that could have come from the script of a Hollywood comedy. I went to the Secretary of Defense's huge office for a meeting with Greek Defense Minister Gerasimos Arsenis. I was informed that William Perry was caught in traffic coming back from the Hill and I should substitute for him in the protocol of greeting Arsenis on the front steps of the Pentagon with an honor guard. I went to the River Entrance and stood in place, and the honor guard stood at attention, but the gate had waved in the wrong black limousine and out stepped a surprised Japanese Ambassador Kuriyama, who exclaimed "What are you doing here?" We laughed and I told the staff "Oh well, try again." They did; we repeated the ceremony and I escorted Arsenis up to Perry's office and began the meeting. What a way to start.

The rest of the work was less humorous. A normal day began with a 6 a.m. run in Rock Creek Park near our little old house in Georgetown, followed by my reverse commute to the Pentagon, where I had reserved parking near the river entrance. I began each day with an early staff meeting with all my deputies. Among the many "routine" tasks were meetings with visiting foreigners, overseeing the offices that managed foreign military sales, attending interagency meetings, testifying before Congress, pleading for funds for International Military Education and Training (a great investment in soft power), and working with the domestic and foreign press. I was not surprised when Walt Slocomb once told me that 80 percent of the policy papers that go to the Secretary of Defense came from International Security Affairs. Once a month, I met with Ted McNamara, my State Department counterpart, and we sorted out the numerous smaller issues where friction had arisen between the two bureaucracies. My relations with Ted were always amicable, and Perry was such a gentleman that he had instructed us not to trespass on State Department jurisdiction whenever possible.

Much of my job could be filed under the heading "alliance maintenance." For example, I was the Defense Department's representative on Air Force One when the president visited Ottawa – mostly alliance maintenance. We also had visits from the defense ministers of Britain, France, and Germany, whom we invited to watch live fire demonstrations at Fort Stewart, Georgia and then held a planning meeting at Key West, the location of Harry Truman's winter White House. In addition to discussing NATO policy, my memory is of a humorous taste-off as the ministers offered examples of their soldiers' boxed meals ready to eat.

The French won. And later, we had to mollify the Italians, who objected to the whole idea of a meeting without them.

I also had to work with my deputies to meet Perry's request for defense strategies for each of six regions. On Europe, there were differences between the Defense and the State Departments. My deputy for Europe Joseph Kruzel, a wonderful Kennedy School graduate, had worked to develop the concept of a Partnership for Peace as a way station for defense cooperation before possible NATO membership. Dick Holbrooke, then Assistant Secretary of State for Europe, held meetings in his office on European security. I outlined an idea of European security as resembling concentric circles, with NATO members at the core benefiting from Article 5 guarantees, surrounded by PFP countries that would benefit from the penumbra of weaker Article 4 assurances, and an outer circle of the Organization for European Security and Cooperation that could negotiate confidence-building measures with Russia. But the White House and Holbrooke wanted to move more quickly.

Japan was another interagency problem, but, unlike the "see but don't touch" approach of the NIC, I could now try to shape policy. I was in charge of producing an East Asia Strategy Report (EASR), as well as attending interagency meetings. For example, at a deputies committee meeting that focused on limiting imports of auto parts and other punitive measures, I reminded the others of the security implications. And when I accompanied Deutch to the White House cabinet room for a discussion of Japanese trade, the tone was similar, and again I made my security points. I was pleased that Clinton referred to them in his summation.

I also accompanied Perry to a meeting of the Defense Science Board, where he laid out his priorities as Russia, Central Europe, Bosnia, and North Korea, yet complained that much of his time was being absorbed by a tier-two issue like Haiti. Operation Uphold Democracy was a military intervention to remove the military regime installed by the 1991 Haitian coup d'état that overthrew the elected President Jean-Bertrand Aristide. The operation, authorized by a UN Security Council Resolution, succeeded in its initial steps on September 16 as the 82nd airborne division was in the air, and a delegation of Jimmy Carter, Sam Nunn, and Colin Powell persuaded the military junta to step down. But that meant that we now owned the problem, and American troops were in Haiti again.

Around the world

Struggles in DC were interrupted by travel. I was accustomed to overseas travel but had no idea how much I would wind up doing for the Pentagon. At the end of 1995, I counted visits to fifty-three countries in fifty-two weeks, much of it accompanied by pomp and ceremony. On one tour of Central Europe with Perry, the airport bands and honor guards of the different countries became indistinguishable. Whereas my travel for the State and Intelligence Departments had more often been individual and on commercial flights, now it was large delegations, large military planes, and helicopters. Fortunately, on some of the trips, the "SecDef" used a giant 747 that carried emergency communications equipment in case of nuclear war. It had a vast reel of antenna wire in the belly that could trail behind the plane in an emergency, and we sat at crew positions that each faced a screen. But the good news was that we also had access to the crew bunks, which, although simple, were horizontal.

Two weeks after taking the job, I accompanied Perry on an eleven-day trip around the world from Andrews Air Force Base to the Middle East to China, Hawaii, and back to DC. The trip to China had been long planned, but after Saddam Hussein moved two divisions to the southern Iraq border, Perry decided to add Saudi Arabia and Kuwait to the itinerary.

After the usual airport reception in Jeddah, a motorcade escorted us to King Fahd's palace, where he awaited us in a long chamber with robed princes seated along the sides. The king spoke for an hour and a half (through interpreters) about Saudi history and security. After an overnight flight, I had to pinch my legs and do isomorphics to stay awake. When we finally broke for a visit to the men's room, I reminded Perry of the key talking points we wanted to get across when our turn came to speak. He smiled and said "What makes you think we will have a turn?" He was right. After more monologue, the meeting ended and we were invited to a huge banquet at the palace of Prince Sultan, the Defense Minister, where the Saudis made clear that they wanted no ground troops, but did want air support. Afterwards, during the motor caravan back to our hotel I noted that the speedometer clocked 115 miles per hour. Fortunately, no camel strayed onto the road. I finally got to bed at 2 a.m., exhausted.

In Kuwait, we visited our troops and ate MREs (meals ready to eat) in a mess hall, before changing into suits for a call on the Minister of Defense. Then back to khakis for helicopter flights to a Patriot Air Defense battery in the desert, and a visit to the USS *Tripoli* hosting marines off-shore. Then back to Kuwait City to put on a suit again for a call on the Emir. The Kuwaitis housed us in a palatial suite with enormous welcome baskets of fruit and flowers, but I had no time to enjoy it. We were soon in the air to China.

In Beijing, we had another airport ceremony, and were housed in the Diaoyutai State Guesthouse near the forbidden city, where we met Foreign Minister Qian Qichen. Winston Lord, Stanley Roth (from the NSC) and I then met with Vice Minister Liu at the foreign ministry to discuss North Korea. He indicated Chinese displeasure with Pyongyang, but said the feeling was mutual and Chinese influence was limited. Later, Perry met Defense Minister General Chi Haotian at an imposing room in the Great Hall of the People and discussed military to military contacts, controlling missile proliferation, nuclear proliferation, and Korea. Chi was a crusty old general who had fought against us in Korea and I enjoyed discussing it with him at the banquet that night. Less successful was a meeting with Prime Minister Li Peng, where Senators Nunn and Warner raised the issue of human rights. Nunn handed Li Peng a letter with names of concern but Li angrily refused to take it. The next day we flew to Wuhan to meet President Jiang Zemin. When human rights came up, Jiang's style was different. He diverted it with the comment that "East and West cultures are like music on the ancient bells of Wuhan." We were then treated to a twenty-six-course banquet, which included scorpions and rendered Manchurian toad fat. Jiang was right about cultural differences!

On to Manila and Leyte, where the temperature was 102 degrees, crowds were dense, and a re-enactment of General MacArthur's landing in October 1944 was planned. In another scene that could have been scripted by a Hollywood comedy writer, helicopters swooped over the beach spraying the guests and banquet food with sand, and the person re-enacting MacArthur stepped out of a landing craft and fell into the surf. They had to do it all over again for the cameras. Fortunately, a lunch on President Ramos's yacht was more successful, and after lunch I went with Admiral Macke to visit USS *Belleau Wood*, which was anchored offshore. With 2,000 marines, 1,000 sailors, and a 400-bed hospital on board, it was a powerful American presence. Our navy was a strong reminder of the American century in the Pacific.

In Seoul, we went to the Blue House to call on President Kim Young-sam and I was pleased to be greeted by two of my former Kennedy School students working there, one of whom was Ban Ki-moon who later went on to become Secretary General of the UN. Perry reassured the president that we were not planning to reduce our 28,000 troops near the demilitarized zone. On the plane to Tokyo, I called Bob Gallucci to learn more about the deal he was negotiating with the North Koreans, though the details of financing had not yet been worked out.

In Tokyo, Perry met with Defense Minister Tamazawa and Foreign Minister Kono, and I went to our embassy where I met with Japanese officials on an agenda to strengthen bilateral defense relations. On the way back across the Pacific, we stopped in Honolulu for a meeting at CINCPAC headquarters, a visit to the battleship USS *Arizona*, sunk in 1941 and still slowly oozing oil, and a celebratory dinner hosted by Admiral Macke. I was now beginning to understand why some people called the world "an American empire," but I considered that overstated. Our presence and influence were global – but far from total. Just ask Pyongyang.

Clinton's trip to the Middle East

I was back in the office for one day, when I was told I would be the Pentagon's representative on President Clinton's trip to the Middle East, starting on October 25, 1994. Presidential travel is yet another story, with more staff, more press, more pomp and circumstance – and more time waiting around. My role would not become important until we reached the Persian Gulf, where the Department of Defense's equities were greatest, but at the early stops in Israel, Damascus, and Jordan, I was no more valuable than a potted palm. Nonetheless, it allowed me to glean information from our defense attachés, and to attend interesting ceremonies such as the signing of the Israeli–Jordan peace treaty at Aqaba, and Clinton's speech to the Jordanian Parliament in Amman, when he pledged respect for Islam. In Jerusalem, I had a corner room in the King David Hotel overlooking the old city and went with a group of senators to hear Clinton give another good speech at the Knesset.

Trip to the Persian Gulf, 1995

On Air Force One to Kuwait, work began as I briefed Clinton in his office at the front of the plane. We then changed clothes to attend Clinton's talk to the troops at Liberty site in the desert, then changed again to meet with the Emir and then fly to King Khalid City in Saudi Arabia. Once again, there was a lot of waiting around. We finally reboarded Air Force One around 2 a.m. I was preparing to sleep, but Clinton came back to the compartment where the officials and senators were sitting and wanted to talk politics. He was optimistic about the coming midterm elections, and described several races that he expected to be Democratic victories. But "even a pro can be wrong": the 1994 election was when the Republican Party not only won but turned right with the so-called "Gingrich revolution."

At Andrews Air Force base, Fred Smith greeted me with papers that needed my signature and the bad news that my father was in terminal decline. I flew to see him in the hospital in Orlando where his bed had a sign "do not resuscitate." The next week, I accompanied Perry to an "unofficial meeting" with Taiwan Defense Minister Benjamin Liu. Because we had no formal diplomatic relations, the session was held in a room at the Four Seasons Hotel near our house in Georgetown. Molly met me there to tell me that my father had died. On Friday, November 4, 1994, I had the odd experience of picking up the *New York Times* and finding myself quoted in a front-page story on Saudi Arabia, while my father's obituary appeared on page 33. I wept.

East Asia and Japan

A week later, I was in the air traveling to Japan again, but this time I led the delegation, and it was about my priority issue. US–Japan relations were at low point, economic friction was high, and many in both Tokyo and Washington regarded the military alliance as a historical relic now that the Cold War was over. A Japanese commission had raised the possibility of relying on the UN rather than the US for security. I regarded this as a mistake given the rise of China and the problem of North Korea. I felt that the US could better engage China if we first repaired the relationship with Japan. The logic was simple. In a three-country balance of power, it is better to be part of the two than isolated as the one.

A chance to shift our policy in East Asia was one of the major reasons I had changed my job and it was also the reason that the first regional strategy report was about East Asia. A first draft was now ready, and I used that for the timing of the trip. I thought we should consult the Japanese before it went final. Japan had complained of inadequate consultation and the feeling that they did not know whom to call when they picked up the phone to Washington. The situation was complicated by the fact that Japan had a new socialist Prime Minister, Tomiichi Murayama, who came from a party that had long been cool toward the American alliance.

I wanted to press ahead with reaffirming the alliance, but not so fast as to create a backlash in Tokyo. I asked Gayle von Eckartsberg, who had been stationed in Tokyo and spoke Japanese, to join me as a special assistant at the Pentagon and manage my press relations with Japan. When I gave an interview that pressed their bureaucracy too hard given their political situation, she would alert me, and I would slow down. Otherwise, I would press forward, as I did with an interview with the

Japanese daily newspaper *Nikkei Shimbun* on the eve of my trip. I was also helped by the experienced counsel of Ezra Vogel at the NIC, and career officials of the State Department like Rust Deming and others. I later replaced my deputy for East Asia with Kurt Campbell, head of my planning and analysis group. At that point Kurt knew little about Asia but he knew what I was thinking, and he knew how to get things done. Subsequently, he went on to become a leading figure in American Asia policy.

After a session with Ambassador Mondale and General Peter Pace, the head of US forces in Japan, I spent the next few days in Tokyo meeting with a wide range of Japanese in and out of government. My message to all was the centrality of the US–Japan alliance for stability in East Asia after the Cold War and the potential destabilizing challenges of China, North Korea, and Russia. My *Nikkei* interview had prepared the ground and I gave other press interviews in Tokyo that Ezra told me went well. When I met with government officials, I covered bilateral issues and suggested a work program leading up to a presidential visit and a declaration the following autumn. When we sat in the official conference room, with its green felt tablecloth, little national flags, and microphones, the officials were cautious given the politics in Tokyo, but at night several took me out for a drink, and their concerns went to the fundamentals. How much could they trust us? As the Chinese market grew larger, wouldn't we abandon Japan for China? I answered no, because Japan was a democracy and was not a threat. It seemed to work.

Returning to Washington, I had to do what the Japanese call "nemiwashi," or root binding, to secure the new policy at home, first explaining it up my chain of command to Slocomb, Deutch, and Perry, and then debriefing my trip to a meeting at the State Department with Winston Lord and Stanley Roth of the NSC. I also called on Ambassador Kuriyama, and on Richard Armitage, who reported that his network was already abuzz with positive reactions. That evening at a dinner at Kay Graham's house for Israeli Prime Minister Rabin, I managed to bend the ears of a few congressional guests about my trip to Japan.

As 1995 began, one of the major tasks was to complete what the Japanese press called the "Nye Initiative." At a January deputies committee in the Old Executive Office Building, which Sandy Berger chaired, Winston Lord and I made the case for a more balanced approach, taking security into greater account. I argued that linking defense to trade as a bargaining chip would hurt our long-term interests on stability in Asia while failing to solve our trade deficit. The deputies from Commerce and STR argued that this would be a policy reversal from the decision to put the economy first, and the press would notice.

They were right. After a speech to the Japan Society in New York, my arguments were quoted in the *New York Times* and *The Economist* as signs of a divided administration. However, I never felt the divisions were unbridgeable. On May 11, editor Fareed Zakaria had called to offer me a chance to publish an article in *Foreign Affairs* to be paired with one they had already accepted from Chalmers Johnson, a California professor and noted Japan trade hawk. The problem was I would have to get it to Fareed within two weeks. Was that possible? I got up at 4 a.m., dictated much of it to be typed up and sent around that morning. I had to fly to a CENTCOM conference in Tampa, but I discussed it with Lord, and accepted his suggestions. I then worked the phones with Laura Tyson and Mike Froman at the National Economic Council in the White House. They were initially reluctant but agreed to clear it if I removed some numbers and softened some comments for tactical reasons. It was published in *Foreign Affairs* as "East Asia: The Case for Deep Engagement."

The following year, Taiwanese President Lee Teng-hui shook up the region by announcing that he would visit the US to make a private trip to Cornell, and this launched what has been called the third Taiwan Strait crisis. China regarded it as a violation of the One China policy, and protested vigorously, eventually firing missiles off the shore of Taiwan; the US responded early in 1996 by sending an aircraft carrier to the area. In the first stages, I received visits from the Chinese defense attaché to protest the visit. The Chinese said they would break off military to military contacts.

September 1, 1995, was the commemoration of the fiftieth anniversary of the end of World War II, with a large international ceremony in Honolulu, Hawaii. Perry hosted an elaborate dinner for the Chinese delegate, General Li Xilin, who came on strong over Taiwan but proved willing to discuss other issues like proliferation and CTB. The next day at Wheeler Field, I sat on a dais behind Perry and Shali and listened to Clinton deliver a good speech acknowledging Japanese Prime Minister

Murayama's apology. We watched 7,000 troops pass in review and, later, from the roof of Fort DeRussy, we watched an equally impressive parade of ships. In between the ceremonies, we conducted bilaterals with Japan and Korea as we prepared to visit those countries. Before flying to Tokyo the next day, I got up at 5 to join Campbell, Karl Eikenberry, and Jo Dee Jacob in climbing Diamond Head to see the sun rise.

In Tokyo, I gave a speech to the Foreign Press Club and then co-chaired a meeting with defense and foreign office officials. At the plenary, the officials demurred about issuing a joint declaration by the President and Prime Minister in November. I adjourned the large meeting and called a small session with my counterparts, the able officials Masahiro Akiyama of the Japanese Defense Agency and Hitoshi Tanaka from Foreign Affairs. They explained that there was hesitation about security on the part of some socialist members of the government. Although I understood their problem, I warned them about the high cost of failure and pleaded for the declaration to nail things down.

The next day, I met with various vice ministers, and then went to visit Misawa, a Japanese Air Base that incorporates a squadron of US F-16s. After a press conference, a briefing and putting on a pressurized flight suit and helmet, I was taken up in the backseat of an F-16 where the pilot simulated dodging missiles from the ground. Sitting in the canopy of an F-16 with nothing but space around you is like riding a horse in the sky: absolutely beautiful. I even got to fly it a little at high altitude and was impressed by how sensitive the controls were. I wondered what my life would have been if I had discovered this at the age of 18!

Back down to earth, I traveled to Seoul inside a normal C-20 passenger jet, and made calls on the Minister of Defense and the Chief of Staff at the Blue House. He was a Kennedy School graduate, and proudly told me there were at least thirty of our alumni in the Korean government. After discussions of host nation support funds and the status-of-forces agreement, I gave a speech at the Seoul Forum where I discussed North Korea and the importance of our alliances with Korea and Japan as stabilizing forces in the region. I was then taken to visit the demilitarized zone at Panmunjom, and looked into North Korea, where all one could see were high buildings and an enormous flag. I was then whisked back to Kimpo Airport by helicopter just in time for my flight to San Francisco and Dulles.

Just when I thought I had the "Nye Initiative" on track, it was almost derailed by the terrible news that three US servicemen in Okinawa had raped a 12-year-old school girl. The Japanese were properly outraged, and there were calls for removal of American bases and revision of the status-of-forces agreement. I learned about it while riding on a plane to New York with Perry for a "two plus two" meeting of defense and foreign ministers of Japan and the US. Perry immediately called General Krulak from the plane and said he wanted a stand-down of forces on Okinawa and a strong response to the incident. At first, this all slowed our progress considerably, but later, the two governments agreed I would co-chair a "special action committee on Okinawa" which would investigate the burden of bases on the island.

In the Fall of 1995, I joined a meeting of Presidents Clinton and Jiang Zemin in the margins of the UN aimed at repairing the relationship. Clinton reassured Jiang that the US was not trying to block their modernization and said that we had important business to conduct in the defense area. Jiang accepted that I would visit Beijing when Clinton suggested it.

But before Beijing, we had to try to get things back on track in Tokyo with another "two plus two ministerial" at the end of October. After a briefing at the embassy, and formal meetings, we went back to Perry's suite at the Okura for late-night drinks with Ryutaro Hashimoto and Koichi Kato, two heavyweights from different factions in the Liberal Democratic Party. They said they had not spoken out more about the alliance because of the Okinawa incident. I pointed out the absence of their leadership meant losing support among young people, and the increase of resistance to bases. I asked them if they really wanted to be alone with China in the region ten years from now. They admitted that they had to take the questions more seriously.

The "two plus two" went smoothly, and Perry and I both did a number of press briefings, speeches, and television interviews. A question came up about whether the US really had 100,000 troops in the region as called for by the EASR. I pointed out that we had 43,000 troops in Japan, plus 14,000 afloat, as well as 28,000 in Korea, and a total of 98,000 in the overall region. The next day we flew to Korea and met with President Kim Young-sam in the Blue House, and then held a large formal meeting at the ministry of defense to hear a variety of committee reports. With more than 100 people in the room, not much new business was done, which I described in my diary as "like bureaucracies mating." Fortunately, we were able to get work done in a smaller meeting in the minister's office.

Two weeks later I flew to Beijing with Robert Einhorn of the State Department to try to restore talks on security issues. An afternoon of discussions at the ministry was followed by a dinner with General Xiong Guangkai, head of military intelligence. As expected, he was tough on the Taiwan issue but expressed interest in the military-to-military contacts and confidence-building measures that I proposed. Einhorn and I took an equally tough stance on the importance of cooperation on proliferation, including the Missile Technology Control Regime.

The next day, I met with Yang Jiechi at the Diaoyutai State Guesthouse. After the usual complaints about Taiwan, we discussed the EASR, as well as proliferation. The same subjects came up the following day at CICIR, a strategic think-tank with ties to intelligence. I repeated a simplified version of our policy on Taiwan: "No de jure independence by Taipei; no use of force by Beijing." They asked me what the US would do if they did use force. I answered that no one could answer that because it would depend on circumstances. For example, if I said we would not use force, they should not believe me because, at the beginning of 1950, the Secretary of State, a much higher-level official, had declared Korea to be outside our defense perimeter and yet, by the end of the year, our two countries were at war there. The moral of the story was "don't risk any adventures." I finished my visits in the Great Hall of the People with Minister of Defense Chi Haotian. I said our policy was engagement, not containment, and our alliance with Japan was designed to shape the environment and provide the stability that undergirds East Asian prosperity. He reminded me about Japan's militarism in the 1930s.

From Beijing I flew to Tokyo, where the original plan had been for Bill Clinton to come for the APEC summit in Osaka and sign a declaration reaffirming the US–Japan Security Treaty (which he eventually did with Hashimoto in April 1996). Clinton canceled his travel because of a budget dispute with Speaker of the House of Representatives Newt Gingrich and a government shutdown in Washington. He sent Vice President Gore in his place. I took a bullet train to Osaka and briefed Gore in his hotel before he and Prime Minister Murayama signed the

Delegation to Beijing in November 1995 with General Chi

declaration. As the press reported on November 20, Murayama and Gore affirmed the security pact and "both men agreed that the bilateral security regime is essential not only to bilateral ties but also to the regional and global communities." The most remarkable thing is that it was signed by a socialist prime minister. And at the end of the meeting, he came over to thank me.

As I wrote that evening: "This has been quite a day. The initiative has survived the perils of Pauline; Hatokayama's death [my first counterpart], the rape case, Clinton's postponement, but it has worked!" As I flew home, I could exhale, but I also suffered from a slight sense of depression – or maybe it was withdrawal symptoms.[9] It was reassuring to get back to the Pentagon and hear from Gerald Hensley, New Zealand's Minister of Defense, that the "EASR had a big effect; even Lee Kuan Yew is more reassured." It looked like my efforts to influence the East Asian balance of power were succeeding.

[9] For a more objective account of the Nye Initiative, see Michael J. Green, *By More than Providence: Grand Strategy and American Power in the Asia Pacific Since 1783* (New York: Columbia University Press, 2017), pp. 465–73.

NATO problems

Of course, I could not focus solely on the "Nye Initiative." I worked with all my six regional deputies on their disparate problems. We were visited by Paul Kagame of Rwanda, and a White House meeting discussed the fighting in Liberia and whether we could protect Monrovia. I also attended a White House meeting on how to promote democracy, met with General Wes Clark, the J5 of the Joint Chiefs about Bosnia, flew to Haiti and then Guantanamo with Deutch, Talbott, and Berger for briefings on those situations, and sat through more deputies' meetings on North Korea. NATO expansion was a hot issue, with interagency differences over the pace. Perry wanted to assure the Russians that further expansion would be slow, but, as I wrote at the time, "my friend Holbrooke is pushing too fast by insisting on consultations this year."

I accompanied Perry to a NATO meeting in Brussels, where the most important negotiations occur not in the plenary, but in the small rooms reserved for bilaterals. Perry outlined new ideas about Bosnia to UK Secretary of State for Foreign and Commonwealth Affairs Malcolm Rifkind in which the UN Protection Force (UNPROFOR) would be extracted and air power used more forcefully against the Bosnian Serbs. However, Rifkind demurred and did not want NATO involved. I met separately with David Omand, a thoughtful British Ministry of Defence official, and he explained his government's concerns over the possible Serbian responses.

I also held bilaterals with Greek and Turkish officials to urge them to develop better procedures for managing their conflicts. We did not want two NATO allies coming to blows in the Aegean Sea. I then flew separately to Ankara to discuss US–Turkish relations with the Minister of Defense and meet with their general staff about conflict management in the Aegean. They expressed skepticism about the Greeks but said they would be willing to meet in the new year. Part of my duty as a visiting representative of the US government was to lay a wreath on the tomb of Kemal Atatürk, the founder of modern Turkey. It was snowing and a long walk up slippery marble steps of the huge structure, but I managed to keep upright.

Upon returning from Turkey to Washington, I received the bad news that I would have to be the Defense Department's representative at

Secretary of State Warren Christopher's meeting with Russian Foreign Minister Kozyrev in Geneva. Although I had fond memories of living in Geneva, I was coming down with a cold and had only one day to rest before returning to Andrews for another overnight flight with Christopher, Tom Donilon, Jim Steinberg, Nick Burns, and others. The sessions in the US mission in the morning and the Russian mission in the afternoon proved interesting. Kozyrev, a moderate in the Russian government, tried ideas about partial membership in NATO and a collective security pact. He said he faced political problems of showing the public and the Duma that it was a "new NATO" that he wanted us to reaffirm. Christopher said that expansion was a given but agreed to further discussions on the process. I wrote that "it looks like Russia will accept if it is done right – and if Russia doesn't change." On Bosnia, Kozyrev commented about a Serbian leader: "Mladic is fighting World War I. They have a strange view of the world." In 1995 with moderates still in control in Moscow, there was a sense of optimism about the future of US–Russian relations.

Six days later, I was in London, where I met with David Omand and others to discuss NATO. He seemed to be in agreement on gradual NATO expansion, but friends I met outside government, like Lawrence Freedman of King's College London and John Chipman of the IISS, were skeptical because of the danger of dilution and taking on ethnic troubles in Eastern Europe. The conversation on NATO continued at the WEF in Davos in January 1995, where I was on a panel with Secretary General Willy Claes. In conversation with Václav Klaus and Vladimir Dlouhy of Czechoslovakia, they said that the hope of expansion was enough for now. I also talked to Kofi Annan about the problems of UN peacekeeping. He agreed that the UN peacekeepers were not equipped to handle fighting, but said they had to be realistic about the probability of being thrown into gray areas by public opinion.

After Davos, I led a mission to the Balkan countries of Albania, Bulgaria, and Romania, members of PFP who had not had a high-level Pentagon visit for some time. Albania was unbelievably poor. When our plane landed in Tirana, one could feel the ripples in the aging runway. The countryside was still dotted with thousands of concrete pillboxes built by the isolationist Communist dictator Enver Hoxha after 1972. The government housed me in his villa with big Soviet style rooms, but no heat! I had to wear extra sweaters to bed that night. At dinner in King Zog's Palace in Durres, I noted that the food served to me and to President Sali Berisha was better than that served to the other guests. In my meetings with various officials, I repeated our message of democracy, stable borders, and human rights. At the formal bilateral working group, we were asked about providing anti-tank and anti-aircraft weapons, and I explained that our current policy precluded it, but the future would depend on the measures I mentioned. All that was part of the American century.

Sofia, my next stop, was an attractive city with tree-lined boulevards and ringed by snow-capped mountains. There were few stores or neon signs, and the former Communist Party headquarters and the Georgi Dimitrov Mausoleum still bore signs of fire and defacement. I called on the Foreign Minister and the Defense Minister and then conducted a bilateral working group in a huge hall behind a little American flag. At a well-attended press conference, the main questions were about NATO, PFP, Bosnia, Russia, and the prospects for military cooperation.

After a short flight, I arrived in Bucharest, where the former dictator Nicolae Ceausescu had destroyed much of the old charm and replaced it with Stalinist buildings. One exception was the Military Club, where we held the meeting of our bilateral working group. It was an imitation Baroque building from just after World War I, and we met under giant paintings of Romanians fighting Turks. I told them that procedures for joining NATO would be "gradual, transparent, and case by case for democratic market economies that had good relations with their neighbors and were capable of contributing to NATO defense." I said much the same to President Iliescu in his ornate presidential palace and he was very smooth in his replies. I said that we had once valued Romania for the problems that it created for Russia, but that was no longer our policy.

From Bucharest, I flew to Paris for consultations with French officials about NATO and Bosnia, and then on to the Munich Security Conference, where Perry gave a speech and we had a series of bilaterals about the usual subjects with various other defense ministers. The Dutch said they felt UNPROFOR was a success and should not be withdrawn, but they would be sadly disappointed by their peacekeeping efforts after the massacre in Srebrenica later in the year.

My next trip to Europe, in March 1995, began in Brussels, where I addressed the PFP ambassadors from Central Europe and then met with Claes to discuss efforts to develop confidence-building measures between Greece and Turkey. Those countries were disputing boundaries in the Aegean Sea where Greek islands are close to the Turkish mainland. From Brussels, I went to Athens and met with Defense Minister Arsenis, who seemed quite open on the subject, but at a defense consultative meeting on the island of Rhodes, the Greek Chief of Staff Khouris, a sour old general with great hostility to Turks, wanted nothing to do with it. It was a tense and unpleasant meeting.

On to Ankara, where I met up with Strobe Talbott and we called on Prime Minister Tansu Çiller at her residence. I also talked with the military chiefs, who agreed with the idea of limiting overflights and avoiding freedom of navigation operations during the tourist season. Even this turned out not to be enough to please the Greeks, and the best we got in the end was a willingness on both sides to accept observers on each other's ships during NATO naval exercises. Such are the chores of alliance maintenance.

Levels of conflict and atrocities grew in Bosnia in 1995. In early July, the Bosnian Serbs massacred 8,000 Muslim men and boys and expelled 25,000 civilians in Srebrenica, a town supposedly under UNPROFOR protection. That proved to be a turning point in policy in the Pentagon. I remember Perry convening a small number of advisors at his home on a Saturday morning, and we all agreed that the current policy was not working. In early August, Perry and Shalikashvili joined other principals at the White House and Clinton decided on a more assertive policy, including the possibility of deploying American troops. Richard Holbrooke would lead a team to get the Serbs to negotiate, and my deputy for Europe, Joseph Kruzel, would be the DOD representative on the team.

Initially, the negotiations were slow, as Kruzel told me when he called me from Belgrade. But airstrikes were greatly stepped up in September after the Serbs shelled the open market in Sarajevo, and by December Holbrooke ably negotiated the Dayton Accords, which resulted in a partial division of Bosnia monitored by a NATO force replacing UNPROFOR. It is interesting that, rather than post-Cold War hubris for intervention, my memory of this part of the American century (as seen from the Pentagon) was one of caution over committing American troops.

In mid-September, I returned to Europe with Perry on a visit to Slovenia, Slovakia, the Czech Republic, and Hungary, where the main topic was PFP and NATO. Our message was the same in each country. Perry explained that a country's progress would be judged by their democracy, market economy, civilian control of the military, interoperability with NATO, and good relations with its neighbors. That was easy in Ljubljana, where Slovenia met those conditions, but led to a tough meeting in Bratislava, where Prime Minister Vladimir Mečiar was displaying authoritarian tendencies. Perry told him that this would halt Slovakia's progress toward NATO membership. It was easier again in Prague with Václav Havel, and in Hungary with Gyula Horn.

The Slovenians took us to their northern border with Italy and a World War I museum (where 100,000 soldiers perished defending an eight-mile stretch) and then to beautiful Lake Bled. In Prague and Budapest, we barely had time to enjoy their old charm. And after a while, tours of training bases and inspections of military equipment begin to look the same. We were always overfed. As someone said, diplomacy means "eating for one's country." And there were interminable gifts and toasts. And wreath-laying ceremonies! When you do four small countries in five days, you have no sooner finished the airport reception with a band and troops lined up in one country than you are off to a similar ceremony in the next, and it begins to feel very *déjà vu*. Nonetheless, such visits have a purpose in structuring expectations and creating ties that Perry called "defense by other means." It was all part of the American century. And before returning home we helicoptered to Garmisch, Germany, where the Pentagon supports multinational officer-training courses at the Marshall Center. There we named a room in honor of Joe Kruzel.

Back home again, we flew to Williamsburg in early October to host a meeting of NATO defense ministers. The plenary discussed NATO enlargement and relations with Russia in the morning and Bosnia in the afternoon. We also held the usual bilaterals and met with the quad (plus Italy this time!) to discuss Mediterranean security. A formal dinner followed at the historic governor's palace, where we were serenaded by "The Airmen of Note." The next day, we took helicopters to USS *Enterprise* for a flight demonstration. There is something very impressive in the launching of thirty tons of airplane in the short distance of fifty yards, or the sonic booms of F-18s sweeping low over the deck and then arcing away to drop flares. Yet another example of the American century.

Informal NATO defense ministerial, Fall 1995

From the Pyramids to the Taj to the Gulf

My travel schedule was frenetic. Between January 6 and February 6, 1995, I was out of the country for twenty-four of the thirty-one days on three trips to ten different countries. The first trip was to accompany Bill Perry to the Middle East and South Asia. Fortunately, Molly was asked to go along to help Lee Perry with her heavy representational duties. Our first stop was Cairo where President Hosni Mubarak received us in his spacious office in the Heliopolis Palace for a wide-ranging discussion of Saddam Hussein, the Persian Gulf, and the Middle East peace process. Perry then laid a wreath on the tomb of the Unknown Soldier (where Sadat had been assassinated), had a military honors ceremony, and met with Defense Minister Tantawi to discuss the particulars of military sales. We then took helicopters to Giza and had a wonderful tour of the pyramids and the Sphinx conducted by their chief Egyptologist, before flying back to Cairo for a banquet at the Officers' Club and a folklore show. By then I was too tired to enjoy it.

In Israel, after the usual ceremony in Tel Aviv, we met with Defense Minister Rabin and took a twelve-minute helicopter ride to Jerusalem, where Perry laid a wreath at Yad Vashem and we called on President Weizman. Perry reaffirmed our commitment to helping Israel maintain its technological advantage. The next day, we helicoptered along the border with the Golan Heights and down the Jordan River, visited a military base, and toured an Arrow Missile facility. A small meeting with Rabin, very different from the large one the day before, raised a variety of sensitive subjects, including Israel's transfer of technology to China and the problem of Iran. Rabin said he feared Iran could get nuclear weapons in seven to fifteen years.

Islamabad, our next stop, was a city of pale buildings set among dark hills and Prime Minister Benazir Bhutto received us in the living-room of her white residence set on a hill with a commanding view. Over lunch, we chatted about her student days at Harvard in the 1970s. I had been her escort when she received an honorary degree in 1989, and she asked why American politics had become so negative. I had no good answer. She also wanted to know if Senator Larry Pressler's amendment would prevent any progress on the sale of F-16s. Again, I had no good answer.

The next day we flew to Peshawar and Landi Kotal in the Khyber Pass, a bleak dry countryside where each house has high walls like a fortress. We had lunch at the Khyber Rifles Mess, where bagpipers wore headdresses that flared up like a cockscomb, and we watched sword and gun dances. At the afternoon meetings, our military hosts expressed their mistrust of India, but we agreed on an agenda for the military consultative group meeting that I would co-chair when they came to DC.

In New Delhi, the grandiose government buildings that the British bequeathed to India were designed in the 1920s to give the impression of a lasting empire, and they looked like a Hollywood set. So did the ceremonial reception that included lancers on horseback. And of course, Perry laid a wreath at the Soldiers' Memorial Arch. At meetings in the South Block with the Minister of Defense, we heard concerns about fundamentalism in Pakistan, as was also the case when we called on

Prime Minister Rao. We worked out an agenda for a US–India military consultative group which I would co-chair when they came to DC. We then flew to Jodhpur to see a mock dogfight of MIG fighter planes and inspect Russian origin T-72 tanks. The best part of the trip, however, was a visit to Agra and the Taj Mahal which was just as stunning as when I first saw it during the Carter Administration eighteen years earlier.

Visit to the Taj Mahal with Secretary of Defense William Perry, 1995

The end of March was marked by a week-long trip to the Persian Gulf with "SecDef" Perry. Our agenda was to reinforce dual containment of Iraq and Iran, reassure countries of CENTCOM's ability to return quickly in a crisis, encourage the Gulf Cooperation Council, and reinforce the NPT. After arriving in Jeddah, we sat in our hotel for "the waiting period" before King Fahd received us in his palace at 11 p.m. – not great if you have been on an overnight flight. Fahd mused about his "days of freedom in California before he became a prisoner in a gilded cage." On substance, he complained that Qatar and Oman had not attended a GCC (Gulf Cooperation Council) meeting and met with Iraqis instead. The next day we toured military facilities in King Khalid

City and then took a bumpy ride over the desert to Prince Sultan's "camp" where we were treated to a feast in a huge open-sided tent and entertained by a herd of white camels and another of black camels criss-crossing in front of us as we sat back and sipped our strong coffee. Beats the usual military band!

From Saudi we flew to Kuwait where we met with the Emir and Crown Prince in the Bayan Palace, and then flew to Al Jaber Air Base to see F-16s and A-10s and talk to the airmen living in a tent city. Dinner that night at the Kuwait officers club had "enough food to feed an army." My suite in the palace was huge, with fifteen pillows on a canopied bed and fresh orchids in a marble bathroom – but I was too tired to benefit.

In Manama, the capital of the small island state of Bahrain, we met the Emir, a little man with a twinkle of a smile, and his brother, the more dour Prime Minister. They were worried about Iran (as well they might be, since Sunnis were ruling a largely Shia population) and did not want Iraq to become too weakened. We then flew to USS *Constellation*, where Perry addressed the crew on the spacious flight deck. One amusing anecdote: the Emir presented me with an expensive wristwatch. I usually wore a TIMEX that cost less than $50. Since government employees are not permitted to retain expensive gifts, my military assistant Tony Aldwell came over and said I had better give it to him immediately to hand over to the government, before I got to like it. I took a quick look and gave it to him. Easy come, easy go.

The next stop was Abu Dhabi in the United Arab Emirates and a meeting with the old emir and his impressive son, Sheik Mohammed bin Zayed. They too were concerned about Iranian expansion, and we discussed prepositioning of American military equipment so as to be ready in a crisis. Our final stop was the small peninsular state of Qatar where the capital, Doha, has very interesting modern architecture. Our hotel was shaped like a pyramid and had great views of the sea. We met the Crown Prince and Foreign Minister from the ruling Al Thani family in a large white marble building with elaborate scrolls in the ceiling and inlaid stones in the style of the Taj. They said that Iran truly feared a US invasion and Perry assured them that was not our intention. In the debriefing with Perry in his conference room on the long plane ride home, we concluded that we had met our objectives.

Latin America

Life did not slow down and that Spring I flew to Peru, Ecuador, and Mexico for consultations and to urge them to send their ministers to a Defense Ministerial of the Americas (DMA) that we were planning in Williamsburg in July. Peru was fascinating. I met with President Alberto Fujimori in a handsome colonial palace next to the Lima cathedral. To my astonishment he was alone except for an interpreter, and took his own notes. I had never seen a head of state do that before. It suggested he was in control but did not trust his staff. I also met with Foreign Minister Goldenberg in the Palacio de Torre Tagle, an attractive Spanish colonial building, to discuss stability after the Peru–Ecuador War earlier in the year. He said Peru had been focusing on defeating the Sendero Luminoso terrorist movement in the highlands and were taken by surprise. (Later in Quito, the Ecuadorians blamed it on Peru.)

After the meetings, the Peruvian army flew me and Colonel Aldwell to Cuzco, a tile-roofed city at 11,000 feet, and then to Machu Picchu at 12,000 feet. I was amazed by the ability of Inca engineering to fit together such huge stone structures with no mortar. I had an excellent local guide as we walked among the structures, and I asked him if the theocratic Inca society could have evolved to a modern society if it had not been colonized by Spain. His guess was "no, because of civil wars," which is ironic given that modern Peruvians and Ecuadorians were killing each other in the Amazon jungles.

Quito is an attractive city sitting in a green bowl surrounded by snowcapped volcanos in the distance and with an attractive colonial sector. I went running despite the 9,300 feet altitude, and I felt it. The Minister of Defense quickly agreed to attend the Williamsburg Conference, so I used my time to ask him how the war had started and how to prevent a recurrence. He said Peru fired the first shot at an Ecuadorian patrol. Ecuador would not attack larger Peru but would make it costly if Peru were to widen the conflict. When I asked people at our embassy what they thought had happened, they said that the basic cause was Ecuadorian paranoia about Peru that went all the way back to the nineteenth century and the national myth of a role in the Amazon leading to aggressive patrolling in a contested area. I do not know the truth, but I was struck by how similar the story was to what I had just heard in Greece and Turkey, and India and Pakistan. Just change the names and places.

From Quito I flew to Mexico City, where Ambassador James Jones, a former congressman, briefed me about the narco trade and the army's involvement, and the fear of what he called "Colombianization." It was interesting that my meeting at the Defense Ministry was chaired by the Foreign Ministry. As one of them later explained, "We want to keep them in their box." The Mexicans wanted reassurance that we were not planning to use the conference to create a regional intervention force, and I told them we would not isolate them, and the purpose of the meeting was to reinforce democracy in the hemisphere. They agreed to attend.

When I returned to DC, I spent some considerable time in preparations with Latin American ambassadors, and John Shattuck of the State Department worked with me on formulating human rights on the agenda. The DMA convened in Williamsburg in July. It was well attended, and all the military delegates pledged support of democracy in the final declaration. The setting was perfect. At the opening dinner in an air-conditioned tent, White House Chief of Staff Mack McLarty spoke and the 82nd Airborne chorus sang. The next day, Perry and Vice President Al Gore spoke. Earlier, I had met with Gore and ministers from Peru and Ecuador. At the final session in the House of Burgesses, Brazil announced it had made progress in mediating between the two countries; the overall declaration had no dissents, and Argentina announced it would host the meeting the following year. The DMA was a great example of how the military can be used for soft power. This role is often neglected in descriptions of the American century.

Africa

Another region that required attention was Africa. I had created a Deputy Assistant Secretary for Africa and I needed to back him up by visiting the region. The good news from South Africa was that, instead of becoming a bloodbath after apartheid, Nelson Mandela had been elected president in 1994 and the situation looked promising. The bad news from the same year was the genocide in Rwanda and the withdrawal, rather than reinforcement, of the small UN peacekeeping force. I was scheduled to visit both countries in the summer of 1995.

We chose to start in Botswana, a small country where we had little strategic interest, but it was a symbol of economic and democratic success. Of course, it helps to be homogeneous and have good leadership. A large portion of their small army had participated in our International Military Education and Training programs that included civilian as well as military topics. Our next stop, South Africa, was very different.

In Pretoria, we called on Defense Minister Modise and Chief of Staff General Meiring and found they were wrestling with integration as well as how to build a civilian defense staff. They asked us about how our Office of the Secretary of Defense worked and about help with integration. We had dinner with Jakkie Cilliers, a white Afrikaner who had fought in Angola but quit in disgust. I asked him what had changed the white apartheid government. He said, "We ran out of moral steam," and the Western boycott contributed to that. But he cautioned that future stability would require a high rate of economic growth to absorb the unemployed population. A sign of the problem was the heightened concern for safety that we encountered when we visited Johannesburg. On the other hand, South Africa was better than when Molly and I had stopped there on our way home from East Africa in 1964.

We flew to Uganda overnight, and I took time to visit my old office at Makerere and stood on the lawn where I had received the letter offering me a job at Harvard thirty-two years ago. We had no official meetings scheduled. I had earlier met with President Museveni when he visited Washington the previous October. He struck me as impressive and intelligent, though he became more authoritarian over time. He asked me what European tribe the name "Nye" came from. Our little team drove across Uganda like tourists, pausing for a photo on the equator and passing through rolling hills where long-horned Ankole cattle grazed peacefully.

When we reached the Rwanda border, we were met by an escort of Rwandan troops with machine guns in a pickup truck, and our little convoy passed long lines of UN World Food Program trucks inching across beautiful green hillsides lined with terraced fields. Kigali itself stretched comfortably over many hills, though some buildings were still devastated. A dinner in my honor in the embassy was attended by many Tutsi officials who had grown up as refugees in Uganda after earlier violence in the 1960s. I asked one of the guests, the respected American anthropologist Alison Des Forges, about the genesis of the current situation. She told me that, as tribal fears accelerated, it became a "kill or be killed" situation in which even longstanding neighbors murdered each other.

While it had some Hutu ministers, the Rwanda government was now dominated by the Tutsi, who had been the primary victims of the genocide. When I met with their leader, Vice President Paul Kagame, he said that they were aiming for justice, not revenge. But putting things back together was not easy. I flew in a UN Huey helicopter to Ntarama, which looked bucolic from the air, but when we landed and visited the church, we found it to be still full of bones and the discarded suitcases and clothing of the people who had fruitlessly sought refuge there a year ago. Amid the terrible smell, I noticed that there was still a picture of the Pope on the wall as well as a poster in French that read "Liberty, Equality, Development." A Tutsi woman who had escaped and survived in a swamp said the killing in her village went on for two weeks, from April 6 to 19. Flying back to Kigali, we crossed an open prison stockade crammed with Hutu prisoners. I thought back to my visit to Auschwitz decades ago with its bins of suitcases, clothing, and hair and wondered how people could do that to each other. We are a strange species.

A flight across Lake Victoria took us to Nairobi, where I had also once lived. Unlike Kampala, where I could easily recognize landmarks and find my way around, Nairobi had grown to be a major city with a population of more than 2 million people. Kenya was not a perfect democracy, but it had a relatively free press and a nonpolitical military. We toured facilities and bases as well as the ministry of defense. The atmosphere of the meetings with defense and foreign ministry officials was very friendly, but they were cautious when I proposed creating and supporting an Organization of African Unity peacekeeping force that might prevent another genocide.

When I returned to Washington and debriefed Perry about my trip, he liked the idea of developing support for an African peacekeeping force and I talked about it with Susan Rice, the smart young Rhodes Scholar who years later became National Security Advisor. Many people feared that Burundi might follow the path of Rwanda and, at a meeting in the Situation Room, I proposed that we offer a logistics and transport package if African states created a rescue force in case of genocide. Unfortunately, not enough African states were interested at the time.

Personal bombshells

My 1995 had begun in South Carolina. Clinton was at an unofficial gathering known as the Renaissance Weekend. He was amiable, charming, seemingly relaxed, and I accepted the invitation to join others to run on the beach with him. After the Republicans gained control of Congress in the November 1994 midterm elections, many were discounting his prospects for a second term. I ventured his chances to be four in ten. I was wrong, but so were others far more expert than me. In February 29, Johnny Apple of the *New York Times* told me Clinton could not be ruled out, but it was most likely that Robert Dole would be president two years hence. And at the White House Correspondents' dinner in April, the thoughtful political analyst Norman Ornstein told me that Clinton could not win the 1996 presidential election. Political crystal balls were invented only to be shattered.

And maybe that is true of all crystal balls. On January 23, I resigned my tenured professorship at Harvard after thirty years. Harvard has a firm two-year rule regarding leaves of absence and my two years were up before I had accomplished what I wanted to do in government. So, I cut the cord. Friends at Harvard had told me that it was likely they would want to rehire me again in the future, but there were no guarantees. And yet, unexpectedly, by the end of the year I was back at Harvard as dean of the Kennedy School.

The first bombshell came on May 2, when Al Carnesale, then Provost at Harvard, called to ask if I would become dean. I had already said no the previous year, but this time I told him I would think about it. One reason was that, on April 19, Timothy McVeigh, an anti-government zealot, had detonated a bomb at a government building in Oklahoma City that killed 168 people, including women and children. Like others I was shocked and saddened at the hostile perception of the federal government. The people I worked with were not making a lot of money, but they worked long hours and were dedicated to the common good.

I had little time to think about the larger issues of government while engaged in the whirlwind of its daily business, but perhaps the deanship would give me a chance to think and do something about it. I talked to Molly and friends like Graham Allison and David Gergen, who argued that it would provide a larger platform for me to think and do something about the big picture that interested me. I took a little 5" x 8" card and drew a line down the middle, dividing the pros and cons, and the Kennedy School came out better than I had expected.

Nonetheless, I felt I could not leave until I had completed my work on US policy toward Japan and Asia. Bill Perry said it was too good an opportunity to turn down, but asked me to hold the announcement until late August. I told Carnesale I would accept after graduation when the gossip mill might have calmed down and allow us to postpone an announcement until August. To my astonishment, it worked. When Molly and I went to the Adirondacks in early June, I lay on rocks in the sun and listened to the river and knew the decision felt right.

Unfortunately, there was a sad sequel. After I returned from Africa in August, Molly and I went to our farm in New Hampshire for a weekend of recovery, before a planned visit to Harvard on the Monday when I was to meet with Carnesale and Neil Rudenstine for a press conference to announce my deanship. August 19 started out as a beautiful summer's day, with a run along the river. After breakfast, however, Fred Smith called from Washington to tell me that Joe Kruzel and two others had been killed in Sarajevo when their armored personnel carrier had tried to pass a stalled vehicle on the treacherous Mt. Igman road and toppled down a ravine. I was devastated because, besides being my deputy, Joe was a friend from Harvard days. I called Gail Kruzel with condolences and told Rudenstine and Carnesale that I had to return to DC and could not attend the ceremony scheduled for Monday. They understood but said that it was too late to stop the announcement that had been released to the press over the weekend.

Monday, August 21 was a hard day. Instead of celebrating at Harvard, I met with seventy-five of my staff in the Secretary's conference room and told them that the announcement of my leaving at the end of the year was true. I then went down to Kruzel's office to talk to his staff. I felt drained, like someone who had skipped his wedding to go to a funeral instead. And at Joe's funeral three days later, I remember a caisson drawn by white riderless horses, a graveside ceremony among trees with cicadas buzzing, Taps, and flag-folding. It was a sad day, but I had to return to the office where other problems had been piling up. Only a week later did I find time to visit Harvard and have lunch with Neil Rudenstine.

But there was still work to do: briefings about Japan on Capitol Hill, dinners at embassies, meeting my old friend John Sewall, now a major general who was about to handle military assistance in Croatia, meetings about the Greeks and Turks, North Korean proliferation, and so forth. I also tried to help Frank Kramer, the able Washington lawyer who would be my successor. And I was bemused when people would ask me about the Kennedy School, since I was too busy even to think about it. Nonetheless I was in touch with David Ellwood, the excellent academic dean, and Republican friends in DC like Gergen and Richard Darman who organized a lunch for me at the F Street Club to meet major figures in conservative politics.

By December, I was down to my last two weeks, and all my dinners were already catered for. I joked that I was going out in a "blaze of calories." On December 8, Bill Perry held an award ceremony in which he conferred on me the Defense Department's Distinguished Service Award with oak leaf cluster, and held a dinner for forty people in the

The Defense Department's Distinguished Service Award ceremony with Paul Nitze and David McGiffert, 1995
Source: Department of Defense

Secretary's dining-room. Many pictures were taken, but perhaps the most interesting was one with former incumbents of the office: Paul Nitze, David McGiffert (my colleague from the Carter years), and Chas Freeman, my immediate predecessor. In thanking people for their generous toasts after dinner, I said: "It's like a funeral but you get to stay alive after hearing the eulogies."

The next day I was back at Andrews to fly to Norfolk with a group of senators to attend the commissioning ceremony for USS *Stennis* (CVN-74), our newest carrier. I went to the State Department for talks with visiting Koreans, worked on the Marshall Center, gave a speech on China at the Asia Society, and played my last game of squash at the Pentagon Officers' Athletic Club with my son Ben (he beat me 3–2). December 14 was the finale. I visited each of the departments in the ISA to say goodbye, and had sandwiches in my giant but now vacant E-Ring office with my staff. They walked me to the car and saluted from the steps of the River Entrance as I drove away.

At our little Georgetown House, Molly and I packed the car to drive north, but before we left, we went across the street to say goodbye to Mrs. Lee, the indefatigable Korean immigrant who ran the little neighborhood store. She gave us a bottle of wine, and we told her she was "a great American." She had sent two children to university; her story was another dimension of the American century, just as important as the Pentagon aircraft carriers I had visited. And for me, a new chapter was starting.

7

The Clinton Years: Kennedy School Dean

When I was first named dean, people would ask me about my vision for the Kennedy School. I would joke that, after the Pentagon, my vision was a fleet of five helicopters. That joke was a way of fending off the question. I wanted to consult with the faculty and others before making any substantive pronouncements. My early days were spent listening – to faculty, staff, students, deans of other professional schools, alumni, donors, and others.

The origins of the Harvard School of Government date back to 1936, when former New York congressman Lucius Littauer gave Harvard $2 million to start a school of public administration. The first students were civil servants who came for a year, took a variety of courses, and earned a master's degree in public administration. In 1966, Harvard decided to rename the School as a memorial to John F. Kennedy. Equally important, it broadened its focus and added a master's program in public policy with a tightly defined curriculum. The School was consistently ranked top, or near the top, of such schools.

New challenges

From the packet of readings that I studied over the 1995 Christmas vacation, I discovered that the School was in good shape, but there was a danger that we would lose our mission of training public leaders and doing research that contributes to the solution of public problems. Because of the Harvard brand, we would always be able to attract good students and faculty, but that was not the only measure of merit. We also needed to walk a tightrope between academic excellence and policy relevance. Harvard already had an excellent Faculty of Arts and Sciences, as well as a business school. We did not want to become a duplicate of either. At Yale, the School of Organization and Management had become a business school, and at Princeton, many regarded the Woodrow Wilson

School of Public and Internatioal Affairs as too academic. Richard Neustadt, a savvy student of politics, warned me that some of the faculty did not buy into the idea of balancing public policy with academic excellence, and simply wanted to be free to do their own research. I told faculty members that I valued research, having done it myself, but that I put a priority on research that had a major short-term or long-term impact on public policy.

On my first day at work, I met with Al Carnesale, the outgoing dean who was now the University Provost, and told him I was worried that the School was in danger of becoming overconfident, losing the essential tension of a professional school. This was confirmed in long sessions with David Ellwood, the academic dean (who years later became my successor), as well as friends like Allison and Neustadt who were among the founders of the new programs. In mid-January, when I lunched with the seven members of the Harvard Corporation, the highest governing board, I told them that I planned to focus on three big problems: the changing market for our product, our internal fragmentation, and our image of being too partisan.

I soon discovered we had a fourth problem, and a big one – money. While Harvard has a large endowment, the Kennedy School did not have a big share of it. Ironically, we had just lost a large contract for training Pentagon officials (no favoritism here!) and I faced an immediate million-dollar deficit. John Dunlop, a former dean and Secretary of Labor, joked that three things tied Harvard together: steam pipes, the financial books, and treaties. While that was amusing hyperbole, Harvard was a very decentralized university, almost like a medieval monarchy dominated by strong barons (deans) who were protective of their fiefdoms. The motto for funding was "every tub on its own bottom." The Kennedy School was a small and relatively new tub, and I spent at least a third of my time on fundraising, guided by an able associate dean, Holly Sargent. She quickly had me on a whirlwind of meeting potential donors.

I sometimes joked that among the wealthy, we had three strikes against us before I even walked in the door: "Kennedy, School, and Government." Fortunately, many of the potential donors turned out to be interesting people who lived in interesting places. And the results were rewarding. During my eight and a half years as dean, we eventually raised some $300 million. This led to a doubling in the size of the faculty, a new degree in economic development, and the creation of five new research centers on economic development, human rights, nonprofit organizations, public leadership, and democratic innovation. I also invested in more scholarships and loan forgiveness for students going into low-paid positions in government and the nonprofit sector. But all this was in the future; in the meantime, I had to get used to rattling a tin cup and asking for alms like a mendicant monk. One amusing tale: when I called on Daniel Rose, the friendly New York real-estate mogul, he was so persuasive in telling me about his own favorite charity helping Harlem students afford college that I wound up giving it money, and still do. It was an expensive call!

People told me that the School was not sufficiently balanced in gender – women tended to see it as an old boys' club. I needed to increase the female proportion of the student body, faculty, and staff. I wanted to fill the crucial position of executive dean with a woman, and because the School was also criticized for lacking political balance, I sought a Republican. I found the perfect candidate in Sheila Burke, a Kennedy School graduate, but at the time she was Bob Dole's Chief of Staff and Dole was running for President. Sheila could commit only conditional on the election. Although it put an extra burden on my time, it was worth the wait. Sheila was perfect and it sent the signal I wanted to the organization.

I hired an able young woman, Victoria Budson, to start a Women and Public Policy Program and eventually persuaded senior political figures like Baroness Shirley Williams and, later, Ambassador Swanee Hunt to come and help. Also, in an age of globalization, we needed more foreign students, and I doubled their proportion to nearly half of the School. When someone criticized the decision to allocate scarce slots at Harvard to foreigners, I replied that not only was our mission global, but the presence of foreign students helped to educate their American classmates.

A major reason I had taken the job as dean was my concern about what was happening to government, and I wanted to pull the faculty together to deal with the issue. Thus, in my first month, I started a faculty study group, the Visions of Governance in the Twenty-First Century. The group met regularly during the Spring, helped by two able young faculty members, David King and Philip Zelikow. It took time to hammer out the shape of the program, but in the summer of 1996 we met at Bretton Woods to discuss papers that would eventually become chapters in a book titled *Why People Don't Trust Government.* Some of the design for the postwar world order had been done at the Bretton Woods Conference of 1944, and the hotel still had brass plaques with the names of the delegates on the doors of the rooms in which they stayed. It was a perfect setting for prolonged conversations both in and out of the conference room. Some of us climbed Mount Washington. I have a picture with Allison and Ellwood that I call the "Three Dean Summit." It would be hard to imagine the faculty spending this much intellectual time together in busy Cambridge, MA, where faculty meetings are absorbed with processes of running the School. The project reinforced the mission of the School, and simultaneously helped my purpose of bringing people together around that mission.

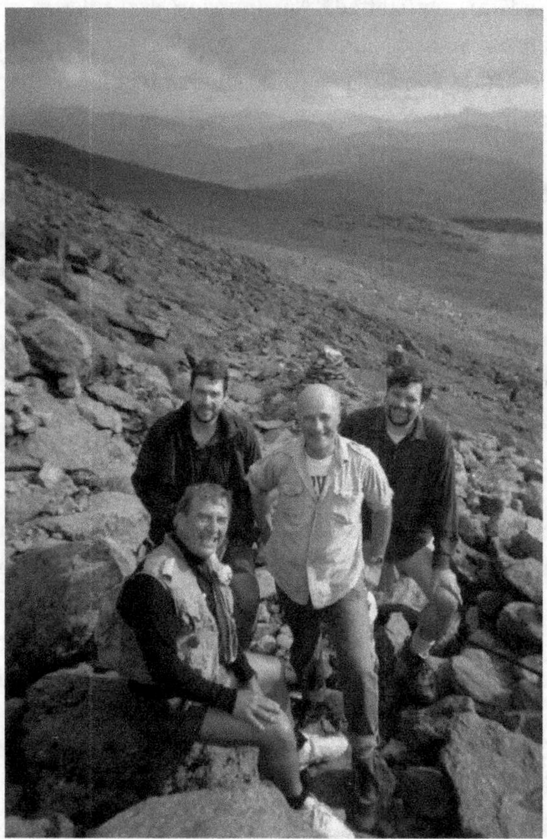

The Three Dean Summit, Mount Washington, 1996

Our research discovered that the percentage of the population who told pollsters that they had a great deal of confidence in government dropped sharply from three-quarters to one-quarter after the Vietnam and Watergate events. But distrust was not just a problem of American government, since there were also declines in other countries and for other institutions such as corporations. There was a general problem with popular trust in institutions. We discovered that people's actual behavior was not as negative as their answers to polls suggested, and that mistrust in government was a mediated behavior. It was interesting to note that the army and the post office, two large federal bureaucracies that were able to advertise, fared better in polls.

Between travel for fundraising, recruiting new faculty and staff, and organizing the Visions Project, my first year as dean was a busy one and we were not adequately staffed. An amusing example: in my first week on the job, my assistant brought me a stack of papers regarding a disciplinary matter that had been awaiting resolution. One student had bitten another, but claimed the School had no jurisdiction for discipline because it happened on graduation day, and he had already been granted his diploma. I told my assistant that a dean had more important matters to deal with than student bites and asked why the dean of students did not handle it. I then learned that there was no dean of students. I promptly hired one, Joseph McCarthy, who was an inspired choice as he saved me not only from student bites but also handled many more important matters. When I saw students in my office hours, I could henceforth discuss more interesting issues.

In June, I attended my first graduation in years, parading in a crimson gown through a Harvard Yard draped with flags and banners and crowded with students and families, sitting with President Rudenstine and the other deans on a dais on the steps of Memorial Church. When my turn came, I ceremoniously pronounced that the Kennedy School students assembled before us were worthy of their degrees. The real work began when we held our own ceremony in the park between the School and Charles River and I shook 550 hands as I handed out diplomas.

Government consulting

Harvard policy allows one day a week for outside consulting, and I used it to maintain my public life. In addition to congressional testimony, and occasional consulting, ex-CIA Director James Woolsey and I co-chaired a classified Intelligence Community study on the risks of terrorism with chemical and biological weapons. Our panel met a number of times at the CIA and we briefed the results at high levels in the government. The then CIA Director George Tenet told me that an earlier report I had supervised while at the NIC in 1994 had helped the government focus on terrorism, but Woolsey and I thought we should try to alert a broader audience. We published a declassified version of our report as an op-ed in the *Los Angeles Times*, warning of the danger that the political system would not respond to the terrorist threat until there was some sort of "domestic Pearl Harbor." We had no idea that our metaphor would become reality.

Another unpublicized public role was participation in a quick trip to Taiwan in early July to warn President Lee Teng-hui not to declare independence. Woolsey, Rich Armitage, Paul Wolfowitz, Ralph Cossa, James Kelly and I met with Lee for an hour and a half in the presidential palace in Taipei. I found him highly intelligent, and he assured us he had no plans to declare independence. (He even referred twice to the importance of the "Nye Initiative.")

Sometimes a public visit was added on to my Kennedy School business. For example, while raising funds in Korea, I also called on President Kim Young-sam in the Blue House, and he told me he was sure the North Korean regime would collapse. Then I went to Tokyo, where I gave several talks and met with Princess (now Empress) Masako, whom I had known when she was a student at Harvard. Then she was just Masako Owada, the smart daughter of my friend Hisashi Owada, before her marriage imprisoned her in the bubble of royalty. It is hard to think of a more difficult job than to be a living flag for one's country. In Hong Kong, I saw my old Princeton classmate Gordon Wu, who, like others, was overly confident about the future of the city when it was returned to China.

A Kennedy School initiative with China grew directly out of my prior work in the Pentagon. As a sign of displeasure with US policy on Taiwan, China had stopped all military contacts and consultations. Bill Perry asked if I could do anything about it in my new role. Working with Robert Blackwill, a former foreign service officer then at the School, we developed an executive two-week program to bring Chinese senior colonels together with American officers. Blackwill had a blowtorch style of management, but he got things done. I raised money to support the program in Hong Kong, and we were able to do privately what had become impossible at the governmental level. The program was a success for several years. I remember conversations with some People's Liberation Army (PLA) officers who toed the party line publicly, but privately said they hoped China would evolve into a democracy in their children's lifetime. Alas, the program ended after one of the participants defected and sought asylum, and the Hong Kong widow who had been providing the funding lost a lawsuit and ran out of money.

Another initiative grew out of conversations with Klaus Schwab, the Swiss dynamo who founded the World Economic Forum and was a graduate of the Kennedy School. Working together, we developed the idea of having the School prepare a series of panels at Davos, as well as sending a number of faculty members and donors to participate in some of the meetings. That program continued throughout my deanship.

In December 1996, I joined the Defense Policy Board (DPB), a federal advisory committee to the DOD. My first meeting focused on North Korea, a sadly familiar topic. There was less optimism about the collapse of the regime than I had encountered in Seoul, but some exploration into opening up the regime through Chinese pressures to introduce market-style reforms. As we now know, this was wishful thinking, but there was a paucity of other good ideas. Experts often said that North Korea was "the land of lousy options."

After the DPB meeting, I stopped by my old Pentagon office and joined their Christmas party. It was great to see old friends but I still felt I'd made the right decision. A week later, after Christmas with our family at our tree farm in New Hampshire, Molly and I flew to a Renaissance Weekend at Hilton Head, where we saw friends, chaired a panel on international hot spots, and talked briefly to Bill and Hillary Clinton about China. In his after-dinner talk, the president said he had two major regrets: having an inexperienced White House staff and underestimating the bitterness of Washington politics.

Innovations

The new year, 1997, proved fruitful for my objective of making the Kennedy School more "woman-friendly." Sheila Burke joined the administrative team, and, in May, we held an International Women's Conference chaired by Shirley Williams. In the Fall term, President Vigdís of Iceland inaugurated the Council of Women World Leaders, which she co-founded with Laura Liswood; our team was also strengthened by the addition of Ambassador Swanee Hunt. In addition, the Women and Public Policy Program was sponsoring more events, and admissions and recruitment were improving.

I tried other innovations too, such as nontenured public service professors – people who had a distinguished role in government but did not fit an academic research profile, as well as senior lecturers who made significant contributions to the School but had more modest research production than required for tenure. I also introduced an annual alumni awards ceremony to celebrate accomplished role models, such as Paul Volcker, former chair of the Federal Reserve, Ian Clark, a top civil servant from Canada, and Mollie Beattie, an environmental activist from Alaska. Another innovation was to increase the number of executive education programs, and to host a dozen Lee Kuan Yew Fellows from Southeast Asia, who would be sponsored by the government of Singapore.

Blair, Clinton, and the Third Way

The Visions of Governance for the Twenty-First Century project was also making progress. Elaine Kamarck, who had managed the reinventing government project for Vice President Gore, took over management of the project. My co-authored book on confidence in government, *Why People Don't Trust Government*, led to several press and TV interviews. In June, I presented a copy to Hillary Clinton, and a few months later she invited me to join a delegation she was leading to meet with Tony Blair on November 1 at Chequers, the UK Prime Minister's country retreat. President Clinton had moderated some of his positions before the 1996 election in a process that some called "triangulation," but he was not the only politician interested in exploring new ground. Clinton joined Blair in explorations of what was called a "Third Way" between left and right in democratic politics, and asked the First Lady to lead the first delegation.

I arrived at Heathrow after an overnight flight and, together with Deputy Secretary of the Treasury Larry Summers, was driven in an embassy car to Chequers, a seventeenth-century brick and stone mansion set among

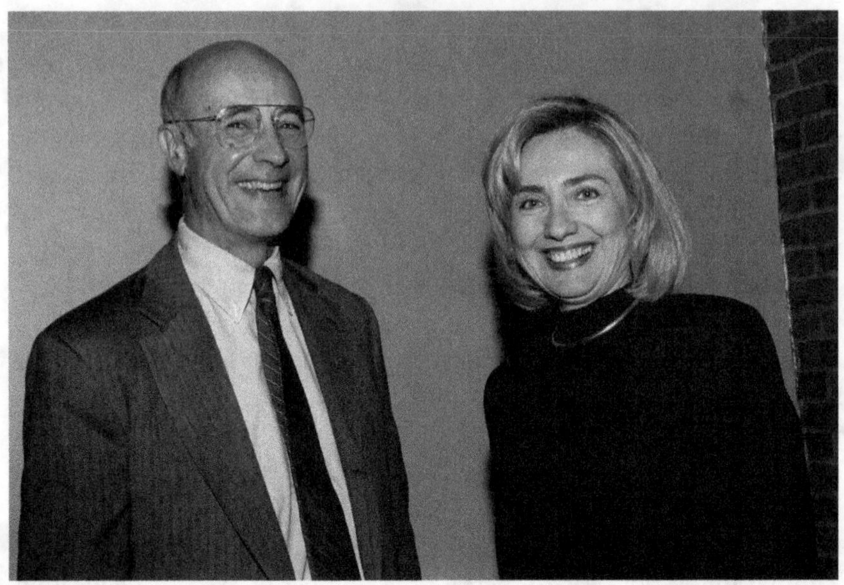

With Hillary Clinton at Harvard Kennedy School, 1996
Source: © Martha Stewart 1996

broad fields dotted with old oaks in the Chiltern Hills northwest of London. Blair greeted us at the massive front door dressed in a blue denim shirt. He was lively, informal, and at ease. I sat next to him at dinner, and he explained how he saw Britain's role as crucial in maintaining good relations between the US and Europe. Among the British participants were Gordon Brown, Peter Mandelson, David Miliband, Margaret Jay, Ed Balls, and Anthony Giddens – as well as Cherie Blair, herself an interesting lawyer. The Americans included Frank Raines, Andrew Cuomo, Al From, Melanne Verveer, and Don Baer. The sessions dealt with how politics was shifting and the need to capture new ideas for the center left; how to deal with the economic and political effects of globalization; how to help those left behind and the problem of growing inequality; and how to reshape government. It was a good discussion with little posturing.

The China puzzle

China also took up a good deal of my time, starting with the executive program for Chinese senior colonels in January and ending with a

Kennedy School Conference on US–China relations in December. A DPB meeting discussed how we did not fully understand China but also, as the analysts reported, China did not really understand us either. My colleague Tony Saich, who spent many years with the Ford Foundation in Beijing, said that China was slowly developing a civil society sector, but that it would remain a one-party state and would continue Deng Xiaoping's moderate foreign policies after his death in February. Among Americans, there were sharp differences of opinion on how we should respond. Where did democracy and human rights fit? For example, in October, Henry Kissinger invited me to a small dinner at his apartment in New York and described the importance of getting along with China, but that brought strong dissent from another guest, Abe Rosenthal of the *New York Times*.

These differences arose again when President Jiang Zemin visited Harvard, and Neil Rudenstine asked me how we should handle the planned protests. I said we should insist that Jiang take some questions from the audience. Jiang answered a few, while thousands of people protested outside Sanders Theatre. In December, the Kennedy School had scheduled a dissident to speak at one of our Forums, and Xiong Guangkai, who was visiting the School, warned me that any embarrassment might cause China to cancel all its programs at the School. I explained several times that speaking at our Forum did not imply endorsement of the speaker, and we had a commitment to remain open to all views. I warned our staff that we might lose our programs, but that it was a bright line we could not cross. China was indeed a puzzle.

Russia souring

On top of everything else, there was Russia, which was changing for the worse. I visited Moscow twice in 1997 and hosted Russians at the School, where we held a conference on the Russian economy. At Davos in February that year, Boris Nemtsov (a liberal politician who was assassinated in 2015) reported that no one was paying taxes and the government was behind on paying wages. In June, Sergei Rogov (whom I knew from my visits to the USA Institute in the 1980s) told me that there was not much sign of democracy in Russia, and everyone was corrupt. And Fyodor Burlatsky (whom I knew from our studies of the Cuban Missile Crisis) told me that Russia had become Tsarist, and few people there were honest. In September, economist Grigory Yavlinsky told a dinner at the School that "Russia is completely corrupt and Yeltsin has no vision." Overall, a very discouraging picture, which alas was prophetic. The benign days of Prime Minister Yegor Gaidar and Foreign Minister Andrei Kozyrev had been replaced by chaos in Yeltsin's later years. People speculated about who would succeed him, but the name Vladimir Putin rarely arose. Russia still had the capacity to destroy us. The US had provided financial aid and advice and created a NATO–Russia Council that brought Russian officers to Brussels, but we could not control its internal conditions. Even at the peak of the American century there were limits to American power.

The Lewinsky affair

After returning home from a trip to Taiwan, I read the news about Clinton's affair with a young White House intern named Monica Lewinsky. "So stupid if true!" I noted in my diary – alas it was and it consumed much of the year in DC. When Tony Blair visited Washington for a second session of the "Third Way" group, hosted by Bill Clinton in the Blue Room, the Lewinsky scandal dominated the headlines. Both Hillary Clinton and Al Gore were there. Bill Clinton had a remarkable ability to compartmentalize his mind and to comment intelligently about abstract policy issues even in times of stress. He fidgeted and drank a lot of coffee and huddled with his political advisors in the corner during coffee breaks, but then returned to the table to make coherent comments on subjects like education and earned income tax credits as solutions to the growing problem of inequality. I doubt I could have done it.

As the year progressed, there was increasing speculation about whether Clinton could complete his presidency. After his televised explanations in August, I wrote that I was disgusted with his self-indulgent behavior, but thought he would survive. After special prosecutor Kenneth Starr's report came out in September, I noted that it said nothing about the original concerns about the Whitewater controversy, which involved investigations into the real-estate investments of the Clintons and their associates; instead, it focused on sex. I thought Clinton had a two-thirds chance of political survival. Later in the month, at an evening at Henry

Kissinger's in New York, Walter Isaacson, the perceptive editor of *TIME* magazine, said he thought the odds were four to one that Clinton would serve out his term. The Republican efforts to impeach Clinton backfired. I wrote that I opposed impeachment because all Starr had shown was "low crimes and misdemeanors. A vote of censure would be more appropriate."

A year later, I went to Washington for an international conference on innovations in government, where Clinton gave the opening address. He came in looking fit and well. He bantered with Gore and Madeleine Albright, and I sat next to him on the platform in the Acheson Auditorium, where he gave a very good speech. Though I remained angry at his behavior, I could not help but be impressed by his charm and intelligence. If he was damaged goods, he did not show it. In March 1998, when former President Ford visited the Kennedy School, I asked him about the effects of "Monica-gate" and he said that he did not think the presidency was damaged. I was struck when I attended the Trilateral

With President Clinton and Madeleine Albright, Washington, 1998

Commission meeting in Berlin that European allies were puzzled by the American fixation on the sexual scandal. They were much more interested in the impending creation of the European Monetary Union and speculation on whether the euro would someday replace the dollar as the world's largest reserve currency.

Rules and red lines

The Clinton scandal encouraged us to clarify a set of rules within the Kennedy School regarding how one should treat romantic relationships between two consenting adults. We decided that power created a red line, and we could not assume full consent when one person had a direct position of power over another. Thus, we set a policy of no romantic relations between faculty and their students, or between supervisors and their staff members. Implementation was not always easy, particularly when the only evidence was "he said; she said." In one case, where I could not be sure but suspected the student was right, I docked the professor's salary and forbade him to meet with students without having his door open. The student later thanked me.

A different type of problem arose when I was notified that a faculty member who raised a lot of money for his research program was spending too much of it on himself. He denied that he had crossed any red lines, but staff investigations showed that he had. I eventually had to fire him for financial irregularities. The process involved hours of discussions with him and with lawyers, as well as one of his donors who offered to fund a chair if we would keep him, and a former cabinet official from Washington who berated me on the phone for nearly an hour.

Technology: new and old

The American century was one of rapid technological change, but the social effects were sometimes slow to catch up. The Nobel Laureate economist Robert Solow quipped in the 1980s that computers showed up everywhere in the economy except the productivity figures. By the mid-1990s, that was no longer true. And their effect was also beginning to be seen in politics.

In 1998, Neil Rudenstine convened the first of two large conferences at Harvard on the Internet and Society. Larry Ellison, co-founder of Oracle, predicted that the Internet would reach half the world's population within a decade. The iconoclastic blogger Matt Drudge said the Internet was "perfect populism" and the day of editors and two sources for a story had become old-fashioned and outdated. Henceforth, there would be no limits. We are still wrestling with that problem.

We took up these themes at our Visions of Government conference at Bretton Woods that summer. As my colleague Dennis Thompson asked in his conference paper with the witty title "E-Mail from Madison," what would happen to Madisonian democracy as the Internet disintermediated the institutions that he had considered to be essential to a stable republic? It was too soon to draw conclusions, but there were many concerns, and we held another conference on the subject at the School in December. Elaine Kamarck and I then edited those papers into a publication, *Democracy.com.*

In addition to these new concerns, my old interest in nuclear technology continued. At a conference convened by the Japanese government, I explained that I would agree with the goal of a nonnuclear world if it were long term and done in a manner that did not raise risks. But India and Pakistan had recently conducted nuclear tests, and there was concern about whether Saddam Hussein was developing nuclear weapons. Rolf Ekéus, the Swedish diplomat working for the UN in Iraq, told me about the problems created by Iraq's evasive behavior, and he felt that the US was right to continue building its case. Furthermore, North Korea chose to conduct a Taepodong missile test that flew over Japan and created great consternation. Friends in the Pentagon, to whom I spoke afterwards, said there had been no progress on North Korea and that if Pyongyang continued to refuse inspections of a new site, it would break the framework agreement negotiated a few years earlier. Some things do not change.

Asia redux

I started 1999 in East Asia. In Beijing, General Xiong told me of China's growing impatience with the US over Taiwan. At the Foreign Ministry, I discussed North Korea with Vice Minister (later Foreign Minister)

Yang Jiechi. He said that Pyongyang was interested in doing a deal with us, and I responded that China should press them to act before a crisis arose. His reply was that China could not do much. He also said the American sanctions on Iraq were counterproductive and we should seek a compromise.

At Zhongnanhai, Defense Minister Chi raised the issue of Taiwan and I asked about North Korea and human rights. Chi's reply was that stability had to come before openness. I heard a similar reply from Vice Premier Li Lanqing. A more liberal retired ambassador told me that democracy was gaining ground slowly, but all elections had to be local because China's population had become too large and illiterate for real democracy. A young government official told me that he and his wife regularly used the Internet through VPNs, and he supplemented his salary by her work in the private sector. Playing off the slogan for Hong Kong of "One country, two systems," he called it "One family, two systems."

In Singapore, I met with my friend and former Harvard colleague Yuen Foong Khong. I asked him about politics and censorship of the Internet. He said speech was free if it was not connected to organizing or action. I raised the question again in my hour-long meeting with former Prime Minister Lee Kuan Yew at the Istana Palace. He said they were pragmatically constructing a nation out of the chaotic bazaar left behind by Britain. Pure democracy would have produced a Chinese communist city-state. He was not worried about the Internet. Controls were for "hoi polloi" and anyone could route around them. "When everyone is computer literate, at that stage we will not have to worry about controls." He said he liked my idea of soft power and Singapore was using it.

My next stop was Tokyo, where I met with several officials, did television interviews, and spoke to a conference about security. Most amusing, Gaiko Press told me that they heard I had an unpublished novel and would like to publish it in Japanese. So, my novel first appeared in Japanese with the title *Dirty Hands*. Some years later, a Japanese journalist asked me if it was because my wife objected to the novel. I laughed and said that sounded much better than the truth that I had set it aside because of the three new jobs I took on in the 1990s.

Kosovo and Russia

The most dramatic events of 1999 included the Serbian ethnic cleansing of Albanians in Kosovo and the NATO bombing of Serbia that began on March 23. After diplomatic efforts by Madeleine Albright and Dick Holbrooke failed to change Slobodan Milošević's policy, and Russia and China blocked UN action, the US and its allies started bombing Serbia without approval from the Security Council. Human rights prevailed and, at a postmortem at Ditchley Park in June, respected international lawyers debated the legality of the bombing. What most participants agreed was that the bombing was moral but not legal, and there was disagreement about whether it was wise.

In Davos two months earlier, Henry Kissinger said he reluctantly supported the use of ground troops but was worried about over-extension. I shared his view and wrote at the time that I was "51–49 in favor." At a March meeting of the DPB, Secretary William Cohen explained why the action was necessary. My own view was that things were getting very messy, and I told Senator Feinstein that we should not bomb unless we knew what came next. I feared ground troops would be necessary. Earlier, at a Trilateral Commission meeting in Washington, people I respected, like Sadako Ogata (later UN High Commissioner), had argued that force would be necessary to solve the humanitarian problem, and NATO Secretary General Javier Solana agreed.

John Shalikashvili ("Shali") and Ash Carter both thought we should plan for ground troops, which Wesley Clark, NATO commander (and my old Pentagon counterpart), also thought necessary. At the same time, Shali said that there was some chance that bombing alone might work if we kept our objectives limited. In the end, by early June, Russian Prime Minister Viktor Chernomyrdin saved us from that decision by persuading Milošević to withdraw his troops if NATO would promise there would be no independence referendum for three years. The bombing of Serbia is sometimes cited as evidence of hubris in the American century after the Cold War. On the contrary, I was struck by how close a call it was and that the key issue was human rights versus realism rather than imperial ambition.

Reality soon closed back in. The Aspen Strategy Group focused its summer meeting on Russia, and the mood was discouraging both in the meeting room and the informal discussions. Most thought that Russia would not collapse but would develop a form of corrupt state capitalism. Later, at a meeting in DC, former NIO George Kolt told me he envisaged a weakening of central government, which was correct in the short but not the long run. In conversations with some of my former colleagues, I was struck that nobody seemed to know much about Putin or to have realized how important he would become. The strategy group debated whether the West had missed an opportunity to rescue Russia in 1992. Brent Scowcroft, who had been National Security Advisor at the time, thought not, but David Lipton (later of the IMF) thought the chances had been 50:50.

Problems of globalization

My own intellectual focus was on "globalization," a new buzzword of the decade. I decided to teach a module on the issue despite the pressures on my time as dean. We also focused the Visions Project on the impact of globalization on governance with attention to trade, immigration, innovation and health, and inequality. As poor workers in the South were being helped, it was at the cost of some workers in the West, who were being hurt. Bob Keohane and I worked on a third edition of our earlier work on power and interdependence and published a *Foreign Policy* article, "Globalization: What's New, What's Not, and So What?" We argued that technology had produced more interdependence at intercontinental distances, but many of our earlier propositions about interdependence as a political tool remained valid whether or not it was global. "So what?" entailed the creation of a wider range of issues on the political agenda. For example, ecological interdependence in the form of global climate change was not a major international issue when we were writing in the 1970s. Jack Donahue and I edited a Visions Project book on the subject.[10]

In January 2000, I was invited to give a Distinguished Visitor Lecture to 500 people at CIA headquarters in the curious auditorium that, because of its shape, is known as "the bubble." I spoke on the problems

[10] John Donahue and Joseph Nye, eds., *Governance in a Globalizing World* (Washington, DC: Brookings Institution Press, 2000).

of globalization. Anti-globalization demonstrators had broken up the World Trade Organization (WTO) meetings in Seattle the previous month, and I had written a mildly critical piece in the *New York Times*, which led Bill Clinton to send me a handwritten note saying he liked my comments about soft power but had not backed away from supporting the WTO. (Later in the year when Director-General of the WTO, Pascal Lamy, came to dinner at the Kennedy School, he said that the Seattle meeting had failed because of differences among the governments, not because of the protests.)

There were anti-globalization protests at the WEF in Davos that year too. Demonstrators broke the windows of a McDonald's and blocked the streets of the snowy alpine village to object to child labor in the hot global South – an act that was itself illustrative of globalization. An Indian delegate admitted that India could do something more on child labor, but rejected the idea of coercion by what he called protectionist labor standards in rich countries. Some argued that international organizations should concern themselves more with ecological standards for trade, while others regarded this as interference by the former imperial powers that had caused the problems in the first place.

I co-chaired a session with Administrator of the UN Development Programme Mark Malloch-Brown, at which a major discussion topic was whether globalization was homogenizing world culture. A French participant lamented that his culture would soon be reduced to merely ten cheeses. I told him I would bet there would still be 365, as Charles de Gaulle had once described. More serious were concerns about the loss of privacy in the age of the global Internet. A Silicon Valley CEO proclaimed that privacy was finished, and we should just "get over it." Clinton gave a well-attended speech on free trade. Afterwards I chaired a lunch discussion with Israeli Prime Minister Shimon Peres, former Swedish Prime Minister Carl Bildt, and Prime Minister Rasmussen of Denmark, who were all concerned about the popular backlash and the problems of governance of globalization. As Helmut Schmidt, former German Chancellor, put it when visiting the Kennedy School in May: "It is hard to be a global leader when you are elected locally."

In August, the Aspen Institute celebrated its fiftieth anniversary with a conference on globalization attended by a thousand people. Among those who spoke were President of the World Bank Jim Wolfensohn,

Jimmy Carter, and Oscar Arias, former (and future) President of Costa Rica and a Nobel Peace prizewinner. My panel discussed governance and institutions. MIT political economist Lester Thurow said that what was new about twenty-first-century globalization was that it was being led by business rather than by governments. Queen Noor of Jordan thought that globalization would increase cultural diversity for Muslim women, but Indian diplomat Shashi Tharoor thought that would be true only for some. More worrisome were warnings from Bill Joy, co-founder of Sun Microsystems, about technological innovation getting beyond human control. I asked the Nobel physicist Murray Gell-Mann whether he thought this was true. He was doubtful. Such were the thoughts on globalization at the turn of the century. It turns out that governments had more staying and destructive power than many people thought at that time.

One potential global problem, at least, did not come to pass as we entered the new century. For some time, computer experts had been warning of a "Y2K Problem" when the world's computers could all massively fail. The government had established a commission to ensure that computer programs would change the date smoothly to the next century rather than shut down. Happily, they succeeded. We gathered our family and some neighbors at our farm and danced as the TV showed the ball dropping over Times Square. My daughter-in-law Kathy, christened the event "Black velvet and hiking boots" as fireworks flashed over the hills.

Political limits

And 2000 was, of course, a presidential election year. Elaine Kamarck asked me to brief Al Gore in his office at the Old Executive Building, and I found him lively and engaged on issues related to globalization. Afterwards, I checked with Rudenstine on Harvard policy on deans' involvement in politics. He said support in the form of private papers and consultations was allowed, but nothing that might imply official endorsement. I told Kamarck to keep my name off any list of endorsers, and I had to say no when the Gore campaign asked if I would agree to be a surrogate speaker. Former Senator Sam Nunn (D) told me in the summer that he thought Gore would beat Senator Bill Bradley for the nomination, but that Clinton would be a drag on him in the general election. He proved to be right on both points.

Some news was bad. In July, the world learned that John F. Kennedy, Jr. had died after his plane had gone missing. I remembered him as handsome and lively and holding bright political promise. He had asked me to write for his magazine *George*, and I had joined him at his father's library just a few weeks earlier. Now he was no more. Another sad death for the Kennedy family, and the end of talk about a political dynasty. A potential leader was gone.

One of my projects as dean was to build a new Center for Public Leadership in the Kennedy School. Public leadership could involve political and government work, but I wanted to develop a concept of tri-sectoral leaders with bridging careers in government, nonprofits, and the private sector. The common denominator was entrepreneurship in adding public rather than merely private value. For some time, I had been wooing philanthropists Les and Abigail Wexner to support the program, and I persuaded colleagues David Gergen and Ronald Heifetz to become the founding co-directors of the Center. The Wexners were smart donors, and I was delighted when they agreed to fund the Center, which, over the years, has flourished.

The Middle East impasse

Early in the new year, I was off to the Middle East to again raise funds. My first stop was Beirut. Although I found the city quite attractive and the campus of the American University very peaceful, I was also struck by the number of shelled-out buildings that remained from their civil war. Lebanon's politics and civic life were equally damaged. Mohammad Safadi, a Sunni member of parliament, held a dinner in my honor and warned me of the stranglehold of confessional politics. An ambassador told me, "You can know Lebanon but never understand it," and another ambassador said that, unlike Singapore, there was no concept of governance. The Ottoman-style bureaucracy was inefficient and corrupt, even though, in their diasporas, Lebanese were highly successful. When I met with President Lahoud the next morning, he was confident of peace, as was Prime Minister Rafiq Hariri when we lunched behind bulletproof glass in his ninth-floor apartment with a commanding view of the city.

But in 2005 Hariri was assassinated. Good governance matters, but the American century could not extend it to the Middle East.

After a short visit to Amman, I was driven to the Allenby Bridge. I had forgotten how small the famed River Jordan of my Bible really is, scarcely as wide as the river on my New Hampshire farm. But it nevertheless took over an hour to cross because of the need to have papers in order before transferring to an Israeli car to take me to Jerusalem. There, I stayed again in the King David Hotel and found it hard not to be stirred by the view out over the walls of the ancient city that had loomed so large in my Sunday School years. Itamar Rabinovich, Israel's ambassador to the US, told me he feared the peace process was getting stuck and Clinton would have to become more involved (which he tried to do but failed before leaving office). On the other hand, a number of participants at a conference held in Caesarea told me that they thought a framework with the Palestinians could be worked out over the next several years. Unfortunately, the optimism of that moment was not justified. On a personal side note, I was pleased when Ami Ayalon, the head of Shin Bet (Israel's internal security service) and a former student, showed me a Hebrew translation of my 1994 article "Peering into the Future" and said he made all his analysts read it.

Optimism about China

When I attended the Trilateral Commission in Tokyo in April, I encountered a good deal of optimism about China. As the economy grew, there were some signs of social liberalization. This period under Jiang Zemin was a contrast to the later authoritarian repression of Xi Jinping. The Asian group had invited Chinese to be "participants" – a move I had suggested three years earlier – and people were bullish about continued Chinese growth. One participant, Zhang Yunlin, said that while China could not be a democracy within a decade, it could be after several decades. Local elections were a start. Some people mentioned China following a "Singapore model" even sooner. There was also talk about the backlash to globalization, but the Peruvian writer Mario Vargas Llosa assured the group that cultural diversity was not under threat.

The economic optimism about China was confirmed during my visit to Beijing in May, but the security issues remained. When I went to Zhongnanhai to call on Li Lanqing, he repeated the usual warnings about Taiwan, but also wanted to raise Chinese concern that our national ballistic missile defense program was destabilizing. The next day, I visited the Ministry of Defense with its long corridor of shiny marble and a deep red rug to spend an hour with Minister Chi and General Zhang. In addition to Taiwan, they also raised questions about ballistic missile defense, both national and regional. They said that, while they would put aside what we had described as the accidental bombing of China's embassy in Belgrade in 1999, they did not feel they had received a satisfactory explanation. On the other hand, both expressed satisfaction with the Kennedy School's program for senior colonels – that was before one of the attendees defected at the end of the year!

The focus of my visit to Beijing was a conference on globalization organized by the *People's Daily* in the Great Hall of the People. Richard Cooper and Joseph Stiglitz talked about economics, and I spoke on the governance of globalization. There were many questions from the floor, and later, at lunch with my academic friends Yuan Ming and Yang Xiyu, I asked them what they heard that seemed new. They cited the idea of information as a key power resource in this new century, and the importance of credibility. The editor of the *People's Daily* commented that credibility must come from the Party, but said he was now allowed to report more than ever before. A brief stop in Hong Kong on the way home reinforced the idea of optimism about the ability of China to adapt.

Europe as a challenger?

China was not the only potential challenger to the American century. In June 2000, I went to a conference on Europe at Talloires on the shore of Lake Annecy. My Harvard colleague Sam Huntington talked about growing differences between the US and Europe, and there was discussion of whether a planned European defense force of 60,000 would be a challenge to NATO. François Heisbourg warned about the US superpower succumbing to unilateralism. I was more optimistic and said we should fear a Europe that was too weak rather than too strong. I did not share the concerns about Europe as a challenge to the American century.

I had a long talk about European institutions with Karl Kaiser, former Director of the German Council on Foreign Relations, and British diplomat Sir Michael Palliser. Enlargement to new members was necessary but was diluting the institutions. The old formula of increasing federalism would no longer work, and we agreed that European governance was *sui generis*; it did not fit any formula. Before returning home, I stopped in Athens, where the Greeks expressed great enthusiasm for joining the Euro zone, and I spoke at a reunion of the various East European fellows who had attended the Kennedy School with the support of the Kokkalis Foundation.

Back to school and politics

September 2000 was the start of the new school year and a chance to take stock of where we stood. In May, Harvard had celebrated the successful completion of its $2.6 billion capital campaign, and the Kennedy School had raised $208 million (compared to its target of $125 million). All those fundraising trips had paid off! As we started the new academic year, our endowment stood at $427 million, and our $100-million annual budget was in the black. During my first four years, the School had grown 15 percent in budget and staff, including the recruitment of some spectacular new faculty members. Even more important, we were on track with the priorities that I had set to accomplish our mission in 1996.

Labor Day meant the start of the election campaign in earnest when the American people, as opposed to the politicos, started to pay attention. During the year, people had been predicting a close race. For example, at the Aspen Strategy Group in August, Senator John Warner told me it was 50:50. There was "Clinton fatigue," and George W. Bush was an inexperienced but attractive candidate. As Walter Isaacson told me, most reporters covering the election would say: "If you were having a beer in a bar, you would rather have it with Bush than with Gore."

I could not be involved because of my job, but I was happy to join Rich Armitage in co-chairing a report on the US–Japan alliance that outlined its importance to our future in Asia. Our aim was to symbolize bipartisan support for the alliance and to elevate it above the fray of campaign politics. We unveiled the report on October 11 at a well-attended meeting in the Mansfield Room in the Capitol. It was the first of several Armitage–Nye reports that we issued in later election years and may have made a modest contribution to the US–Japan relationship. It certainly received a lot of attention in the Japanese press.

That afternoon, I spoke at a Kennedy School Conference on Innovations in Government held at the National Press Club, and then met with our alumni. As I was taking a cab to the airport, I managed to catch the end of the Bush–Gore debate. It was a very different experience from 1988 when I had been present as a professor, not a dean, and spoke in the spin room after the Dukakis–Bush debate. Two weeks later, when I went to Paris to a meeting of deans hosted at Versailles by Sciences Po, I was struck by a piece of graffiti that read "La vie est poesie" – life is poetry. How true!

November 7 was election day and I voted for Gore. Listening to the returns was like riding a seesaw. An early call of Florida for Gore was reversed, but by the time I went to bed Gore was ahead. I was up early the next morning to find out the result but there was still no answer. Gore had won the popular vote, but the electoral college depended on a recount of disputed votes in Florida. The next four weeks were a roller coaster. On December 8, as I was splitting firewood at our farm in New Hampshire, I learned from the radio that the Florida Supreme Court had ruled in Gore's favor on the recount, but the next day the US Supreme Court voted 5–4 to stay the recount, and a week later decided by the same margin in favor of Bush. What was interesting was how the legitimacy of the court decision was widely accepted, helped by a graceful concession speech by Gore. That evening, the Kennedy School held a dinner for the new members of Congress following our practice of meeting at the School after elections, and there were no recriminations. It was a dramatic contrast to what would occur twenty years later.

Summing up Clinton

How can I sum up the Clinton years? I am proud to have played a part. Bill Clinton never articulated a complete vision for the post-Cold War world, but he ultimately embraced a strategy very similar to that charted by George H. W. Bush. In September 1993, Tony Lake declared the "defining feature of this era is that we are its dominant Power"; we must "prevent aggressive dictators from menacing the post-Cold War order, and ... aggressively promote free markets and democracy." Clinton put his own brand on it with the term "engagement and enlargement." By this he meant engaging with former enemies and enlarging the domain of free market democracies by using market forces more than military might. Clinton warned that "we cannot police the world." The real hubris in the post-Cold War American century comes after Clinton.

Clinton relied heavily on economic change. His prudent fiscal policies and domestic economic initiatives prepared the US to prosper in a globalizing economy, and he went against public opinion (and many Democratic party advisors) to pass the North American Free Trade Area (NAFTA) legislation that he had inherited from Bush, as well as to complete the Uruguay Round of tariff reductions and to launch the WTO and support China's entry.

Rather than try to create a Cold War policy of containment of a rising China (which was unlikely to succeed given the attitudes of other countries that I have described), Clinton hoped to integrate China into the liberal international order. While he was overoptimistic about the extent to which trade and growth would liberalize China, Clinton's policy was not as simple as it might seem. It also involved a realist strand that reaffirmed and strengthened the US–Japan security treaty as an insurance policy, which I helped initiate. Clinton also invested major efforts in peacemaking. Had Rabin not been assassinated in November 1995, there might also have been an agreement between Israel and Syria. One of the final acts of Clinton's presidency was a Camp David meeting where he tried unsuccessfully to mediate between Yasser Arafat and Israeli Prime Minister Ehud Barak.

Russia was another top priority for Clinton, and he spent a great deal of personal time on it. He made major efforts to develop a relationship with Yeltsin, to provide aid and encourage investment, and to expand the Group of Seven advanced economies to a G-8, with Russian membership. But after seventy years of communism, Russia had neither the economic nor the political institutions to successfully absorb Marshall Plan type aid, and as corruption grew and Yeltsin became physically and politically weaker during the decade, he became too frail a foundation to build upon.

Clinton's initiative to expand NATO to include former members of the Warsaw Pact went beyond the Pentagon's more modest Partnership for Peace program, which I advocated until Clinton made his decision. In 1999, NATO admitted Poland, Hungary, and Czechoslovakia. Although Yeltsin accepted this at the time, Putin later pointed to NATO expansion as proof of Western perfidy. The difficult counterfactual is what the world today would look like if NATO expansion had not stabilized central Europe.

Clinton replaced Cold War containment with a view of expanding market economies and encouraging democratic evolution summarized by engagement and enlargement. In terms of his personal motives, it is not accurate to describe Clinton as succumbing to post-Cold War hubris, though some in his administration overestimated American power. He was prudent in his implementation, relying more on economic change and institutions than on military force. When he did use force for interventions, it was prudently applied for humanitarian purposes, though his goals also included promotion of democracy. He pursued both peacekeeping and peacemaking as major foreign policy objectives.

At the end of his term, the American and global economies were growing, alliances with Europe and Japan had been strengthened, relations with major powers of Russia and China were reasonable, and international institutions strengthened. Efforts had begun to deal with climate change and missile proliferation.

Clinton was a superb politician with an important ability to relate to people and pull them together. He used flattery (as we all do), but was also able to convey a sense of sincerity. For example, in a speech at Harvard, he paid a nice tribute to me and included that his daughter was reading my books at Oxford. Watching him work a rope line and shake hundreds of hands even when tired was amazing. Where Clinton fell short was in his personal indiscipline and its wider effects. His looseness with the truth in his personal affairs undercut trust in his presidency. On January 20, 2001, David Gergen flew from Washington to join us with a small group of friends in New Hampshire. He had advised Clinton in the White House (and, before that, three other presidents). We sat around the table and tried to sum up Clinton on the eve of Bush 43. I ventured that historians would probably judge Clinton as a "B+" president who could have been an "A" if he had had more self-restraint. David's response summed it up: "You are right, but then he would not have been president in the first place."

8

The Bush Years

In my 2013 book *Presidential Leadership and the Creation of the American Era*, I concluded that George H. W. Bush ("41") had one of the best foreign policies of the American century – proving that I could be analytically nonpartisan despite my earlier political efforts in the Dukakis campaign. But I wrote that, despite sharing half his father's genes, George W. Bush ("43") had one of the worst. Unlike his father, he had no experience in foreign affairs and came into office with many advisors who had a view that America could do whatever it wanted in a unipolar world. They failed to understand the limits of American power.

Unipolar hubris

Although there were early signs of it in the Clinton Administration, it wasn't until the Bush years that the "sole superpower" succumbed to hubris. Before joining the administration, Paul Wolfowitz (who became Deputy Secretary of Defense) told me that all we would need in Iraq were 50,000 troops, while Ken Adelman, Director of ACDA (Arms Control and Disarmament Agency), predicted publicly that the invasion would be "a cakewalk." Secretary of Defense Donald Rumsfeld told a 2003 Army conference (which I also addressed) that he did not understand what soft power meant. This hubris was evident well before the events of 9/11. On a three-month leave of absence from the Kennedy School deanship, which I spent at All Soul's College in Oxford, I wrote a book whose title summarized my views: *The Paradox of American Power: Why the World's Only Superpower Can't Go It Alone.* It was to become my most widely read work (other than my textbook, which ran to ten editions) – selling more than 100,000 copies and making it onto the *Washington Post* and *The Economist* lists of "best books of the year."

The year 2001 was a turning point in the American century. For the first forty years, our grand strategy focused on containing the

Soviet Union with the help of allies in a bipolar world. After the Soviet collapse, we had our unipolar moment and Clinton tried a strategy of engagement and enlargement of democracy. In 2001, this approach switched abruptly to a "global war on terrorism." As mentioned in the last chapter, as consultants to the NIC in 1996, Jim Woolsey and I had produced a classified report warning about a massive terrorist attack, and we published an op-ed predicting that the country was unlikely to prepare adequately until we suffered another Pearl Harbor. But neither of us predicted that terrorists would use commercial aircraft as piloted cruise missiles or would so quickly change the national agenda. Before September 11, 2001, the Bush Administration had not given high priority to terrorism, but 9/11 was like pouring a five-gallon drum of gas onto a campfire in a dense pine forest. Terrorists are like ju-jitsu players: they cannot defeat governments, but they can use the theater of terror to set the agenda and shock the stronger player into using his strength to damage himself. That was what Al-Qaeda did to Bush with his invasion of Iraq.

Despite the close election result in November 2000, I was relaxed about politics as the new year started. I even recorded that "Bush looks like a moderate with a good foreign policy team. We'll see." Sadly, I was wrong. By May, I noted that "Bush ran as a moderate but has pandered to his conservative base. He talked of humility in foreign policy, but practices arrogant unilateralism," Even before the shock of 9/11, the US was succumbing to the hubris of being the sole superpower. As French Foreign Minister Hubert Védrine put it, the US had become a "hyperpower." I later came to know Védrine and realized that he was not anti-American but a hard-core French realist.

Before September 2001, much of the agenda in world politics focused on the backlash against globalization that some critics treated as synonymous with Americanization. At Davos in January that year, Paul Kennedy and I had shared a session where he said I had been right in our debate about American decline a decade earlier. At the Trilateral Commission in London in March, I spoke about governance of globalization and the democratic deficit in international organizations. As the statesman Harlan Cleveland once phrased the problem: "How do you get everyone into the act and still get action?"

The view from Europe

My Kennedy School agenda was full of tasks such as recruiting faculty, developing a new five-year plan, and raising money; avoiding a deficit during the "dot.com recession" in the economy; and planning for our annual Bretton Woods conference on visions of governance. The external visiting committee reported to Harvard's Board of Overseers that "the Kennedy School is in its best shape to accomplish its mission in its history."

Thus, in April, I felt comfortable in taking a short sabbatical and accepting an invitation to spend three months as a visiting fellow at All Soul's College, Oxford to work on my book. Returning to Oxford was a delight. All Souls was founded in 1438 and devotes its endowment to support of advanced studies. It provided me with a flat in Iffley, a small village on the Thames marked by an ancient Romanesque church and houses with thatched roofs. From our windows, we could see the spires of Oxford, and if I did not want to take the bus, I could cross the Iffley Lock and walk up the Thames or bike to town along the old towpath in a half hour or so. On a trip to London, I met Bill Emmott and Clive Crook at *The Economist* (my favorite weekly), and then filmed an interview with Tim Sebastian for the BBC's TV program *HARDtalk*. Much of it involved his complaints about US unilateralism. I then gave a lecture at Chatham House on "Globalization and Its Discontents."

On a visit to Berlin, a few weeks later, there was much discussion of European federalism and the new Euro money that would become the official currency the following year. Some saw Europe as a future challenger to the American century. British politician Peter Jay told me that European federalism was a French plot to create a nation to balance American power, but Germans such as Karsten Voigt and Karl Kaiser assured me that Germany did not see it that way, and they were skeptical about the idea of a federal Europe. I agreed with them, viewing Europe as an ally rather than a threat to the American century. But some Europeans were overconfident.

At the Aspen Institute in August 2001, Antony Blinken and Felix Rohatyn, former Ambassador to France, presented papers on Europe; Rohatyn said we should not be misled by the behavior of French radicals who had set fire to a McDonald's restaurant, because the younger generation of businessmen were pro-American. Diplomat James Dobbins said that European complaints about US unilateralism had to be weighed against European unilateral actions that isolated the US on issues like the International Criminal Court, the Kyoto Protocol on climate, and the treaty to ban landmines. On NATO expansion, the group was about evenly split, but no one expected a divorce from the US.

9/11 and its fall-out

Some events are so dramatic and emotional that one can visualize them and remember where one was at the time decades later. The academic year had started well and the 11th of September was a beautiful autumnal morning like any other. I had gone for my morning run and was working on some footnotes for the book, when my assistant Jeanne Marasca called about a plane hitting the World Trade Center in New York. Like many people, I assumed the first plane was an accident, but as I commuted to work and heard reports of a second plane hitting the World Trade Center, I knew the nightmare of a domestic Pearl Harbor had now occurred. Some Kennedy School staff members and the central university administration urged that we close the School and send people home. But I disagreed. Having people watch horror on TV alone in their apartments was worse than any risk of an attack on the Kennedy School, and the police said there was no imminent risk. Instead, we should try to try to maintain a sense of community. So we did what we knew how to do best: we assembled a Forum to try to make sense of what we were experiencing. I was joined by Allison, Gergen, and the terrorism expert Jessica Stern. The Forum was packed, and we warned against stereotypes, and overreactions that would harm civil liberties. I was later told that the Forum had a good effect on the School.

At home that evening, Molly and I listened to President Bush speak about remaining "a beacon of freedom." I was scheduled to travel the next day, but all flights were cancelled, so I wrote op-eds and did television interviews instead. We held a number of discussions at the School, but there was so much uncertainty. I wrote on September 14 that "even if we get Bin Laden, there will be others, and have we thought through a 'war on terrorism?' We will have to use force, but what comes next?"

With planes grounded, Senator Kerry was unable to return to DC, so he invited me, John Deutch, and Ash Carter to his house on Beacon Hill to think about what a war on terror might mean. I said I feared "the rhetoric of war may divert us from the many civilian things we need to do." The next day, I held our third public Forum on 9/11 with David Pryor (former senator), Kim Campbell (former Canadian Prime Minister), and Ash Carter. We worried that expansive bombing of Afghanistan might kill too many civilians and make the terrorism problem worse. I also worried about Bush having framed it as a military issue. I made the same points at a Council on Foreign Relations teleconference on terrorism, and I worked on a chapter for the book they were preparing on terrorism. At the School, we made plans for an executive program on domestic preparedness run by Juliette Kayyem.

Within a few weeks, I was able to resume travel. The airport security lines were impossibly long and items as small as nail clippers were confiscated. Flying over New York, I could see plumes of smoke still drifting up from the wreckage of the twin towers. At the Nixon Center in DC, the neoconservative Richard Perle called for the destruction of state sanctuaries for terrorists, with precision bombing of Afghanistan and Iraq. Others, like Iran and Syria, he said, would then fall in line. He also suggested that, if the Saudis did not let us use their bases, we should put them in Israel instead; that we should not let our alliances and coalitions shackle us; that we only needed a few states to be on our side; and that it was a mistake to allow NATO to invoke Article 5 about coming to our defense. My diary entry that night was a short and resounding: "No!" Later, Perle conceded that some of his early remarks may have been "incautious," but he told me his position did not change. He believed we should remove Saddam regardless of what other countries, including our allies, thought.

The situation became even more complex in late September when someone began mailing deadly anthrax powder to congressional, press, and other offices, which killed five people. It later turned out to be domestic terrorism by a disgruntled government scientist, but at the time the threat seemed infinite because it was amplified by the false rumors that always occur in crisis situations. I told Jeanne not to open any letters or packages that seemed suspicious, but to bring them to me to check the sender. The School did have one incident of a letter with powder, which was taken away by responders in Hazmat suits, but fortunately it turned out to be a false alarm.

Governor Tom Ridge was appointed the first director of a newly created Office of Homeland Security in the White House, and Richard Falkenrath from our faculty went to work for him. The office had trouble getting going. My colleague Ernest May said Ridge ran the risk of becoming an auxiliary press secretary rather than a planner. Al Hunt of the *Wall Street Journal* was concerned that Ridge got off to a poor start by spending too much time on the shifting facts of anthrax mailings rather than on building up his planning capabilities. Later, General Barry McCaffry made a similar point at a Kennedy School meeting. I tried to convey these thoughts to Falkenrath and others when I visited their offices in late November. Within two months, Kabul and the Taliban government had fallen to American military power. Welcome as that was, the fact remained that we were not showing similar aptitude on homeland security.

As a symbol of solidarity after 9/11, the next Davos meeting moved to New York. The annual evening party was held on the floor of the Stock Exchange near Ground Zero. But many Europeans were unhappy with Bush's policy, particularly after his speech that lumped the disparate countries of Iraq, Iran, and North Korea together as an "Axis of Evil." I shared the criticism and in various television interviews, such as BBC and CNN, I called it "a rhetorical bridge too far."

Problems of peace

In December 2001, I was invited by the Norwegian Nobel Committee to give a paper at a symposium to celebrate the 100th anniversary of the Nobel Peace Prize. Fourteen former laureates, fourteen representatives of organizations that had won the prize, and eight scholars attended, among them my colleague Amartya Sen who went on to win a Nobel Prize in economics. My paper was on the rise and fall of great powers. Elie Wiesel was the commentator, and responded favorably.

I was struck, however, by the gap between the academics and the activists. We shared many of the same values, but had different approaches to the truth. I found much of their thinking rather unsystematic. Based on a single comment, Bishop Desmond Tutu argued that US Blacks had different views of 9/11. He condemned the idea of bombing in Afghanistan and said that Bush, Saddam, and Bin Laden were all God's children. I regarded that as only a half truth. Jody Williams, a former Nobel Peace prizewinner who had successfully led the effort for a treaty to ban landmines, said that only civil society could save us. We needed a legal rather than a military response to Bin Laden. My response was "OK, but exactly how do we catch him?" She commented that I was a "typical academic." But even among the activists there were differences between the pacifists and those like Wiesel who said that, but for World War II, he would not be there. Peace is not simple, not even among peace prizewinners.

In the ceremonies the next day in Oslo City Hall, UN Secretary-General Kofi Annan gave a good speech about humanitarian values and how to achieve them. That night I wrote: "Why do I get so annoyed by utopian preachers when my values are closer to theirs than to right-wingers like Richard Perle? Is it their sloppy thinking? But for all my commitment to reason, it is values that matter most. But how to combine them?"

Track 2 with India

Early in 2002, I flew to India to co-chair a "Track 2" dialogue between the Aspen Strategy Group and an Indian delegation convened by the Confederation of Indian Industry and its Director General Tarun Das. The idea had been suggested by Ambassador Robert Blackwill, who was searching for ways to strengthen US–Indian ties in the aftermath of 9/11. Such dialogues are called "Track 2 diplomacy" because, while the participants are close to governments, they remain disavowable.

We met in Udaipur, in a beautiful seventeenth-century marble palace in the middle of a lake, and we were greeted with bagpipes and rose petals. Henry Kissinger and industrialist Ratan Tata opened the session, and politician Jairam Ramesh spoke of India's growing role in the world and the importance of the US dropping its Cold War habit of thinking of India and Pakistan as connected by a hyphen. Only recently, the Pakistan military had launched incursions into Rajasthan, and India had mobilized, but we had a common interest in not wanting nuclear Pakistan to become radical or a failed state. At the same time, some Indians felt

Pakistan's strategy was to bleed India by low-intensity conflict. Improved Indian relations with China might help to moderate Pakistan. Although some of the speeches felt left over from the past, when Blackwill later hosted me and Kissinger at his Roosevelt House embassy in New Delhi, we all agreed that there was a new US–India relationship.

When the group met a year later at Jaipur, Indian strategist K. Subramanian put it bluntly: "India had decided that it dislikes the US less than it dislikes China." When we discussed our nuclear relations, which were still tense, I suggested a compromise in which India would say it would act as if it were a member of the NPT and the Nuclear Suppliers Group, join the Proliferation Security Initiative, and help us on Iran. In turn, we would treat India as if it were a weapons state under the NPT. At a subsequent meeting in Washington in December, S. Jaishankar (later Foreign Minister) told me that my suggestions at Jaipur had helped outline a nuclear deal. Sometimes, Track 2 diplomacy can help.

Cutting back

After returning home from India, I encountered one of the less pleasant aspects of leadership – firing people. Given the downturn in the economy, the School was facing a 3 or 4 percent shortfall in our $100 million budget, and I promised the Harvard Corporation that I would cut $2.5 million in our expenditures. Working with executive dean Bonnie Newman (former senior aide in the Bush 41 White House) and academic dean Frederick Schauer (a smart lawyer), we developed a plan to cut thirty slots by attrition and make terminal payments to twenty-five others. I decided to get the news out quickly and addressed an all-staff meeting. I took the blame for allowing expansion to exceed the economic limits set by the economy. I also announced cuts in the budget of the dean's office. While not everyone was happy (including me), McKinsey consultants reported to the Corporation in July that our promise would be met.

The invasion of Iraq

Over the summer of 2002, reports of an impending invasion of Iraq intensified. The columnist Jim Hoagland told me there would be an invasion by January. It was a constant topic of discussion in the corridors of the Aspen Institute, with my co-chair Brent Scowcroft expressing skepticism about invading Iraq and publishing his view in mid-August. Former Secretary of State James Baker also published an op-ed in August about the importance of a multilateral approach, with which I agreed. In early September, Pakistan's leader General Musharraf visited the School and said he thought bin Laden had been killed and that an invasion of Iraq would be a mistake.

In September 2002, I met with Sir Michael Quinlin, formerly the top official in the British Ministry of Defence and a devout Catholic who wrote a very thoughtful book on just war. He said he could support air strikes but opposed an invasion. I agreed about patience and a multilateral approach, but did not rule out the use of force if proliferation was imminent; I opposed the idea of an occupation that tried to turn Iraq into a democracy.

I was increasingly worried about what I considered would be a self-inflicted wound in our struggle against terrorism, and on October 21 I published an op-ed in the *Financial Times* with the headline, "Owls Wiser than Hawks About Iraq." It presented my case for a patient multilateral approach. Henry Kissinger called to say he agreed, but felt that action had to begin that winter because of temperatures in the Gulf, and also to avoid the issue becoming involved in the political climate of the US 2004 presidential election. I made my same argument on an NPR program a few weeks later, but obviously to no avail. In November, in the aftermath of 9/11, Bush captured the Senate as well as the House in the midterm elections. It was faint consolation that eight of our Kennedy School graduates were elected to Congress.

In December, the School held a public Forum on Iraq. Christopher Hitchens, a left-leaning British public intellectual, argued that war would be just given the repressive nature of Saddam Hussein's regime, but my friend Brian Hehir, a Catholic priest, argued that, based on just war theory, war was not yet necessary. I went to New Hampshire for our usual family Christmas vacation, but also to read some books. Charles Kupchan's *The End of the American Era* overestimated Europe's military weight and underestimated American staying power. Andrew Bacevich's *American Empire* leveled some important criticisms, but overstated his case. David Rieff's *A Bed for the Night*, about the failures of humanitarian intervention, made telling points about good intentions, but did not answer the question of what we should do when we could. As I listened to Christmas carols while reading before the fire, I wondered about the effects of organized religion when so many millions were killed in its name(s). But if not religion, would it just be something else? I walked under the bright stars before going to bed, worrying, wondering, and feeling insignificant in their infinite splendor. Kant was right!

Much of 2003 was consumed by Iraq. I started the year thinking the odds of war were 70:30, but that war would only be legitimate if it were multilateral. At Davos, I moderated a panel comprising Senator Joe Biden, Richard Haass from the State Department, and Kenneth Roth of Human Rights Watch. Questions from the audience were skeptical, but, as one person said, it made anti-Americanism seem a little less sharp since Americans too were split over the policy.

Colin Powell gave a good speech, arguing that the burden of proof was on Iraq to show that it did not have weapons of mass destruction; the Archbishop of Canterbury asked him what America's policy was doing to its soft power. After Davos I went to Rome to give a speech to a conference at the Vatican and said that it was a mistake to put the Iraq problem ahead of the threats posed by Al-Qaeda or North Korea. Much would depend on the UN inspection report by Hans Blix and whether an intervention was multilateral or not. At the beginning of February, Powell's testimony to the UN Security Council was not compelling enough to generate a second resolution of UN support.

A few days later, I had dinner with Kofi Annan in New York. He said he expected a vague second Security Council resolution, but it was important to keep the focus on disarmament rather than regime change. John Negroponte, US Ambassador to the UN, reckoned a second resolution seemed less likely than it had the week before. My friend John Ruggie, who had worked at the UN, thought France might support a second resolution if we gave the UN inspectors another six weeks, but French diplomat Jean-Louis Gergorin said President Jacques Chirac would veto it because an intervention would lead to a new wave of terrorism. We will never know, but in any event, it might not have mattered. At another meeting in New York, when a deputy National Security Advisor was asked what the administration would do if Saddam Hussein agreed to disarm, he replied that they would find other resolutions to enforce, including those on human rights. As Richard Haass wrote later, Bush had already made up his mind.[11] The motives were mixed, but along with legitimate concern about weapons of mass destruction, some in the administration had illusions about transforming the Middle East through democratization.

Still the public debate continued. The *New York Times* published an article (with my picture) entitled "Liberals who support the war," but all the nuances of my position about multilateralism and imminent threat of proliferation were dropped. Ironically, the same day the *Washington Post* published my op-ed advocating that we should take more time for the UN inspectors to report or we would wind up with the right war in the wrong way at the wrong time. On March 19, President Bush announced the beginning of hostilities. Our thoughts were irrelevant. So much for the importance of public intellectuals.

Leadership and soft power

In July, I attended the 100th anniversary of the Rhodes Trust, where Bill Clinton, Tony Blair and Nelson Mandela all spoke in London's ancient Westminster Hall. Cecil Rhodes (1853–1902) was an imperialist and a strange man (as described by his biographer, my friend Robert Rotberg).[12] He died at the young age of 48 lamenting that there was so much left to do.

A month later, I hosted Lech Wałęsa at the Kennedy School. He said he had never intended to become a leader, but he had led a strike at a dangerous time in Poland and others had followed. Now he felt the revolution was over and his type of leadership was no longer needed or wanted. That contrasted with Turkish leader Recep Erdogan, whom I met at Davos at his request. He was intent on convincing me that he was a moderate rather than extreme Islamist. I had three such meetings with him over the years, including a lunch in my office when his son graduated from the Kennedy School in 2004. I must admit I did not expect him to become as authoritarian as he did. Maybe the answer lay

[11] Richard Haass, *War of Necessity, War of Choice: A Memoir of Two Iraq Wars* (New York: Simon and Schuster, 2009).

[12] Robert I. Rotberg, *The Founder: Cecil Rhodes and the Pursuit of Power* (Oxford: Oxford University Press, 1988).

in power rather than Islam. As Lord Acton said: "Power corrupts and absolute power corrupts absolutely." Erdogan became more authoritarian as he became more powerful.

I discussed Bush's leadership with Dick Darman and he described George W. Bush as totally different from his father and competing with him. (I once asked Scowcroft about the relationship between father and son, and he said one had to read Shakespeare to understand it.) In any case, as Darman put it, "Colin Powell did not play to Texan biases." At the Carnegie Endowment, I debated with Newt Gingrich about strategy – a surprisingly cordial event given Gingrich's reputation for bombast – and his classic comment about soft power was "How can a Texan speak softly?" No two presidents in recent history shared more genes than the two George Bushes, yet no two were more dissimilar in leadership style. That puzzle led me to contemplate writing a book on leadership after I stepped down as dean and returned to teaching.

In the meantime, I spent the summer months drawing together my thoughts for a book on soft power. I felt Americans underplayed it and this was part of our problem in Iraq. We could not attract the terrorists, but it was essential to win the hearts and minds of those in the middle whom the terrorists sought to recruit to their cause. As our intelligence agencies later confirmed, our invasion of Iraq had made the terrorism problem there worse. In August, terrorists detonated a bomb at UN headquarters in Iraq and killed Sérgio de Mello, the able Brazilian diplomat who headed the mission.

In September, Colin Powell invited me and a small group of outsiders to a dinner on the eighth floor of the State Department, where he made clear that he understood the importance of soft power. At the same time, his deputy, Rich Armitage, was scathing in his description of Rumsfeld's arrogance. Obviously, we had no difficulty in defeating Saddam's army with our superior hard power, but only at the price of great damage to our soft power as we became bogged down in a quagmire reminiscent of Vietnam. I tried to spell this out in *Soft Power: The Means to Success in World Politics.*

Resigning as dean

In September 2003, I announced my plan to step down as dean the following June and return to teaching and research. I jokingly told the faculty: "I want the irresponsibility of being a professor again like the rest of you." Not only did I enjoy teaching, but I wanted to regain the 40 percent of my time that went to external representation and fundraising. I felt I was leaving the School in good shape. In eight years, I had doubled the size of the faculty, tripled the number of executive programs, created five new research centers, and balanced the budget. In the months that followed, French Ambassador Jean-David Levitte presented me with a medal for becoming a Chevalier des Ordres de Palme Académiques, and the Kennedy School held a large dinner to celebrate my retirement, with video tributes from Presidents Carter and Clinton. I was also honored at Princeton, where I was awarded the annual Woodrow Wilson Prize for distinguished service by an alumnus. In addition to government service, Princeton President Harold Shapiro cited my "big ideas" related to transnational relations, power and interdependence, and soft power. As I

In the dean's office, 2004
Source: Joseph S. Nye Personal Archives. Harvard University Archives

noted at the time, however, even when honored, humans seem never to feel totally secure. This was brought home when Molly and I attended the opening of a Gauguin show at the Museum of Fine Arts, where she was a senior associate. I was struck by the questions that Gauguin painted at the bottom of his monumental scene of primitive life in Tahiti: "Where do we come from, what are we, where are we going?" Good questions.

The 2004 election

The election year began with Bush attracting only 48 percent approval in the polls. Things were going badly in Iraq. A PBS documentary called it tactically brilliant but strategically flawed. Getting rid of Saddam was the easy part; governing Iraq was the hard part. General Eric Shinseki had been criticized but proven right in his estimates about the large number of troops that would be required, and Rumsfeld and Wolfowitz had been badly wrong. But Rumsfeld arrogantly dismissed complaints about chaos in Iraq with the flippant statement that "freedom is untidy." In March, Robert McNamara spoke in the Kennedy School Forum about the errors he had made in Vietnam. He was critical of the Iraq war, but told me privately that he did not think it proper for him to attack Bush by name. I was puzzled by this deference to the presidency. McNamara told me that Kennedy would have exited Vietnam after re-election, and that, by 1965, he (McNamara) had warned LBJ that there was a less than 50 percent chance of winning. But, after too many negative memos, Johnson stopped listening to him.

A few weeks later, the UN inspector David Kay told another Kennedy School Forum that he thought Saddam had pretended to have weapons of mass destruction in order to enhance his power both at home and abroad. Our leaders, particularly Dick Cheney, were not telling lies in terms of what they believed, but they greatly exaggerated far beyond what the intelligence actually said. And the result was a disaster. When I was interviewed by broadcaster Jeremy Paxman on the BBC TV program *Newsnight*, he asked me whether I thought the pictures of torture at the Abu Ghraib prison had undercut American soft power. Of course, he was right. When I went to the Trilateral Commission in Warsaw in May, I found that views of the US had dimmed, even among friends. And the same was true when I was introduced by former Prime Minister John

Major to give the annual Ditchley lecture in July. Iraq was undermining the foundations of the American century.

I had been doing some marginal work for John Kerry's presidential election campaign, but, as my deanship ended, I felt I could do more. At an event for Kerry in Cambridge, I told him that I thought he should announce his plans for exit from Iraq as soon as possible. Ash Carter made a similar point. At a meeting hosted by the dean of Princeton's School of Public and International Affairs Anne-Marie Slaughter, Kissinger was critical of Bush for not making the occupation multilateral, but said our presence was necessary to make a statement about our power to deter others. I said that we could offer the Iraqis a year or two of training, but then get out. I made the same points to Susan Rice and Rand Beers, who were advising at Kerry's campaign headquarters in DC. I told them that when I had visited French officials at the Quai d'Orsay earlier in the Spring, they had vowed there would be no French troops in Iraq.

The Democratic Party held its nominating convention in Boston that summer, and I played a small part by giving surrogate talks on foreign policy to various groups, attending events, and meeting with foreign visitors. Elaine Kamarck got me a pass to the convention floor and backstage at the Fleet Center, and I was pleased at how many of my former students stopped to say hello. I watched Kerry's speech, and he did a good job of outlining a centrist position in American politics. It was hard not to catch the excitement of a convention again, and I drove home elated. Nonetheless, I wrote that night that I thought the odds were 50:50. When the Aspen Strategy Group met in August, we heard from the pollsters Charlie Cook and John Zogby that Kerry might be able to win. They said the country was polarized, the 5 percent of undecided voters were inattentive, and views on Iraq were already "baked in."

Of course, we discovered the answer on election day. I awoke at 6 a.m. the next morning, turned on the radio and learned that Kerry had lost. My reaction was sad but not shocked. Before the election, Kurt Campbell had told me he expected I would be offered an important position if Kerry won. That was not to be. The country was now burdened with four more years of Bush's foreign policy. I had recently read my friend Niall Ferguson's *Colossus: The Rise and Fall of the American Empire*, which diagnosed why Americans are not good at imperialism. I wondered why he thought we should even try.

Puzzles of leadership

In 2005, I went to the University of Oxford as the Winant Visiting Professor, with a fellowship at Balliol College, but I wasn't sure what I would do there. I had just read Sidney Guberman's fascinating biography of our Princeton classmate Frank Stella, who had risen quickly to fame, but never stopped reinventing his art. It was the first time in twelve years that I hadn't had a set agenda. How would Oxford turn out? Was I still creative? Could I reinvent myself as Stella had done? I should not have worried about Oxford. That year, I spent two pleasant terms there, and then returned to spend part of the Trinity (summer) term as a visiting professor over the next six years. My experience as dean and as creator of a Center for Public Leadership had piqued my curiosity about what made good leadership and how it could be taught. I also wanted to explore how to apply my concepts of soft, hard, and smart power to individuals as well as countries. I did so when I published *The Powers to Lead* in 2008. I concluded that there are too many variables to support a strong theory of leadership, but, like love and power, it was too important to ignore.

I was still trying to puzzle out the contrasting leadership of the two Bush presidents. Leadership requires both emotional intelligence – the ability to manage one's emotions and relate to others – and contextual intelligence – the ability to adjust one's skills to different followers and different contexts. I concluded that leadership is an art, not a science, but, like other arts, such as playing the piano, it can be taught and learned, and there will be varying degrees of proficiency. There are theories of music that may help make a great piano player, but not as much as teaching and practice. But I am jumping ahead. First, I had to plunge into the murky water of leadership theory and learn to swim.

Oxford was a delight. Even in January, I was greeted by green grass, primroses, and snowdrops as I did my morning run in Christ Church Meadow. Andrew Graham, Master of Balliol, and my friend Adam Roberts, a senior professor, welcomed me to my first meeting of the Senior Common Room. I was amazed at how much administrative detail the dons discussed compared to our faculty meetings. Vice Chancellor John Hood, an impressive though controversial leader, asked me if I would like a contract to consult on the establishment of a Kennedy-like school at Oxford. I said I would do it for free, and over the next few years met often with Ngaire Woods, the smart and effective New Zealand Rhodes Scholar who went on to become the founding dean of Oxford's Blavatnik School of Government, on whose advisory board I later served. In general, my view was that the Kennedy School should not try to create foreign branches but should share our intellectual property and experiences to help others develop their own schools of public leadership. We did this in Oxford, Singapore, Berlin, and Dubai.

Teaching leadership

I taught a course at Harvard on presidential leadership in the Fall of 2005, which involved such complicated figures as Woodrow Wilson, the two Roosevelts, and Richard Nixon. When we came to George W. Bush, I warned the class that we should aim to avoid political preconceptions and try to judge him on his systems for information and learning. In my opinion, Bush seemed strong on risk and perseverance but weak on contextual intelligence. He was better on vision than on diagnosis. When a student said he thought Bush was evil, I said no, but one could accuse him of being culpably negligent.

As for personality and emotional intelligence, the author Bob Woodward had described Bush to me as "transformational" by temperament; while some, like James MacGregor Burns and other leadership theorists, praise that characteristic, it can be a mixed blessing. Teddy Roosevelt was transformational and succeeded. Wilson was transformational but lacked emotional intelligence and failed. Toward the end of the Harvard term, Michael Ignatieff, the thoughtful Canadian who headed our Carr Center for Human Rights, told me that he was going to resign and return to Canada to try to become Prime Minister. He knew the risks, but felt his life would not be complete if he did not try. Ultimately, he failed, but I have always admired him for trying.

At Davos that year, I was asked to address the Young Global Leaders about the meaning of "success." I said it required balancing concentric circles of goals. For me, the core was family and friends with surrounding circles of nature and creativity, and public service outermost. In contrast, for a great leader like Gandhi, service to others was at the core. Each person had to make his or her own choice of priorities. Otherwise, one becomes a prisoner of events.

Divisions over Iraq

After the 2004 presidential election, General Barry McCaffrey told a group at the Kennedy School: "We are one step away from failure in Iraq." But Bush assured the *Washington Post* that the outcome of the November elections had vindicated his Iraq policy. He then gave his second inaugural address, which stressed promotion of democracy as a means of legitimating the invasion of Iraq. I found it depressing.

At a conference at Ditchley, Britons and Americans discussed intelligence failures and successes in Iraq. An important American official said he thought our intelligence had been polluted by exiles like Ahmed Chalabi, who had their own political networks among the neoconservatives. The British reported that they had stopped four significant terrorist plots in the past two years. Both sides said they did not think the effectiveness of the intelligence liaison between our two countries had been diminished by events, and had not felt pressure at the working intelligence level. British defense expert Michael Quinlan told me that Blair had decided in Spring 2002 to back an invasion of Iraq not as a result of intelligence, but because of Bush.

Was Iraq an intelligence failure? John Deutch, a former Director of the CIA, told me he felt that the process was corrupted by excessive political pressures and expectations. In my view, analysts did not deliberately falsify, but intelligence analysis requires sorting through vast amounts of unconfirmed information. As one of my former NIC colleagues put it: "Imagine analysts with piles of raw intelligence reports, one pile that suggests Saddam has weapons of mass destruction and another that suggests he does not. If the policy people are constantly pressing you for more details about the first pile, you spend less time on the other one." That is why good intelligence managers should set up procedures to ensure attention to the second pile. In addition, the 2002 National Intelligence Estimate on Iraq was done under pressure of time, and relegated dissenting analytic details to footnotes even when the agency looking at the second pile had the most expertise on the subject.

But none of this deterred the administration. In early June 2005, Condoleezza Rice invited me to a dinner at the State Department which included various foreign policy experts, including John Gaddis, Bill Kristol, Anne-Marie Slaughter, and others. Rice stressed the transformational objectives of Bush's leadership and asked us which one thing each of us would like to see in foreign policy. Kristol and Gaddis said ridding the world of tyrants. I said what I wanted most was a policy that restored our soft power. I also attended a Council on Foreign Relations meeting where Senator Biden, just back from Iraq, said he was pessimistic, but the situation was not hopeless. Shortly afterwards, Vice President Cheney gave a major speech on how we were winning in Iraq. When I went to the reunion of American Rhodes Scholars in Philadelphia, Ash Carter said we should get out of Iraq, but Wes Clark urged a drawdown to a level of 50,000 troops that could be more sustainable.

In January 2006, John Gaddis, Joshua Muravchik, and I were invited to the White House to discuss foreign policy with three thoughtful staff members: Peter Wehner, Michael Gerson, and Peter Feaver (my former student). Naturally, they defended the Iraq strategy; Gerson said that Bush deeply believed in the democratic element of the policy and regularly pressed for elections in Iraq. I was worried about the excessive rhetoric compared to performance, and thought they should be focusing more on the rise of Asia.

In August, I went to Riyadh, where I met with a number of officials and gave a lecture at the shiny white marble Cultural Center. Afterwards, I was entertained at dinner outdoors by a group of princes sitting in a circle. They generally felt the US had made a mess in Iraq, but that we should not get out. The next day, Prince Faisal bin Salman arranged a tour for me of old Riyadh with its souk and museum. I was told that in 1939 (shortly after I was born) the palace was made of mud, water was cooled in camel skins under the stairs, and the foreign office was one room. How the country had changed in the American century!

At home, people were increasingly critical of Bush's Iraq policy. At a Kennedy School meeting, Deutch had debated with his old boss James Schlesinger, who wanted to leave 30,000 troops in Iraq to train and keep the peace. At the summer meeting of the Aspen Strategy Group, Dov Zakheim talked about the dangers of an impending civil war, which we could not solve. The Middle East expert John Waterbury said that US–Arab relations were the worst he had seen in forty years, and Hank Crumpton, the CIA official who skillfully managed the 2002 defeat of Al-Qaeda in Afghanistan, told a Kennedy School group that it would be impossible to defeat terrorism without some degree of soft power.

Bob Blackwill described how Bush had been a realist until 9/11, but that the shocking event transformed him. Now, however, Bush had lost our post-9/11 national unity. On November 7, in the midterm elections, the voters repudiated him by returning Congress to the Democrats, and, soon afterwards, Bush fired Rumsfeld. At the end of the year, James Baker chaired a commission on Iraq that concluded we should, "train and back out." But Bush chose otherwise. The following month, he rejected their advice and instead announced a new surge of troops. It was a bold step, which staved off disaster on his watch but just kicked the problem to the next president.

US politics heats up

As 2006 progressed, attention began to focus on the 2008 presidential election. In March, I attended a small lunch in Boston to hear Democratic Senator Evan Bayh of Indiana, who was young, positive, and had won five races in a Republican state. He advocated leaving Iraq in six months. In April, analyst Juliette Kayyem invited me to meet Mark Warner, another young and positive Democrat. In fact, I wrote that my surprise at their youth was probably a comment on my age! Bush's polls were suffering because of Iraq, and the conventional wisdom was that Hillary Clinton was likely to be the Democratic nominee. At our Trilateral Commission meeting in Tokyo in April, Tom Foley, former Speaker of the House, said he bet that John McCain would beat Hillary in the presidential election. At that stage, there was no talk of another up-and-coming young senator named Barack Obama.

I was torn between Clinton whom I knew and Obama whom I did not know, but liked from what I had read about him. I felt that he might be better for our soft power, but, as James Traub quoted me saying in the *New York Times*, I worried about his lack of experience in handling national security crises. Susan Rice asked if I would like to meet with Obama and I told her I was still on the fence. Later in the year, a former student Liz Sherwood asked if she could list me as a Clinton supporter. I said yes, though it was a close call. Obama was rising in the polls and I'd have been equally content to see him win. For me, the choice concerned experience versus freshness: the first African American or the first woman president? I wanted "all of the above." Who could win the general election and who would be better at handling a crisis as president? I hoped Obama would win, but I felt that Clinton would prove more adept at handling crises.

In March 2008, I decided to vote for Obama in the Massachusetts primary, feeling that we needed change from the Clinton/Bush/Clinton cycle. But the outcome of the primary contests was not clear until Hillary conceded in early June. At that point, I thought the odds of Obama becoming president were 51:49 because the economy was heading downward. But I had been wrong before – and I was not alone. A famous Republican pollster told me near the end of the previous year that he thought the outcome in 2008 would be that Democratic Senator John Edwards of North Carolina would defeat Mitt Romney of Massachusetts. Like my ill-fated 1968 prediction of Rockefeller versus Kennedy, he did not even come close. Humility should come first, but that is rare when politics is involved.

Russia and Gorbachev

Winter of 2006 found me in Moscow, where I spent a fascinating week and spoke at the Academy of Public Administration, Moscow State University, Spaso House, and other locations. My interlocutors tended to be pessimistic about Russia's future. One said the average Russian had been happier in 1980 than today, and liberal ideas do not work everywhere. Some said the 1991 revolution had destroyed institutions and power had now become personalized, and corruption was rampant. Another said that although they now had private property and some degree of freedom of speech, they had no real democracy. Yet another described their system as "managed democracy." Ambassador William Burns told me that although Russia had been helpful on Iran, the Russians resented being neglected and were suspicious of our activities in Ukraine – all this years before Putin's invasion.

The highlight of my visit was my speech at the Gorbachev Foundation and my interactions with the former Soviet president. I went to a concert in his honor at the new music hall, where artists, musicians, and dancers sang "Happy Birthday" and went on stage at the end to thank him for giving them back their artistic freedom. However, an aide told me that when Gorbachev had spoken not long before that at Stavropol, people had shouted insults about him destroying the Soviet Union. He shouted back: "I gave you the right to shout."

I sat in my hotel room pondering these thoughts while looking at the sun glint off the gold domes of the Kremlin as I polished my talk on "Lessons of the Cold War." Afterwards, Gorbachev said he liked my talk and was very personable and outgoing. I noted: "He leans into you while he talks and seizes your elbow like a politician." He said he had no regrets. An amazing historical figure, truly transformational, but not exactly in the way he intended (which was to save the Soviet Union). Nonetheless, I admired him.

Unfortunately, relations with Russia continued to sour. Gorbachev later came to a symposium at the Kennedy School, and some members of his group, such as Sergei Rogov, said that Russia was thinking of withdrawing from the INF (Intermediate-Range Nuclear Forces) treaty

Kennedy School symposium with Graham Allison and Mikhail Gorbachev, 2007
Source: © Martha Stewart 2007

and that arms control was unraveling. At the same time, the Kennedy School was teaching a group of Russian generals in an executive program.

Meeting Qaddafi

In February 2007, while again at Oxford, I had a visit from Bruce Allyn, formerly of the Kennedy School, who was working for Michael Porter's Monitor Group, which had a contract to develop a plan for change in Libya. Allyn offered me an honorarium to lecture and meet government officials in Tripoli and held out the prospect of a possible meeting with Muammar Qaddafi, who had spoken with the democratic theorist Ben Barbour on a prior visit. The prospect of meeting the mercurial leader while I was writing a book on leadership was too interesting to pass up. After two days in Tripoli, I was due to fly to the UK. I had met Seif, Qaddafi's son, and had given the public lectures, but there was no sight of Qaddafi himself. On the afternoon of my scheduled departure Allyn knocked on my hotel door and told me to come quickly. A car whisked us past several fortified walls into a vast park in the middle of the city where camels, horses, and goats grazed, and Qaddafi presided in a huge Bedouin tent that overlooked the ruins of the office building the US had bombed in 1986. The setting was surreal.

Inside the tent, Qaddafi was dressed plainly in a traditional robe and had a table on which his staff had spread out five of my books. We proceeded to discuss development, the Arab world, Wahhabism, human rights, and democracy. He insisted that his "bottom-up" direct democracy was more effective than our representative type, and he gave me a signed copy of his "little green book" in which he had laid out the theory. The conversation lasted for two and a half hours, and I was about to miss my flight to London. At the airport, guards and procedure were delaying me, so I pulled out the green book, showed them Qaddafi's inscription, and they waved me through. Soon after in London, I gave the Liddell Hart lecture on the future of power and was awarded an honorary doctorate from King's College. As I rode back to Oxford with Sir Michael Howard, the great British historian of war, I wondered at what had been a truly strange set of days.

Soft power and smart power

Back home, at a conference in Washington on democracy and the Arab world, the columnist Charles Krauthammer gave an optimistic view of Bush's war as a moral cause. I disagreed, and said it was destroying American soft power. I was interested that two European parliamentarians, Joschka Fischer of Germany and Ana Palacios of Spain, said they had read my book and agreed.

The administration was still not doing well in combining hard and soft power. To address this, John Hamre, President of the Center for Strategic and International Studies (CSIS), suggested that Rich Armitage and I co-chair a bipartisan CSIS commission on "smart power" – the successful combination of soft and hard power. It included a number of former members of Congress. Senator Bill Frist was particularly impressive on the soft power benefits of health assistance in Africa (an area where the Bush Administration led successfully). After several meetings, we released the commission report in November at the National Press Club, and Armitage and I testified on the Hill. Shortly before, Admiral James Stavridis described how his Southern Command was reorganizing to promote soft power, and, shortly afterwards, Secretary of Defense Robert Gates gave a speech urging that we invest more in our soft power and put more money into the State Department. I had the feeling that my concept was beginning to have a practical as well as an analytical effect.

In April, Armitage and I testified before the Senate Foreign Relations Committee. Needless to say, I was pleased when Republican Senator George Voinovich said he had read my book and wanted the US to invest more in soft power. Democratic Senator Bob Menendez also asked about soft power. Republican Senators Richard Lugar and Chuck Hagel asked about reorganizing more effectively for foreign policy.

China was also becoming more interested in soft power. In 2007, Hu Jintao declared they should invest more in their soft power, but I felt they were limited by their insistence on tight Communist Party control of everything. The year before, I had lectured on soft power at Fudan University and was struck how it had grown, but sorry to see a large new statue of Mao, whom I considered a bad leader. The students' questions were good and I asked them about democracy. They replied that it was desirable but posed too great a risk of instability for China today. At the same time, they said they needed more freedom to think creatively, but, they added, "look at what we are saying. Twenty years ago, it would have put us in jail." Ironically, one of their professors, Wang Huning, went on to become the chief ideologist of the Politburo and used that position to implement Xi's suppression of creative thought.

I spent the summer working on my leadership book in which I aimed to apply the concepts of hard, soft, and smart power to individual leaders. I rediscovered how I enjoyed the work of trying to shape ideas and never knowing where it would come out. At one point, I asked myself: "Why do I do it? Curiosity? A new challenge? Desire to be creative? Will anyone read it? Or, like the novel, do I just want to do it?"

The mood in Europe

Early in 2008, I took a trip to Russia, France, Britain, and Switzerland. The TOTAL advisory board met in St. Petersburg and I told them I thought the chances that the US would bomb Iran had receded to the range of one in a hundred. On the future of Europe, the general consensus was that the federalist dreams of a few years ago had ended, but, ironically, given the outcome of UK's Brexit referendum some years later, the former British Home Secretary Leon Brittan was more optimistic about Europe than his French counterpart Hubert Védrine. The highlight of the visit was dinner in the eighteenth-century Yusupov Palace, and a ballet in its private theater – a spectacle so beautiful it brought tears to my eyes. Russian soft power in action!

In Paris, I switched to the ornate dining-room of the Quai d'Orsay for a conference on Europe's role in the world. French Minister of Foreign and European Affairs Bernard Kouchner said France's role in NATO had to be coupled with a strong European defense capability. Later, in a walk in the gardens, he told me that the US should leave Iraq. An Indian delegate suggested that Europe was losing relevance because it was not plugged into elite networks in Asia the way the US was. That was a source of American soft power and it was combined with hard economic power. On the way to Davos, I read an *International Herald Tribune* story that portrayed the US as a crippled giant, but when I arrived at the WEF, I discovered that their annual competitiveness index ranked the US in first place. The next month, at a Ditchley conference, the general consensus was that Europe could not get its act together.

Trilateral affairs

Another problem that took my time was the future of the Trilateral Commission. David Rockefeller had started it in the 1970s as a way to respond to globalization and include Japan in Track 2 discussions, which were then primarily trans-Atlantic. The Commission was designed to tie Europe, Japan, and the US together at the informal Track 2 level. Now, some members were arguing that, with the end of the Cold War and the economic success of Japan, it should be wrapped up. I considered the discussions to be valuable and that, instead, the Commission should be broadened to include other Asians, including China and India. In April, I talked to Paul Volcker, former North American chair, Peter Sutherland, the European chair, and David Rockefeller. They persuaded me to succeed Tom Foley (who was ailing) as the North American chair, and I presided over my first international executive committee meeting in Washington. After lengthy discussions, my view was accepted, and I received many congratulations for saving the institution. Now the question was whether I could make it work. Over the next decade, we broadened the membership, both internationally and in gender and generation. I felt I had succeeded in 2018 when I handed over to Meghan O'Sullivan on the tenth anniversary of my chairmanship.

Cyber conflict

My attention was increasingly drawn to cyber conflict as a new dimension of security and world affairs. I attended a conference on the subject at MIT organized by John Mallery; he and Admiral William Studeman, former CIA Deputy Director, urged me to spend more time on cyber issues. I told them I was too old a dog to learn new tricks, but Studeman argued this was going to become a major issue in foreign policy and, as a foreign policy expert, I should not leave it to the technocrats. His prediction was correct. In the annual list of security challenges issued by the Director of National Intelligence, cyber moved from not making the list at all in 2007 to topping it a few years later. I was also concerned about climate change. At an advisory board meeting for the Oxford Martin School, Sir Nicholas Stern had made a compelling case that market forces and conventional discount rates could not alone solve this serious problem. But I could not take on two new fields at once, and I chose cyber.

I knew I had a lot to learn but I welcomed the challenge. I could never be a cyber native (like my grandchildren), but I could aspire to being a cyber immigrant who could translate traditional political concepts into the cyber world, albeit with a heavy accent. In 2011, when I published *The Future of Power,* I included a chapter on cyber power along with military, economic, and soft power. Later, I wrote academic articles on nuclear lessons for cyber security, cyber deterrence, and a regime complex for governing cyber activities. For two years, I served as a member of a Global Commission on Internet Governance chaired by Carl Bildt, former Prime Minister of Sweden. And after that I served on a Commission on Stability in Cyberspace chaired by Michael Chertoff and Latha Reddy. I never lost my heavy accent as an immigrant to the cyber world, but I was never bored.

The 2008 election approaches

As the presidential election approached, the main discussions concerned the wars in Iraq and Afghanistan. Obama had criticized Iraq as a war of choice, but accepted Afghanistan as just and necessary. Earlier in the year, Rory Stewart (a future Tory Cabinet Minister in Britain) had joined the Kennedy School to run our Human Rights Center. He told me he thought we should get out of Iraq and scale back our objectives in Afghanistan, where he had traveled extensively. I made similar points at a conference at the Center for New American Security but Bill Kristol disagreed, saying we were not being assertive enough, an opinion that was shared by retired General Jack Keane and Republican Senator Lindsey Graham.

At a meeting in Princeton (which accompanied my fiftieth reunion), Ambassador Barbara Bodine said we should get out of Iraq over the next two years. At the ASG, Bob Blackwill told me that Iraqi Prime Minister Nouri Al-Maliki was incompetent and beholden to Iran, which had more influence than we did, and it would take several years to withdraw. As though this was not problematic enough, relations with Russia were deteriorating. In April, it had launched a serious denial of service cyberattack against Estonia, and in August it invaded Georgia.

In September, the international situation became even more dire with the financial crisis that followed the bursting of the bubble of speculative investments in real estate. On September 15, Lehman Brothers, the US financial services company, went bankrupt, triggering a 4.5 percent one day drop in the Dow Jones Industrial index. Some economists predicted a deep and extended recession. Former Treasury Secretary Larry Summers told me he thought the odds were one in four. Economist Martin Feldstein said a half a trillion-dollar stimulus package would be necessary, and Paul Volcker blamed the crisis on Wall Street financial engineers who were too clever by half.

I played only a minor role in the presidential election, occasionally giving surrogate speeches, but I was overjoyed when John McCain gave a gracious concession speech and Obama was declared the winner on November 4. This was, I wrote, "a glorious day for America! An African American president. I did not think I would ever see it. The idea of America lives even if we have not always lived up to it in our history. Reminds me of the joy I felt over Brown vs Board of Education."

The next day I flew to London where Peter Mandelson, President of the UK's Board of Trade, said that soft power had been restored overnight, something that could only happen in the US. Ambassador Wolfgang Ischinger told me "Obama will affect Germany the way JFK did." I gave a speech about Obama at the European regional meeting of the Trilateral, where the only sour note came from the comments made by Russians like Karaganov and Chubais about the growing mistrust of the West in Russia. Comments on Afghanistan were divided. Deutch urged that we scale back our objectives, but Toria Nuland of the State Department said we were on our way to success.

Just before Christmas I had a call from my friend Jim Steinberg, the incoming Deputy Secretary of State, asking if I was willing to become ambassador to Japan. I told him I would have to discuss it with Molly, who was not enthusiastic, and would prefer something closer to our grandchildren. During the year, we had been visited by all our nine grandchildren and I delighted in taking them to collect the eggs, fish for sunnies, take the trash to the dump, sit in my lap and "drive" the tractor as I mowed the meadow, or swim in the ice pond after a long day's work. Grandchildren turn out to be a very good interim answer to Gauguin's questions: "What are we, where do we come from, where are we going?" And Tokyo was a long way away!

Assessing Bush

When Barbara Bush, former First Lady, visited the Kennedy School and spoke at a forum in September, 2002, I found her to be a warm and spirited woman. I asked her if she had thought her son would become president, and she replied yes, but she never knew which one. In my view, the wrong one made it.

George W. Bush deserves credit for good intentions. He told the American people after the 9/11 shock that they should not take their anger out on innocent Muslims, and he was sincere about democratizing the Middle East, but the worldwide feeling of deception about Iraq and the fact that his rhetoric so exceeded the grasp of what American power could do meant that the outcomes were often the opposite of what he intended.

Unipolarity had relaxed the Cold War constraints on American foreign policy, and there were very few countervailing forces that could balance our power, but the unipolar moment unleashed the danger of hubris. Clinton's interventions were mostly undertaken reluctantly (or not at all in the case of Rwanda). His strategy of enlargement and engagement placed more emphasis on economic globalization and institutions. He promoted democracy by using market forces rather than imposing it by military might. Bush was morally brave in the case of the surge, cosmopolitan in his policy toward Africa, and a far-sighted realist in his relations with India, but all this was overwhelmed by his blunder in Iraq. His weak emotional and contextual intelligence undercut his goals. Jonathan Powell, former Downing Street Chief of Staff, once told me that Tony Blair sought out multiple streams of information but felt Bush was insufficiently curious and that hurt his performance. Powell thought Blair should probably have waited for a broader coalition before going into Iraq, but they feared that Bush would go it alone anyway. It turned out to be a disastrous decision for the popularity of both leaders. And Bush's use of Wilsonian rhetoric after the event to justify his action helped to generate a public reaction not unlike what Wilson himself had engendered nearly a century earlier. Not a great presidency for the American century.

9

The Obama Years

I was optimistic about Obama's leadership as his presidential term got under way. He promised youth, vitality, and progress on race relations – all good for American soft power. At the same time, he faced huge problems. The recession of 2008–9 might turn into a depression, the two wars in Iraq and Afghanistan were unresolved, terrorism and a chaotic Middle East posed a continuing threat. During these years, I was an advisor on the Defense Policy Board and the State Department Policy Advisory Committee, as well as an occasional consultant. I focused largely on great power relations, Asia, alliances, soft power, and cyber issues, while maintaining my role in various nongovernmental organizations.

False alarm

In early January 2009, a major Tokyo newspaper, *Asahi Shimbun*, ran a front-page story that I would be the next ambassador to Japan. I was inundated by congratulatory emails and press inquiries to which I replied, "No comment" or "Rumors are just rumors." Answering friends was awkward because I was ambivalent and had told Steinberg that I preferred something nearer to my grandchildren. He told me I was on the list for under-secretarial jobs in Washington, but being a white male made that difficult. My friend Graham Allison advised against Tokyo and said I had more to contribute at home. In early March, Steinberg called to tell me that the nomination would be announced in the next two weeks, and when I went to Tokyo for the Trilateral Commission meetings, Prime Minister Tarō Asō asked: "When are you coming?"

It was not to be – much to Molly's relief. According to the *New York Times*, I was caught in a contest between the State Department and the White House political staff which felt they had already made too many concessions to Hillary Clinton. John Roos was chosen instead, a

California lawyer and large donor who became a fine ambassador and whom I visited whenever I went to Tokyo. All's well that ends well, but American political processes can be messy.

The limits of social science

By contrast, I turned my attention to academic work, to learning about cyber, and I began a new book that incorporated cyber with my prior work on military, economic, and soft power. It was a very pleasant surprise when a 2008 report of a poll of several thousand international relations scholars ranked me as the sixth most influential scholar over the previous two decades and the most influential scholar on foreign policy.

The economic situation was gloomy during the "Great Recession" which had originated in Wall Street. Some thought it spelled the end of the American century. But who could replace us? In 2015, Polity published my *Is the American Century Over?* in which I examined the possible contenders. Acting as an entity, Europe (then including the UK) had a larger economy than the US, and China was growing at double digit rates. My colleague Jeffrey Frankel speculated that the euro might replace the dollar as a reserve currency by 2015. At the June meeting of the Trilateral Executive Committee, some participants felt the economic crisis had dealt a devasting blow to American prestige, and trade would be increasingly cleared in currencies other than the dollar. Among my economist friends, Marty Feldstein saw China overtaking the US economy by 2025, but Dick Cooper disagreed and saw no alternative to the dollar as a practical matter. Cooper turned out to be closer to the mark, but we now know that Chinese leaders thought more like Feldstein and interpreted the financial crisis as proof of American decline. They dropped Deng Xiaoping's cautious approach and switched to a more assertive foreign policy.

The clashing economic predictions led me to wonder about the limits of social science. For all their pretensions to being a science, macro economists were not much better than political scientists at prediction. Too much must be assumed. I wrote that social science understands small islands of data well, but must take enormous leaps of theory-faith to get from one island of data to another. I included my own predictions of American non-decline, which rested on assumptions about our entrepreneurial culture and openness to change. But would that continue? The increasing exploitation of shale gas and oil by entrepreneurs was beginning to have an important effect on reducing our dependence on energy imports, while earlier in the decade many people said we had passed "peak oil." Social science is important, but must be accompanied by humility. I was reminded of this at Oxford in May 2009 when I participated in the Vice Chancellor's review of the social sciences. Oxford was evolving from a confederation of medieval colleges into a university where central professional departments were growing stronger, but there was still a long way to go.

American power was dented by the financial crisis, but it remained crucial in Asia. While China may have interpreted the crisis as proof of American decline, most of Asia wanted access to China's market as well as an American presence to balance Chinese power. This was illustrated during a visit to Hanoi where I met with Prime Minister Nguyen Tan Dung and toured the simple former home of Ho Chi Minh who had been the villain of American politicians during the Vietnam war. On the surface, Vietnamese relations with China seemed smooth, but at a dinner in the home of Nguyen Ahn Tuan, one of the important guests asked me a revealing question: "Do you know why our country is shaped like an S"? I said "No." He replied: "It's from the weight of China on our spine for thousands of years."

Afghanistan

In addition to the economy, hanging over everything in 2009 was the problem of Afghanistan, where the "good war" was going badly. At the Munich Security Conference in February, I heard President Hamid Karzai (in his trademark emerald green cape) give a good speech, but I wondered if he could follow it with actions. Talking in the corridors to Dick Holbrooke, whom Hillary Clinton had put in charge of the "Af/Pak" region, I noted a sense of caution in my normally ebullient friend.

Experts were divided. Rory Stewart said the best strategy was a lighter footprint for a longer duration with some 20,000 troops defending Kabul. Similarly, Bob Blackwill argued that we should let the Taliban control the Pashtun areas in the south. At a Council on Foreign

Relations board meeting in October, military expert Stephen Biddle said he backed General McChrystal's counterinsurgency approach with 90,000 troops. He saw no middle option. On November 5, General James Jones, National Security Advisor, brought in a group of outsiders to discuss Afghanistan and told us that Obama had held eighteen hours of meetings on the subject, and that the price tag of a full counterinsurgency was "a bridge too far." It was more feasible to think of a "build-down" over three to four years.

Obama gave a speech that split the difference, combining a limited surge with a date for withdrawal. I was skeptical and regarded the Nobel Peace Prize award to Obama as "premature." The DPB meeting in June coincided with Obama's firing of General McChrystal and his replacement in Afghanistan by David Petraeus, but, as some of us observed, can anyone do counterinsurgency when there is no governmental structure? The slogan "clear, hold, build" assumes something to build upon. At a later Ditchley conference on intervention, Ambassador Karl Eikenberry and Rory Stewart both said that Obama's surge in Afghanistan had been a mistake.

By the time of our Aspen summer meeting in 2011, Obama had given a speech announcing a withdrawal of 10,000 troops with the goal of withdrawing another 30,000 the following summer. Ambassador Paul Bremer said this would make nation-building difficult. Jim Dobbins said that although we should be cautious about nation-building, it sometimes had to be done. On the other hand, former students of mine who had served in Afghanistan argued that we should restrain our objectives to keeping 10,000 troops solely for training and counterterrorism purposes.

A few years later, the ASG again focused on Afghanistan. Few people believed that we could sustain the 400,000 troops that would be needed for a full counterinsurgency operation, but there was division about the implications for human rights. What would happen to Afghan women if we were to leave? Madeleine Albright argued that we should not succumb to cultural relativism; all people have equal rights. I said I agreed that people are equal in that sense, but they are embedded in cultures that vary greatly and change slowly. Foreign policy is about trade-offs among objectives and about prices and timing. General Douglas Lute, who was in charge of Afghan policy in the White House, said no one was talking about a "lights out" scenario, but about how to dim and leave with the lights on. We had to make sure that our money and assistance did not merely destabilize a society marked by communalism and corruption – as some put it, a "criminalized patronage network." While Lute said our discussion was more refreshing than what he heard in Washington, it was, of course, inconclusive – and the problem remained unresolved through the duration of Obama's presidency.

European disunion

At the beginning of the financial crisis, some thought the euro would replace the dollar, but in fact the opposite occurred. In 2009, when I attended the Trilateral Commission meeting in Dublin, Peter Sutherland hosted me and Mario Monti, the future Italian Prime Minister. He confessed that he was worried about the euro given that the weakness of the Greek economy in the aftermath of the financial crisis loomed like a "dark cloud." At the plenary meeting there were many concerns about whether the problems of the Greek economy would spread to the other Mediterranean countries. Optimism about the euro replacing the dollar had vanished. On a more light-hearted note, Irish President Mary McAleese hosted us for dinner. As I wrote in my diary that night: "What would my poor Irish grandmother have thought of (1) an Irish president; (2) a woman; (3) her grandson having dinner with her? How the world changes!"

But the situation in Europe did not change. In 2012, I was struck by the continuing unease about the euro and European unity. Any suggestion that Europe might replace the American century had vanished, as I discovered from talking to Javier Solana (former Secretary General of NATO) and David Miliband (former British Foreign Secretary) about the subject. Miliband worried about the development of a two-tiered Europe with first- and second-class members. Solana also worried, but thought the tensions could be managed as a "two-speed Europe." I attended a dinner hosted by Mark Leonard's European Council on Foreign Relations at the Swedish embassy in London, with Jonathan Powell, Douglas Hurd (former British Foreign Secretary), economist Jim O'Neill, and human rights activist Mabel van Oranje, all of whom were worried about Europe's loss of soft power. Powell thought the malaise was manageable, but others worried what would happen if there was a run on the banks in Southern Europe.

During an earlier visit to the Kennedy School, Turkish Foreign Minister Ahmet Davutoglu had described Turkey's role in Europe. He'd read my book and said that Turkey was gaining soft power from its geographical position as a democratic bridge from Europe to the Middle East and Turkic Central Asia. Earlier, in September, the DPB had spent a day discussing Turkey, and the consensus was that urbanization and a pious lower middle class meant the end of the domination of Ataturk's Europeanized elite and the rise of a nationalistic Islamic base for Erdogan's populism. Democratization did not mean liberal democracy, and Turkey would be a difficult ally. Erdogan fired Davutoglu and proved the prediction correct.

Later, in 2015, I went to Berlin for the Trilateral Commission meetings. On my early morning run near the Brandenburg Gate, I ruminated about how much terrible history had occurred in such a small space. At the meeting, Karl Kaiser and Thierry de Montbrial correctly predicted that Europe would evolve with an inner core anchored by the euro, and an outer ring with Britain in a separate orbit. German Chancellor Angela Merkel addressed us in the Reichstag building and, as I was about to introduce her, the sound system failed. To lighten the moment, I quipped: "I have always been impressed with German technology." Merkel did not skip a beat, and quipped back in perfect English: "The exception always proves the rule."

The Putin problem

Russia became a growing problem. At a meeting at the Kennedy School in 2014, economist Igor Yurgens warned that Putin felt disillusioned with the West and power had gone to his head. A DPB meeting described Russia as being in economic and demographic decline; Putin resented this account, and would make opportunistic moves to disrupt the international situation, which now included threats to interfere in Ukraine. But given the competition with China, how far did we want to isolate Russia? At a meeting of the Trilateral Commission executive committee in DC, there was a long debate about including Russia in our meetings. It was finally resolved by allowing the European group to include whichever Russians they found acceptable. Former Prime Minister of Finland Esko Aho warned me not to expect Putin's successors to be any better.

At a Forum at the School in September 2014, by which time Russian involvement in Ukraine was clear, Carl Bildt and Mario Monti recommended sending economic and nonlethal military aid to Ukraine, but Niall Ferguson warned about sanctions being ineffective and not alienating the Russians. Indian participants made clear they would not isolate Russia. A State Department official told us that the administration was split on the issue of lethal aid to Ukraine. Scowcroft said that maybe we could have done more, but he doubted it would have made a difference. Blinken told me that Obama was trying to maintain regular communication with Putin. And when John Kerry met with the Foreign Affairs Advisory Board to discuss the mess in Syria, he pointed out that the problem could not be solved without Russia and Iran. Foreign policy is not simple!

In early 2015, Fred Kempe, President of the Atlantic Council, asked what, in my opinion, would be the big security issues facing the Council in the new year. My response: "A resentful declining Russia; a rising nationalistic China; and Islamic terrorism now represented by the proto government of the Islamic state." John Sawers, former head of MI6, told me that 2004 was the year that Putin decided that reformist "color revolutions" were a Western plot that must be resisted. At the Munich Security Conference, Russian Foreign Minister Sergei Lavrov uttered his usual untruths about Ukraine, and Sergei Karaganov, my friend from the 1980s, blamed the West for breaking the rules in Kosovo, Iraq, and Libya. Deputy Secretary General of NATO, Sandy Vershbow, warned that he saw little hope of appeasing Russia while paranoid nationalism was so widespread. Senator Lindsey Graham urged lethal aid to Ukraine, but Merkel said no. When I went to Paris, French Foreign Minister Laurent Fabius invited me to his elaborate office in the Quai d'Orsay and we discussed Ukraine. Putin had agreed to a ceasefire of sorts, named the Minsk Process, but it was not clear whether it would be worth much – as we found out in 2022.

The Arab Spring

At the Munich Security Conference in early 2011, the big topic hanging over the conference was the so-called Arab Spring events in the Middle East, which had started off in Tunisia and were spreading to other countries such as Libya and Egypt, where demonstrators used the Internet to organize protests in Tahrir Square. German political scientist Volker Perthes said he felt optimistic for the first time in thirty-five years about the possibility of a middle way between dictators and Islamists. Ambassador Frank Wisner addressed the conference by video and said that the US sought an "orderly transition to democracy." Within the week, however, Egyptian President Hosni Mubarak resigned, and the army took control. I wrote that it was a remarkable success for a nonviolent protest, but "I wonder if it will really lead to democracy. Let's hope." Of course, those hopes were dashed. There were limits to American power. When the DPB met in March to discuss the situation, there was some optimism about Tunisia and Egypt, but pessimism about Yemen and Libya. Some drew analogies to the democratic revolutions of 1848 in Europe, but those events had also led to disappointments.

On March 17, the UN Security Council authorized a "no fly zone" to protect civilians in Eastern Libya under the new doctrine of the "Responsibility to Protect" (R2P). I wrote a blog supporting Obama's decision to join the action, but worried about its limits. In the end, Qaddafi was caught and killed in October 2011, but the R2P resolution was badly damaged, and civil war still reigns in Libya.

A mess in the Middle East

That summer, the Aspen Strategy Group discussed the Middle East. Richard Haass, President of the Council on Foreign Relations, predicted decades of turmoil and few levers to influence it. Dennis Ross, Middle East expert who had served both Republican and Democratic presidents, was slightly less pessimistic. There was disappointment that Mohamed Morsi's Islamic Brotherhood had won the Egyptian election and dismay about some of the steps he was taking. The biggest problem was Syria, where President Bashir Assad had used chemical weapons against insurgent populations. I felt that Obama should respond with cruise missiles. Sometimes a careful use of hard power is essential. As things developed, in 2013 Obama decided to seek a mandate from Congress, but it was not clear whether there were enough positive votes – as was the case also in the British Parliament. When Putin suggested sending UN inspectors into Syria, Obama was saved from his worst nightmare, but Putin later manipulated the situation to Russia's favor, and Obama's credibility had been dented.

No one had good answers on Syria. At Munich, Kofi Annan said that we should have integrated Russian and American forces in a UN peacekeeping mission, but it was now too late. John McCain blamed Obama for failing to enforce his 2012 "red line" against the use of chemical weapons. Some suspected that Putin would never leave because Assad was a useful pawn. This was confirmed at a Harvard seminar by former Russian Foreign Minister Andrey Kozyrev, who described Putin as "a KGB street fighter who respects only force and lacks soft power." Syria, plus Obama's battles with Congress over government closedown, led sensible commentators like journalist David Ignatius to label him "too timid."

An Iran war?

The year 2012 began with another Middle East issue looming large: Iran. Some observers thought there was a 25 percent chance of an Israeli attack by the end of the year. In early February, at a board meeting of the Council on Foreign Relations in DC, Richard Haass and Gideon Rose put the odds even higher; I hoped this would not be the case because it could reinforce the Islamist narrative in the region. Fortunately, as we discovered later, the Obama Administration had already begun quiet diplomacy on a nuclear agreement.

In 2015, I attended a meeting in New York with Foreign Minister of Iran Mohammad Javad Zarif. The dialogue was very reasonable, and in July the administration announced an agreement to restrict Iran's nuclear program in return for a loosening of some sanctions. I signed a letter of former officials supporting the agreement organized by Ambassador William Luers because I did not see a realistic alternative. Israel, however, opposed it. When former Prime Minister Ehud Barak visited the Kennedy School, he said we should have bombed Iran instead. At the Aspen Institute in August, the majority of the ASG supported the agreement; Diane Feinstein told me she was annoyed that Senator Chuck Schumer, among others, would not support it. All this came to naught, however, when Donald Trump later withdrew from the agreement.

Pivot to rising Asia

Chairing a Ditchley conference on the tenth anniversary of the 9/11 attack, I said that I regarded it as a lost decade. As the terrorists intended, the event had changed the agenda of world (and American) politics and hurt our soft power. Nonetheless, it was not clear that it would be viewed as a larger turning point in the eyes of future historians. I thought the rise of China and decline of Russia would prove to be more important to the future of the American century. Obama wanted to pivot to Asia, but friends told me that most meetings in the Situation Room were bogged down in the Middle East.

My personal focus during the Obama years was heavily on Asia. In December 2010, Aspen held a strategic dialogue at the Central Party School in Beijing. Vice Minister Fu Ying said they were divided on whether the US wanted cooperation or containment. When Americans raised the question of whether China claimed the South China Sea as a "core" interest, we were told they were internally divided on that as well. But they were not very forthcoming when we raised issues like cyber theft of intellectual property or cooperation in constraining North Korea. In Shanghai, I lectured at a school of public administration and the Shanghai Institute of International Affairs, and was entertained on a dinner cruise on the Huangpu river with its contrasting shores of the old European Bund and the modern skyscrapers of Pudong. On to Taipei, where I met with President Ma at the palm-lined presidential palace, and he told me he felt their strategy was working. Taiwan's soft power was an asset, but they also wanted F-16s. On my return to Washington, I found US officials concerned about growing Chinese nationalism and complaining about China's lack of cooperation.

In 2011, I went to Beijing to attend a conference organized by Lu Mei for the China Development and Research Foundation. I was particularly impressed by Vice Minister of Finance Liu He, who was a Kennedy School graduate and became a key figure in economic policy. Informally, Chinese friends told me that Hu Jintao was a weak leader, and Xi would be the same because the Standing Committee did not want a strong leader. My friends in China worried about a rising nationalism and hubris. They clearly underestimated Xi.

In Delhi, the ASG held its fifteenth strategic dialogue. We called on Prime Minister Singh, who, like his National Security Advisor Shankar Menon, wanted to talk about relations with China. I recommended a "Goldilocks policy" – not too hot and not too cold. At the meetings, Jairam Ramesh described the difficulties that India faced in trying to live with a global limit of 450 parts per million of carbon dioxide, as had been discussed at international climate meetings. Economist Montek Singh Ahluwalia spoke of India's need to maintain a high rate of economic growth to cope with its increasing population. No one in India was optimistic about the situation in Afghanistan.

In December, I co-chaired an Aspen Track 2 dialogue in Delhi. The Indians hoped we would keep 10,000–20,000 troops in Afghanistan, and were concerned about Pakistan, which one of them termed "too nuclear to fail." They also believed that China was using Pakistan to contain them. Menon said that an Israeli or American air strike on Iranian nuclear facilities would be a big mistake and ignite the region. On the other hand, they were optimistic about India retaining a high rate of economic growth at around 7 percent. That proved to be achievable, but when I walked from my modern hotel to visit Humayun's Tomb, a red sandstone and marble masterpiece, I was appalled by the poverty of people scavenging in garbage dumps not far from shops that sold Gucci and Hermes luxury items. India was progressing, but still had a long way to go.

When Xi Jinping visited Washington in the Spring of 2012, everyone was curious about the new leader. Earlier, former Prime Minister of Singapore Lee Kuan Yew had told me that the incoming Chinese president would be a stronger leader but still not in full control of the PLA. I joined a group of experts to brief State Department Deputy Secretary William Burns, but there was no consensus. At a lunch, Xi spoke well and when Vice President Biden criticized China's performance on human rights, Xi responded that "we are not perfect, but making progress." Later, at the DPB, Secretary of Defense Leon Panetta told us that he was impressed in his private conversations with Xi. Alas, these early hopes did not turn out well. On an amusing side note, during the visit I was asked by high officials if I would be interested in replacing Ambassador Roos when he stepped down. I said "No!"

After a visit to Macquarie University in Australia to help inaugurate their Soft Power Advocacy and Research Center, I continued on to

Beijing where I had been asked to lecture on soft power at the School of Marxism at Peking University. Over lunch, I asked the dean why they studied Marxism when China was now developing capitalist markets. His reply: "Markets are for economics; Marx is for politics." Later, after my lecture, the dean told the students that my definition of soft power was too political, and China preferred a more cultural approach. A little later, I pursued the theme at a dinner with a member of the Central Committee and, after a few drinks, he confessed: "We are Confucians in Marxist clothing." After Beijing, I took the impressive modern bullet train to Jinan and Shandong University, where I again lectured on soft power. I was impressed by the boldness of some students who asked about what I thought of censorship of the Internet and the "Great Firewall of China." As one put it: "If we are so confident, why do we have censorship?" When I returned to Harvard, I had an office visit from the son of Bo Xilai whose parents had been arrested, and he wondered if he could help them by going back. I advised him to stay out of the government's clutches.

The Senkaku conflict

In October, I became involved in the Senkaku/Diaoyu Islands dispute. The uninhabited islands are claimed both by Japan and by China, which argued that Japan seized them illegally in a war in 1895. The US took no position on the underlying historical claims, but since the islands were included in the Okinawa territory that the US returned to Japan in the 1970s, they were covered by the US–Japan security treaty. The last thing the US wanted was to be involved in a fight over the uninhabited islands, but nationalists in both countries stirred the pot. In 2012, the Japanese government bought three of the islands from a private citizen, allegedly to prevent their purchase by a nationalist group, but China objected to the change in the status quo and increased its forays into the area. Hillary Clinton asked four former officials, Richard Armitage, Stephen Hadley, James Steinberg, and me, to visit Tokyo and Beijing to try to calm the waters. In Tokyo, we met with Prime Minister Yoshihiko Noda and explained why the US was neutral on the underlying claim, but would stand by our commitment under the security treaty. We also explained our position to a group of opinion-makers who were assembled by the embassy.

In Beijing, we met with Premier Li Keqiang as well as State Councilor Dai Bingguo, who said that rightwing forces were rising in Japan. China wanted a new type of great power relationship with the US that would restrain such forces, and the islands should be under joint control. We explained why that was not possible and returned to Tokyo to debrief Noda and Japanese officials and urge them to keep calm. Armitage and I stayed on for more meetings. We had updated our Armitage–Nye report on the alliance to maintain bipartisan unity before the US election, and we discussed it at several venues in Tokyo. When we returned to Washington, we debriefed Secretary Clinton and other officials on our talks. The island dispute was not resolved but nor did it escalate out of control. It is impossible to know whether our trip helped, but sometimes in diplomacy, as Woody Allen once said, the main thing is just to show up.

Year's end

In any event, as 2012 came to an end, I felt things were going well. In December, forty-five newly elected members of Congress arrived at the Kennedy School to attend a course on their new duties and major issues. Edward Luce of the *Financial Times* and I outlined the pros and cons of the argument that American power was in decline.

I was not quite ready to retire, but beginning to contemplate it. In the Fall, I had attended the annual meeting of the International Studies Association in San Diego and participated on panels on the information revolution and cyber power with an impressive group of younger scholars. Afterwards I told Bob Keohane that I had a feeling I should bow out of such meetings, but he said, "No, young people need sensible seniors as models and your standing has never been higher." His advice was reinforced when a poll ranked me #2 as the "scholar who had done the most interesting work over the past five years." I said I felt I was overrated and not up to the youngsters in the field, but I did not want to give up and felt reinvigorated by teaching. But when should one bow out? On a sadder note, the next year I went to Lafayette College with Jimmy Carter to pay tribute to my former student Robert Pastor who was suffering terminal cancer. He was an ebullient man, but had no choice.

With Bob Pastor, and Jimmy and Rosalynn Carter at Lafayette College, 2013

Back to Asia

As Obama was being reinaugurated in 2013, I was returning to Asia for more Track 2 dialogues. In Delhi, Indians and Americans agreed that our relationship was bound to succeed because of China, but that it would not become a formal alliance. And we mostly agreed about keeping a small residual force in Afghanistan. But there were also uncertainties. Indians were concerned about their unity as "a land of twenty-two languages" and about raising their economic growth rate from 5 to 7 percent in the face of a growing population. Within a decade, India would become more populous than China.

On to Beijing, where the smog was a choking 500 parts per million and everyone was masked. At a conference at Peking University, friends warned that Hu Jintao and Dai Bingguo had kept a lid on things, but Xi Jinping was more nationalistic and less liberal, cracking down on opinions on the Internet, where social media was burgeoning. Vice Minister He Yafei said that the conflict in the South China Sea was a problem of "face" and they had to find a way to de-escalate it. Chen

Gang, a former Kennedy graduate who was chair of the Beijing City Council, told us of his efforts to save the innovative "798" contemporary art installation in the face of criticism from the old guard.

In Japan, I was told of their fear that Xi was changing policy in a more nationalistic direction. In a meeting with Prime Minister Shinzo Abe, I argued that Japan needed to improve its relations with South Korea if it wanted to pursue deterrence of North Korean nuclear use. For years, memories of Japan's aggression in the twentieth century had limited defense relations, but a recent effort at resolution had collapsed when Japan insisted that Korea take down a monument to "comfort women" (sex slaves), which it had built near the Japanese embassy. Abe said he was willing to try, but Japanese pride was a dominant issue for his followers. Pacific defense was hindered by nationalism in both our alliances.

Later in the year I traveled again to Japan to address students at their national defense university, take part in the Mitsubishi advisory board meeting, and attend a CSIS dinner with National Diet members convened by the Nikkei editorial board. With John Hamre, Steinberg, and Armitage, I again called on Prime Minister Abe, who was gracious, but nothing had changed in terms of relations with Korea. At dinner at his home, my friend Yukio Okamoto, a thoughtful retired diplomat, told me that nationalism was growing, and Abe would visit the Yasukuni Shrine to honor the war dead because that was what his followers wanted.

In December 2013, in Beijing, Foreign Minister Wang Yi had invited me to a private dinner with only a junior note-taker present. Wang wanted to quiz me about how China could increase its soft power. I pointed out that raising hundreds of millions of people out of poverty and celebrating a gorgeous traditional culture, as demonstrated by the Shanghai Exposition a few years earlier, were important sources of attraction for China. At the same time, as long as it had territorial disputes with its neighbors, and as long as its insistence on tight party control over civil society and human rights continued, China would face serious limits on its soft power in Asia and in the West.

At Davos in early 2014, I went to a party for Boris Johnson, then Mayor of London, and an odd type of leader. His speech was full of puns and as unruly as his hair. I had known his father Stanley at Oxford. As I wrote that night: "What a piece of work, both of them." It was hard to believe he would go on to become Prime Minister! I then joined a China-televised panel with Lloyd Blankfein (Senior Chairman of Goldman Sachs), Nick Clegg (Deputy Prime Minister in the UK's coalition government), and Wang Dalian, reputedly the richest man in China. When I explained that territorial disputes were limiting China's soft power, Wang Dalian criticized me for "hurting the feelings of the Chinese people." Later, the Chinese TV interviewer apologized to me and said that Wang's comments reflected Xi's new nationalistic approach. Another Chinese said that relations with Japan would not improve until Japan apologized for World War II the way Germany had. When I later chaired a panel with Wang Yi, he asked me privately if Abe's recent article about an analogy to 1914 was serious. Optimism was diminishing.

Japan was again on my agenda in 2015. China had dropped Deng's moderate foreign policy and Abe responded by talking about amending Japan's pacifist constitution. Formal amendment was not possible politically, but he worked with the Diet to make clear that "collective self-defense" fit within the constitutional concept of self-defense. When several of us called on him in his office on July 14, he seemed calm and collected, even though he had just come back from seven hours of debate on the subject in the Diet. And his approach seemed to work.

My next trip to Japan in the Fall was very different. After attending the Mt. Fuji Dialogue on US–Japan relations, I was invited to the Imperial Palace to receive the Order of the Rising Sun from the Emperor. I rented a formal morning suit, took a limousine to the palace, bowed to Abe and Chief Cabinet Secretary Yoshihide Suga, then waited in a large room with 100 Japanese and two other foreigners (a scientist and a congressman). Finally, a small man appeared, gave a short speech in Japanese, then walked along the rope line exchanging bows rather than handshakes. It was a very Japanese ceremony.

Before that, I was focused on China. In the summer of 2015, I had given an interview for the Xinhua News Agency which said that, while I was well known in China, there was some debate over whether I was a hawk or a dove. I told them I was an owl. At a meeting at the Berggruen Institute in New York, the Australian expert Hugh White said that the US should ask China what it wanted in exchange for co-leadership of the world. I argued that this would be a mistake because it would undercut the alliances that were central to our position. Former Australian Prime

Minister Kevin Rudd, who knew Xi, described him as a nationalist authoritarian.

I ended the year with another trip to China. Before a meeting of the ASG with the Central Party School, I took the bullet train to visit Qufu, the birthplace of Confucius, where there is a square mile of Kong family tombs dating back seventy-seven generations. I was shown the damage done by Red Guard youth in the 1960s campaign against Confucianism. I asked my Chinese escort what the current role of Confucianism was and he said: "It is part of our culture but not an ideology or religion." With that, in two hours, the train took me from 478 BC to the booming metropolis of twenty-first-century Beijing.

At the conference, there were various ideas for cooperation. I said we could accept the rise of China if they accepted our permanent presence in the Western Pacific. I asked them whether they would feel safer with or without the US–Japan alliance. They were ambivalent and accepted that the US was here to stay, but the mood was less accommodating than it had been the previous year. A friend told me privately that there was a political crackdown on expression and corruption and the PLA was using nationalism in the South China Sea as a means to protect itself in domestic bureaucratic fights.

Earlier that year, in April 2015, Prime Minister Abe had visited the US and I hosted him at a Forum at the Kennedy School before heading to Washington for the festivities there. Biden and Kerry hosted a lunch for him at the State Department, and I was surprised to find myself seated at the head table with Henry Kissinger, Madeleine Albright, and Colin Powell. I was even more surprised when Abe came over and thanked me (in English) for all my help. That evening was the state dinner at the White House. The hall was filled with cherry blossom and a Marine band in scarlet jackets was playing. In the receiving line, I told Obama that I had just published a new book, and he quipped that "everybody knows about Nye's soft power."

Cyber conflicts

In addition to the Asian balance of power, I was trying to wrap my mind around the new topic of cyber security. My first meeting of the Defense Policy Board had focused on the cyber threats to security, and Defense

Attending a reception with President Obama and Japanese Prime Minister Shinzo Abe at the White House, 2015

Secretary Robert Gates told us the Pentagon would need to reorganize to meet the threat. Later, a subgroup of the board went to the National Security Agency at Fort Meade, where the Director, General Keith Alexander, showed us some of their impressive capabilities, but warned that, "if we can do it, they often can too."

In June 2013, I gave a paper at the EastWest Institute's conference on cyber security in London. The warnings were dire, with some experts predicting attacks worse than Stuxnet, which the US and Israel had launched to disable the Iranian nuclear centrifuge program. Secretary of Defense Leon Panetta had warned against a "cyber Pearl Harbor." Chris Painter, the top American cyber diplomat, told me we had a short time to develop cyber norms before it was too late. That summer I gave a lecture at the Aspen Institute on what lessons cyber experts could learn from the history of societal reactions to the introduction of a disruptive nuclear technology a half century earlier. I pointed out that it took crises and nearly two decades before the first international agreements were reached.

When classes started at Harvard in January 2014, I took the plunge and offered (with Alexander Klimberg's help) a course about the international implications of cyber technology. I also began working on a scholarly article on the subject for publication later in the year. In May that year, I went to Stockholm as a member of Carl Bildt's Global Commission on Internet Governance. As Tony Blair had said during a visit to the Kennedy School, the Internet made democratic leadership more difficult because the political extremes trend most strongly. And international cooperation on cyber was still in its early stages. Like my students, I had a lot to learn, but I was pleased that my course received high marks in the end-of-term evaluations.

In 2013, a sharp disagreement had arisen with our allies when whistleblower Edward Snowden revealed numerous NSA classified communications. The US response that "everyone spies" did not alleviate the anger. It was true, but the Americans had greater capabilities. A week later, former NSA Director Mike Hayden discussed the problem at a small meeting at Harvard. Reformed procedures could settle the domestic issues, but how could trust be restored internationally? The NSA had recklessly bugged Angela Merkel's cell phone just because they could, and there had seemed to be zero risk – unless one considered the possibility of a disloyal insider like Snowden. Later in the year at a national cyber conference convened by the Hewlett Foundation, many suggestions were made to improve security through public education, but no one had an answer concerning disloyal insiders.

Amusingly, when I went to London in 2014, I was invited to the Cabinet Office for a discussion of cyber security. As I tried to cross the Mall, it was blocked off for the Queen's opening of Parliament. I missed my appointment while a crowd waited for a little old lady to drive by in a horse and carriage. Only in Britain could a twenty-first-century issue wait for an eighteenth-century parade. At least it was a good one – and good for British soft power too!

While in London, I also attended a meeting of Carl Bildt's Global Commission. We discussed fragmentation of the Internet, conditions for trust, and the prospect of cyberwar. Pindar Wong of Hong Kong tried to convince me that blockchain technology would be a means of security more important than its current use for Bitcoin. But the looming question was whether we would make the investment in redundancy and resilience that would mitigate inevitable attacks. It was hard to accomplish when the early days of the Internet had emphasized connection, not security, and the commercial model was "move fast and break things." These questions remained on the table when the Commission met later in the year at The Hague (including a visit to Europol to see how they handled crime), Accra, and Bangalore. Bildt was an excellent chairman, but answers were scarce.

During the summer of 2015 I began work on a scholarly article on "deterrence and dissuasion in cyberspace." Some analysts stated that deterrence did not work in the cyber domain. I disagreed and said it worked in different ways and with different thresholds from nuclear deterrence. I published an article in which I argued that we could not be sure that deterrence was the reason that we had not experienced a "cyber Pearl Harbor," but we did know that on actions below the level of war, deterrence sometimes worked and sometimes failed.

One of the interesting cyber events of 2015 was a conference that John Mallery organized at MIT with seven Chinese and one Russian official. The Chinese were surprisingly forthcoming about their interest in finding normative limits. Obama and Xi had signed an agreement to restrict cyber espionage for commercial purposes and the Chinese initially observed it. Russia and China had also agreed to a set of UN norms limiting cyber conflict, but Russia violated them almost immediately with its interference in Ukraine's electrical grid and its interference in the 2016 US presidential election. Obama waited until after the election to announce that there would be punitive sanctions, but incoming President Donald Trump dismissed the issue as not real. The prospects for compromise were dimming.

Almost the end

My personal life at this time was also eventful. February 2011 saw the publication of *The Future of Power* and *The Economist* welcomed it with a strong review. At the Council on Foreign Relations, Richard Haass hosted a debate about the book and the question of American decline between me and Gideon Rachman of the *Financial Times*. A few weeks later, the *Washington Post* said "Nye is a master of his field at the height of his powers," and in *Foreign Affairs* it was written that "Nye is the preeminent theorist of power in world affairs today." That was the good news. The bad news was the constant travel and speeches in dozens of cities that go into a publisher's book tour. In ten days in England in May 2011, I counted seventeen talks as well as three BBC interviews. I grew very weary of traveling and of talking about the book.

Toward the end of 2011, I went to DC for a ceremony for my inclusion in *Foreign Policy*'s list of the "Top 100 Global Thinkers." I was also pleased when a German blog listed me as the twenty-eighth most influential international intellectual (Al Gore, Jürgen Habermas, and Peter Singer topped the list). Then *Foreign Policy* listed me as the most influential academic on policy and the fifth most influential as a scholar. Ranking high on both lists at the same time was rare, but, as I wrote at the time, "this means what?" Academic integrity and political influence are sometimes hard to combine, but it seemed I had threaded the needle. Even so, after giving an eighteen-minute TED Global talk to 700 people on the future of power, I asked myself: "Am I being too optimistic, even as I try to stay balanced?" Later, on a hike in the White Mountains of New Hampshire with Bob Keohane, I asked him for his opinion. After a few miles of discussion, we concluded that we were not far apart on the issue of decline, but he was a modest pessimist, and I was a modest optimist.

In the Spring of 2011, I was honored with a *Festschrift* – a German academic tradition to celebrate a professor with a volume of essays, but some in American academe developed the idea of a living *Festschrift* or conference instead. My former students Peter Feaver and David Welch organized a two day "Nye-fest" with more than 100 former students and colleagues at the Kennedy School. Among the many toasts, Peter Katzenstein, Professor of International Studies at Cornell University, said I had deepened the study of power; Keohane called me a "rooted cosmopolitan with peasant roots"; and Anne-Marie Slaughter and Holly Sargent praised what I had done to advance women at the School. Philip Zelikow cited my Enlightenment faith in reason, but also the way I had founded policy networks and "labs" like the Aspen Strategy Group. Gideon Rose said I had set a model for how to take people and ideas seriously. It was overwhelming! My only regret was that, given the book tour, I had so little time to savor it.

I decided to cut my teaching (and salary) in half. I enjoyed teaching, but not grading. I realized that good feedback is essential to learning, and I felt professors should personally write a comment on each of their students' exams. I also made it a point of principle not to miss classes. I wanted to release more time for travel and writing, but in a way that would make it possible to continue having contact with students. That became my arrangement for the next seven years.

I dabbled a bit in politics. When Michelle Nunn, a former student, said she would run for Senate in Georgia, I thought it was a very gutsy move and sponsored a fundraiser that was attended by Massachusetts Governor Deval Patrick, Senator Ed Markey, and Congressman Joe Kennedy. Later, I joined in sponsoring another fundraiser for New Hampshire's Senator Jeanne Shaheen that featured Patrick, Governor Maggie Hassan from New Hampshire, and Massachusetts Congresswoman Katherine Clark. Alas, in the November elections, the US Senate went Republican, but at least Shaheen won. And when the newly elected members of Congress went for orientation at the Kennedy School in December, I was pleased to see that two of them were graduates of the School, including my former student Seth Moulton.

The highlight of several summers during the Obama years was a week of fly fishing for salmon in Alaska's glorious Tongass wilderness fifty miles east of Wrangell, and not far (in Alaska terms) from where I had worked in the copper mine in 1956. We stayed in a Forest Service A-frame cabin under huge old-growth hemlocks and spruce dripping with moss and with long views of snow-capped mountains on the Canadian border. Each day we motored up the roiling muddy glacial Stikine River to clear tributaries where we would hike upstream to fish. We caught countless fish, the largest being a 47-pound king salmon on a five-ounce flyrod. All were returned to spawn. It wasn't just the fishing that was great: one day, we took a boat close to a glacier and chipped ice off one of the little icebergs that it had calved. That night I had a gin and tonic with 10,000-year-old ice! I also fished a pool on a river where a wolf came so close to me that a friend took our picture; it was not clear which of us was more surprised.

On December 7, 2015 it almost all ended. Molly and I were traveling along Interstate 93 returning from New Hampshire to Boston, when she screamed at me. I was driving at about 70 mph and had lost consciousness; we were heading down a steep embankment into the woods. It was too late to control the car, which rolled over and hit several large trees. When the thudding ended, I called out to Molly, unbuckled my seat belt, and managed to crawl out through the back of the car. I found her with the passenger side door blown open. She had cuts on her head and legs and had broken three ribs. I had superficial cuts and bruises, but thanks to air bags and Subaru engineering, I was able to sit up in front of the ambulance that took us to Concord Hospital.

Later, doctors discovered that my heartbeat had dropped so low that I had blacked out – a problem that was eventually solved by inserting a pacemaker. While Molly recuperated in the hospital, I called our son Ben who worked in Boston, and we went back to the scene to rescue personal possessions including art work we were transporting for Molly's gallery friends. The next day, feeling sore and bruised, I taught my class, and a week later I presented my cyber paper at a faculty seminar. It was a terrifying experience that almost ended everything, including this book, and I felt awful about endangering the most important person in my life. It reminded me what fragile and temporary creatures we are and how much of our fate rests on chance.

The rise of Trump

The year 2016 was Obama's final one in office, but it might better be known for the rise of Trump, since it was he who dominated the news. In the Republican presidential primaries, Texas Senator Ted Cruz beat Trump in Iowa; some thought Trump had peaked but he went on to win the New Hampshire primary. In my new year's musing, I wrote that we were going through a bad spell in politics, but we had seen worse in the 1930s and 1960s and would probably recover. I said this to former Brazilian President Cardoso during a meeting of the TOTAL advisory board in Rio later in the month. He said that Brazil was going through a similar wave of nationalist populism but warned that "it will take years to dig out of this hole." At that time, watching the joyous well-behaved parades preparing for Mardi Gras, it was hard to believe that Brazil was in trouble. But he turned out to be right about both countries. President Dilma Rousseff was impeached in August 2016 and was succeeded by a rightwing populist, Jair Bolsonaro, who modeled himself on Trump.

At the end of February, Trump won the South Carolina primary and Jeb Bush dropped out. In early March, Trump and Clinton each won seven of their respective party's primaries. Mike Chertoff suggested to me that "we are now entering a new era of American politics." Trump continued to succeed, despite his more outrageous statements. As Republican consultant Mike Murphy told a meeting at the Kennedy School: "Outrage attracts attention, and 24/7 media attention provides the equivalent of free advertisement. Politics has always had an element of theater, but now it is driving out policy." My worry was that it was also driving out the important norms of self-restraint, much as had occurred in ancient Rome before the decline of the republic. My role as a participant in politics was limited to occasional calls with the Clinton campaign foreign policy team, but, as a citizen, I was concerned.

As Matthew Schlapp, Chairman of the American Conservative Union, explained when he spoke to the North American meeting of the Trilateral Commission: "Many people foresaw the populist wave, but few foresaw Trump and his ability to ride it." Tom Pritzker, Chair of Hyatt Hotels Corporation, once told me that Trump had a reputation in the business world for lying and cheating, completely unlike business magnate and philanthropist Warren Buffett, who generated trust. But it worked for Trump in a polarized political environment, even though *Politifact* reported that 60 percent of his claims were untrue compared to 12 percent for Hillary. On foreign policy, his anti-alliance and mercantilist statements, not to mention the nasty aspersions he cast on poorer nations, represented an upending of American foreign policy. As the polling expert Sam Popkin said to me, even if the chances of his election are only one in six, that is still Russian roulette.

At the Aspen Institute in August, few of our Republican members defended him; indeed, a group of fifty Republican foreign policy experts signed a letter saying Trump was too dangerous. I was writing a monthly column for *Project Syndicate*, and I devoted that month to Trump's lack of emotional intelligence in terms of mastering his own emotional needs and relating to others. All to no avail. Even a tape disclosed in October in which Trump boasted of groping women and getting away with it because he was famous did not derail him. I described it as a sickness caused by reality TV and social media culture.

On election day, November 8, the *New York Times* put the odds of Hillary winning at 85 percent, and she did indeed win the popular vote by 2 million, but Trump won the electoral college. Ironically, if 100,000 votes had changed in three states, Hillary would have become the first woman president. She conceded graciously and Obama asked for reconciliation. There was still some grumbling in the foreign policy elite. In Washington, at a tribute held by the ASG for Brent Scowcroft to honor his stepping down as my co-chair (to be replaced by Condoleezza Rice), Brent said that, while Trump's election was a disaster, Republican members should serve if asked. A few disagreed, however, saying they could never serve under such a man.

Assessing Obama

How to summarize Obama's term of office? It started on a high note. His rhetoric and behavior did much to restore American soft power that been damaged by the Iraq war, and his accomplishments were solid though not spectacular. Ironically, despite his efforts to reduce American involvement in the troubled Middle East and to refocus attention on the rising region of Asia, Obama found that, in foreign policy, the urgent often drives out the important. He was unable to persuade Israel to forgo its settlements in the West Bank or to get the Palestinians to engage deeply in a peace process. In Iraq, he had to reverse his position as ISIS strengthened. But Syria was his biggest problem.

In August 2012, he casually declared that the use of chemical weapons would be a "red line," but a year later, when Assad used chemicals and Obama was unable to obtain allied or congressional support for an air strike, he accepted a Russian compromise proposal for international removal and inspection of Syrian chemicals, and that decision became an oft-cited symbol of weakness. Obama armed moderate opponents of the Assad regime, but he resisted pressures to set up safety or no-fly zones in Syria when it was unclear whether the beneficiary might be the Islamic State. Some realists applauded this prudence; but other critics argue that his caution had bad consequences, including the rise of ISIS.

Despite his problems in the Middle East, Obama had several foreign policy accomplishments on global issues. First was the successful handling of the global economic crisis, when he made effective use of the Group of 20 in the early days of the crisis. His efforts to negotiate an agreement on global climate change led to a degree of success at Paris in 2015. He negotiated a replacement of the Strategic Arms Reduction Treaty that cut the American and Russian strategic arsenals, and convened summits on nuclear security, but his efforts to denuclearize North Korea proved unsuccessful.

Closely related to these global issues was Obama's handling of relations with an ever more powerful China. He had twenty-four face-to-face meetings with Chinese Presidents Hu Jintao and Xi Jinping, and was able to bridge differences on climate change and cyber norms that had appeared intractable. At the same time, Obama maintained close alliances with Japan, Korea, and Australia, and improved relations with India to help maintain the balance of power.

Obama also tried to reset relations with Russia and developed a good working relationship with Dmitri Medvedev, but he had more difficulty when Vladimir Putin returned to the presidency in 2012. Putin saw American support for color revolutions in the former USSR, the revolutions in the Middle East in 2011, and the 2014 revolt in neighboring Ukraine as threats to his authoritarian regime. His hybrid war in Eastern Ukraine and the seizure of Crimea led to a serious worsening of relations and sanctions from the Obama Administration, but not of sufficient strength to serve as an effective deterrent.

Obama has sometimes been criticized for being prudent to a fault, but in this he was like the first rather than the second President Bush. Revolutionary times may produce opportunities, but they can also produce nasty surprises and unintended consequences (as Obama discovered in Libya and Syria). He was attentive to the implications of new technologies like drone strikes and cyberattacks, showed respect for liberal values and procedures, and made efforts to use and develop international institutions. Above all, Obama respected truth, and broadened moral discourse at home and abroad on major global issues. This was in sharp contrast to his successor.

10

Trump, Biden, and Beyond

The four years of Donald Trump's presidency were a challenge – to me, to the country, to the world. Trump was a difficult president because of his low contextual intelligence regarding international affairs and a high level of narcissism that limited his emotional intelligence. He had not been filtered by the American political process, and the presidency was his first political office. He had run his family's New York real-estate business since 1971 and hosted the reality television show *The Apprentice* from 2003 to 2015. Forbes estimated his net worth to be $3.1 billion.

Trump's unique background produced a highly unconventional political style. Success in reality television meant keeping the attention of the camera and that was often accomplished by statements that were more outrageous than true, and by breaking conventional norms of behavior. Trump also learned how to employ the new social media platform of Twitter to dominate the agenda and bypass the traditional press. Like him or not, he was a brilliant communicator and far more original than any normal politician.

The new president also intuited and mobilized a populist discontent about the uneven economic effects of global trade on parts of the country, and resentment of immigration and cultural changes, particularly among older non-college white males. His populist, protectionist, and nationalistic statements earned him free media coverage far in excess of the traditional paid political advertisements. Many people expected that, after the close election, Trump would move to the center to broaden his political support – as most politicians would do. Instead, he continued to play to his loyal base and used that base to threaten primary campaign challenges against those who differed with him, so that Republican congressional figures feared to express open criticism. Many of those who openly opposed him lost their primaries, and mainstream Republican foreign policy experts who had signed an anti-Trump letter during the campaign were excluded from the new administration.

Trump's initial foreign policy appointments were impressive nonpolitical conservatives like former Exxon CEO Rex Tillerson in the State Department, General James Mattis in Defense, General H.R McMaster as National Security Advisor, and General John Kelly as Chief of Staff. I initially felt reassured, but Trump eventually discarded them all. Instead, he governed as he had campaigned, and became a very unconventional president who challenged the basic premises of American foreign policy and the American century.

To the delight of some and the concern of others, Trump was different. Policies were often announced, and cabinet secretaries fired, on Twitter. The result was an administration with frequent changes in top personnel and contradictory policy messages that undercut his top officials. While this approach caused problems for Trump with the courts, the press, and America's allies, what he lost in organizational coherence he made up for in his almost complete domination of the agenda. Unpredictability was one of Trump's political tools. As his former Chief of Staff Reince Priebus told the Trilateral Commission when it met in Singapore, Trump did not care about process, he just wanted to own decisions by using tweets, surprises, and extreme positions.

Trump's political views were eclectic rather than traditional Republican. He had long expressed protectionist views on trade and a nationalist resentment based on a view that allies took unfair advantage of the United States. During his political campaign, he had become the first major candidate to challenge the post-1945 consensus on the liberal international order – a subject on which I published an article in *Foreign Affairs* early in 2017. While he softened some of his security iconoclasm after becoming president, many of Trump's campaign themes continued to guide his foreign policy. He suggested that Japan and Korea might develop their own nuclear weapons to replace their American alliance; he also withdrew from the Paris Climate Accords, rejected the Trans-Pacific Partnership trade pact that Obama had negotiated, weakened the WTO, renegotiated NAFTA, imposed national security tariffs on steel and aluminum imports from allies, launched a broad set of tariffs against China, withdrew from the nuclear agreement that Obama and US allies had negotiated to limit Iran, criticized NATO and the Group of 7, and praised authoritarian leaders who were involved in human rights violations. Trump's first National Security Doctrine, issued in December

2017, expressed skepticism about multilateral institutions and global commerce and focused attention on great power rivalry with China. It was more moderate than some of his verbal statements; one of its primary authors told me he doubted Trump had read or understood it.

The Trump Administration also invested less money and rhetoric in developing American soft power. Polls (as well as an annual *Soft Power 30* index published in London) showed that American soft power declined considerably in 2017. Tweets can help to set the global agenda, but they do not attract if their tone and substance are offensive to foreign publics and leaders. Trump also paid less attention to human rights, which had traditionally been a source of American soft power. Although he used air power to punish Syria for chemical attacks on civilians and tried to persuade Saudi Arabia to limit its bombing of civilians in the Yemen war, Trump's speeches lacked the embrace of democracy and human rights that had been espoused by every president since Carter and Reagan. Even critics who applauded Trump's tougher position on China faulted him for not working with allies in responding to Chinese behavior. In addition, while global rules and institutions can be restraining, the US had a preponderant role in their formulation and was a major beneficiary of global alliances. Moreover, the US had greater soft power than China, but Trump's style undercut those advantages.

A statement signed in August 2016 by fifty Republican former national security officials stated: "A President must be disciplined, control emotions, and act only after reflection and careful deliberation … Trump has none of these critical qualities. He does not encourage conflicting views. He lacks self-control and acts impetuously. He cannot tolerate personal criticism. He has alarmed our closest allies with his erratic behavior."[13] They and others argued that Trump's personal temperament made him unfit to be president.

As a political leader aggregating power, Trump was clearly very smart, but his temperament in governing ranked him low on the scales of emotional and contextual intelligence that had made an FDR or George H. W. Bush such successful presidents. As Trump's ghostwriter said: "Early on, I recognized that Trump's sense of self-worth is forever

[13] "Statement by Former National Security Officials." Letter in *Washington Post,* August 8, 2016.

at risk. When he feels aggrieved, he reacts impulsively and defensively, constructing a self-justifying story that doesn't depend on facts … Trump simply didn't traffic in emotions or interest in others … A key part of the story is that facts are whatever Trump deems them to be on any given day."[14] Trump's personal needs often distorted his motives and interfered with his policy objectives. In 2019, Graham Allison, David Sanger, and I took the CEO of a high-tech firm fishing, and he regaled us with a description of an Oval Office meeting with Trump. The meeting was to discuss important international security aspects of a new communications technology, but Trump would digress to comment on Biden's make-up and the "horseface" of a woman who had criticized Trump.

Trump's temperament also limited his contextual intelligence. His lack of experience in government and international affairs contrasted with that of most of his predecessors, but equally striking were the limits of his efforts to fill in the gaps in his knowledge. His constant need for personal validation led to flawed policy that weakened American alliances – for example, after his summit meetings with Putin and Kim Jung Un in 2018. Unwillingness to confront unwelcome evidence was culpable negligence.

In addition, Trump showed little concern for limiting damage to others, and he narrowed rather than broadened moral discourse both at home and abroad. His lack of respect for institutions and truth led to a loss of soft power. He was not a traditional isolationist, but he presided over a period of retrenchment that reflected popular attitudes. Trump altered the American century by rejecting the liberal international order. He promised to "Make America Great Again" by a narrow transactional approach and disruptive diplomacy that challenged conventional wisdom and much that I had worked on throughout my career.

Early in 2017, the Trilateral Commission met in Washington. Treasury Secretary Steven Mnuchin was only partially reassuring on trade, but former Chair of the Federal Reserve Ben Bernanke and Director of the IMF Christine Lagarde were upbeat about the international economy. Naturally, all the foreigners wanted to know about Trump. I chaired a

[14] Tony Schwartz, "I Wrote the Art of the Deal with Trump." *Washington Post*, May 16, 2017.

session on "Trump's America" with journalist Andrea Mitchell, diplomat Paula Dobriansky, and co-Chair of the Carlyle Group David Rubinstein. We cautioned foreign guests not to expect normal politics, but also not to overestimate the wave of populism or underestimate the checks and balances built into American institutions. In May, Ban Ki Moon came to see me in my Harvard office to solicit my opinion before he returned to Korea to meet with President Moon Jae In. I counseled patience, and I said I thought some day we would look back at Trump as a serious road accident but not a fatal crash. When I attended the annual North Pavilion Dialogue at Peking University, led by Professor Wang Jisi, Dai Bingguo invited former CIA Director John Negroponte and me to a private lunch to discuss Trump. As we told Dai, Trump was something new, and all we could counsel was patience.

Retirement

In 2017, I celebrated my eightieth birthday and retirement from regular teaching. My role in government ended when the new administration dropped me from Pentagon and State Department advisory boards (as nomally happens with a political change). I continued to write, speak, and serve on a reduced number of boards, but I was now primarily an observer. However, my curiosity about the world and America's place in it remained as strong as ever, as I tried to make sense of Trump's radical changes and how they affected the American century.

I started the year as a visiting professor at Schwarzman College, an island of American residential collegiate life that Steve Schwarzman had funded in Tsinghua University in Beijing. His idea was to emulate the Rhodes experience by having selected students from around the world and China live and study together. I had sat on a selection committee with him in New York, so I was pleased to see it in successful operation. The discussions were quite open and we could use the Internet freely. On the other hand, friends told me that Xi was tightening party control in general. And, needless to say, there was great curiosity about Trump.

In February, I attended the Munich Security Conference, and sat next to General John Kelly at breakfast. I was reassured by his balanced approach, and by Vice President Pence's speech reaffirming American commitment to NATO. Similarly, Republican Governor John Kasich of Ohio reaffirmed our alliances. I was pleased when I heard that Trump had replaced the erratic General Steve Flynn with H. R. McMaster as National Security Advisor. Also in Munich, Dutch Foreign Minister Koenders introduced the new Global Commission on Stability in Cyberspace (GCSC) on which I had been asked to serve.

The Asian balance of power

My interest in Asia continued. In March, I went to Honolulu to attend the board of the Pacific Forum and speak about Asian security. Admiral Harry Harris, a former student, invited me to lunch in his huge office lined with flags and with commanding views out over the bay and Pearl Harbor. We discussed Japan's slow strengthening of its defense posture, as well as the perpetual problem of North Korea, where the rhetoric had been ratcheting up. At a later meeting of the Trilateral Commission there were alarming estimates of war with North Korea, which some observers placed between 25 and 50 percent. I said war would be too costly for the Korean people, and we would have to learn to live with and contain a nuclear North Korea.

In the Fall, the Aspen Strategy Group met with its Indian counterparts for the twenty-second time. The Indians were more openly anti-Chinese than in the past, but many were pro-Trump because he was being tougher on Pakistan and was keeping troops in Afghanistan. But there were also reports claiming that many Delhi elites were convinced that the US was in decline. Later in October, I flew to Tokyo, where everyone was puzzled about Trump, but Shinzo Abe had been re-elected and some said this meant he had pre-empted populism in Japan. Abe also proved to be a skilled manager of the Trump relationship by playing to his vanity. In general, participants at the Mt. Fuji Dialogue felt that the US–Japan alliance was in good condition, in contrast to Europe.

In 2018, I flew to Singapore for a meeting of the Trilateral Commission. Officials told me that Singapore had altered its higher education strategy along the lines of the report of a committee I had been part of a decade earlier. And at a dinner celebrating my stepping down after ten years of being chair, toasts were raised to me for having saved the Commission and for rejuvenating and diversifying it. It is nice to see one's work recognized.

When an American asked Singapore Foreign Minister Balakrishnan whether the US could recover its position in Asia after Trump, he replied that the damage to our credibility was lasting, but, in the end, it would depend on whether the anchor of the US–Japan alliance remained intact. Fortunately, our Japanese members said it had broad support and there was no alternative. At home, Armitage and I were preparing another bipartisan report on the alliance to help protect it in a congressional election year.

The ASG meetings of that same year focused on China. Foreign policy strategist Michael Pillsbury had a somewhat alarmist view, while Allison cited war games that showed the US could not defend Taiwan. On the other hand, political scientist Tom Christenson argued that China did not pose an ideological threat like the Soviets in the Cold War, and economists Larry Summers and Dick Cooper warned against overestimating the Chinese economy.

At the end of 2019, I also returned to Tokyo, where I gave speeches, attended the Mitsubishi advisory board, and met with politicians at dinners and at the Mt. Fuji Dialogue. I had to present my views at a panel on American politics and I said my guess was that Trump had a 45 percent chance of re-election, but warned that my predictions were suspect because there were too many wild cards in the deck. When I traveled on to Beijing for the North Pavilion Dialogue, my Chinese hosts were still puzzled, but one of the Russian participants, Andrei Kortunov, said Russians had no ambivalence about Trump. They did not like him, and the Russian meddling in the 2016 election should not be viewed as an effort to elect Trump but as a chaotic payback for what Russia saw as the US role in the Maidan demonstrations in Ukraine that had toppled a pro-Russian president.

Some people praise Trump for his tough policy toward China, but he never had a clear strategy for Asia. A State Department official said that Trump had badly misjudged Kim Jong Un when they met in Hanoi. The head of policy planning in the State Department told me that Trump had got China's attention on trade issues, but lacked an overall China strategy. Fortunately, our alliances in Asia were too resilient for Trump to destroy.

European anxieties

Europeans were more concerned than Asians about Trump. The hubris that many Europeans had felt two decades earlier had vanished, and many were anxious about the future. I flew to Bratislava in May 2019 and attended a Global Security Conference that focused on US–Europe relations. Several Republican attendees warned that Trump did not like Europe and saw it as a rival, but that view was not true of a number of important people in the administration. I had dinner with Catherine Ashton, the European Union's former High Representative for Foreign Affairs, and found her quite pessimistic. Europeans had been shocked by Trump's withdrawal from the Iran nuclear agreement and his levying of tariffs against allies on security grounds. In addition, she was discouraged by the attitudes about Europe in post-Brexit Britain.

Returning to Europe a month later, I had breakfast with George Walden in the great dining-room of the Oxford and Cambridge Club, with its 16-foot-high portraits of ancient dignitaries. Walden, a former Tory MP, was gloomy about British politics and what he called second-rate leaders. At lunch, with the editors of *The Economist*, I learned that a second referendum on Brexit was unlikely, and that Britain had no strategy. The mood was not much better at Oxford, where I stayed again in Nuffield College and attended the Blavatnik International Advisory Committee. A Ditchley conference focused on cyber problems, particularly coping with artificial intelligence used for political disruptions and fake news. I also made a brief visit to Athens to give a speech for Kennedy School Kokkalis Program alumni, including several from Turkey. Turkey continued to be a problem. I was pleased when the Sabanci Foundation honored me in Istanbul with a generous prize for my work on international relations, but I was dismayed by Erdogan's populist authoritarianism.

At the seventieth anniversary of the Treaty of Washington, which established NATO, polls showed strong congressional and public support for the institution, but Trump disdained both it and the European Union. In August 2019, the ASG opened with a panel of four former national security advisors: Condoleezza Rice, Stephen Hadley, Tom Donilon, and Susan Rice. I proposed a hypothetical to them. What if Trump got all NATO countries to spend 2 percent on defense, if regime change occurred in Iran, and if China negotiated a favorable trade deal? Would historians view him as a success? Their answer was "no" if it came at the price of destroyed alliances, institutions, and trust. Trump's distrust of our allies was not making America great again.

In 2019, I was honored with the Centennial Medal of the Graduate School of Arts and Sciences, which meant I was to attend Harvard Graduation for the first time in a decade. The speaker that year was Angela Merkel, a remarkable European leader, and, as we looked out from the platform to the banners, gowns, and sea of faces, I congratulated her on her sense of humor. She replied: "I don't know how anyone could do this job without it!"

Harvard graduation ceremony, with German Chancellor Angela Merkel, 2019

AI and cyber

Our Aspen sessions that year focused on the impact of artificial intelligence on international affairs. Eric Schmidt said that China would equal or exceed the US in AI by 2030 (which was Xi's stated goal). Military experts told us that weapons controlled by AI would be the wave of the future and that any platform that could be seen could be destroyed by swarms of autonomous vehicles. Experts on democracy worried about manipulation of social media and covert information wars that would destroy trust. Could humans develop rules of the road for the new technology based on self-interest? These questions also arose at Stanford, where I participated in former Secretary of State George Schultz's meetings on governance and security. Discussions included Europe's worries about its declining population, populist reactions to immigration, and the fact that Europe had no tech companies in the top fifteen.

At Stanford with George Schultz, 2019

In May 2019 I went to DC for a meeting on AI and international relations sponsored by the National Academy of Sciences and the Royal Society. Stuart Russell, Professor of Computer Science at Berkeley, estimated that real quantum computing was still a decade or two away, but that the competition between China and the US was already hindering cooperation on AI for areas like medicine and aging where all could benefit. A young scholar asked me what I thought about our growing knowledge. I replied that the older I got, the less I thought I knew. The numerator went up but so did the denominator. Still, the search for integrative understanding is insatiable.

In June, I went to The Hague where the GCSC was meeting. Members were concerned that the degree of cooperation that had characterized the UN meetings on cyber in 2015 was now shrinking under Russian and Chinese assertive demands about sovereign control of the Internet. The Commission members from those countries had little to say. The GCSC wrapped up its work in 2019 in Addis Ababa, where we presented our eight basic norms to a meeting of African states in the OAU building. After the meeting, Mike Chertoff and I walked to the "Red Terror Museum" which has displays memorializing the half million people killed during that period of Ethiopian history. From Addis, I flew to Kampala to see my old haunts from five decades earlier. My friend Olara Otunnu, former Ambassador to the UN, drove me around Makerere and the Kasubi Tombs and I felt right at home. He warned me, however, that corruption was eroding education and institutions. I noted that Uganda today has a population of 40 million compared to fewer than 10 million when I lived there. Demographics were outpacing technology.

The year of Covid

In 2020, the world was struck by Covid. The virus that emerged in Wuhan at the beginning of the year disrupted everyone's plans and cost millions of lives. Oxford published my new book, *Do Morals Matter? Presidents and Foreign Policy from FDR to Trump*, and I spent the first two months on book talks and media appearances in Boston, Chicago, Washington, and New York. But by March, when the scope of the pandemic became clear, that was the end of that.

The disruption was a personal cost, but the disruption of Trump's plans was a national benefit. Initially, I believed Trump was likely to be re-elected because of his incumbency and a strong economy, and I worried how this would erode our democracy at home and our standing abroad. It was not clear who among the Democrats could beat him. The Biden/Harris combo was, I noted, "the best bet, but there was low public enthusiasm." Trump's fumbling and mishandling of the pandemic contributed greatly to his undoing in November that year. To give him credit, he made a good decision to use government funds to accelerate the development of MRNA vaccines, which began to be distributed in early 2021. But he also misled the public about testing and promoted false remedies. In doing so, he damaged his credibility.

Molly and I went to Stanford early in the year, where I participated in seminars on AI and cyber security, and enjoyed more conversations with George Schultz, who, like Kissinger, was amazing at his age. But the dark shadow of Covid was lengthening. On February 28, the PBS *Newshour* estimated that Covid would infect a third of the population, and columnist Peggy Noonan wrote in the *Wall Street Journal* that Covid would be a game-changer. She was right – but Trump called a press conference and declared it a Democratic hoax.

Though I continued with a planned trip to promote my book in Los Angeles, we soon learned that Harvard and then Stanford were limiting the size of meetings, so we canceled our trip to Hawaii, where I was to present the book at the ISA. It was sad to shorten everything to come home, but a good thing we did. Five days later, the Bay Area ordered everyone to shelter in place. By then we were in New Hampshire, isolating on our frozen farm. On March 25, Trump announced that he wanted everyone back to church and work by Easter. Dr. Anthony Fauci, his Covid advisor, said he doubted this would be possible, and was criticized by the president. In March, polls showed a majority still trusted Trump, though Biden was two points ahead in early polls.

In a very short time, my world turned upside-down. From being someone who traveled frequently, I went to being a stay-at-home for a year and a half. The early days were marked by great uncertainty about how long Covid would last and what precautions were necessary. I remember going to fill my car with gasoline and using rubber gloves and wipes to handle the pump nozzle. I realized that my travel plans to Europe in the Spring would be cancelled. The stock market had tanked, and some analysts thought the recession might last for two or three years. But I did not realize what an important role the Internet would play. With Zoom and other systems, I found myself in constant contact, and giving even more speeches than usual because personal travel costs had been reduced. Some weeks, I could go to Brazil, Europe, and Asia without ever setting foot in an airport or spending a drop of jet fuel. In a Zoom meeting with Beijing, I argued that the response to Covid represented a failure of top leadership in both China and the US, and I published a *Project Syndicate* column on the failure of cooperation – to no avail.

At the personal level, Molly and I bought some day-old chicks which we raised in a box under a heat lamp in our house. Their happy chirping, as well as the seedlings germinating on the sunny windowsill, restored a sense of hope. I took my various granddaughters fishing, and the youngest asked me if I was afraid of dying. I said: "No, it is like a big sleep. The thing to fear is prolonged pain or losing your mind." But since 75 percent of Covid deaths were among people over 65, I wore a mask and tried to avoid going into stores as much as possible until vaccines became available. Just before the lockdown, I remember speculating about the future with the Keohanes. Would our grandchildren see the same progress in their lifetimes as we had? Bob said no. I said yes on health, wealth, and social mores, but I was worried about technology, war, and climate change. For the past seventy years we had lived in a "Whig" period of history with a built-in expectation of progress. But was that simply a secular expression of faith, like any religion, meant to lighten life? Were we approaching the end of the American century?

Populism and politics

I continued to worry about Trump's populism and his erosion of the norms of self-restraint that make democracy work. Trump had not been the first to discover the powers of populism. As Richard Hofstadter wrote in 1965, there had always been a paranoid strand in American politics. George Wallace, Newt Gingrich, and others had already exploited the white nationalism that followed the profound social changes of the 1960s and '70s, but Trump became its master. No one knew where he was going.

I attended a day-long celebration of Robert Putnam's important work in social science, and he made the case that another progressive era was possible based on generational change. Ronald Inglehart agreed on the importance of generational change, and William Galston pointed out that, in contrast to the 1960s, today's protesters turned to politics rather than destruction. And while immigration was fueling populism in many countries, it had not disrupted Australia or Canada. The future of nationalist populism and its effect on politics was hard to predict.

By April 2019, Biden had become the twentieth candidate for the Democratic nomination. I thought he was too old (like me), but I would support anyone who could defeat Trump. The 2020 political year heated up after Labor Day, and polls showed Biden with a lead. David Brooks wrote a prescient column saying he doubted Trump would accept such an outcome. "What then?" On the eve of the November election, I wrote: "How can a culture produce the Declaration of Independence and also enshrine slavery in its constitution? Produce Lincoln and the Gettysburg Address, yet follow reconstruction with lynchings? Produce King and Obama as well as Trump, a mendacious bully who boasts of molesting women? Now the test is whether our culture will remove him peacefully."

The previous year Trump had faced impeachment for his efforts to interfere in Ukrainian politics to help his political position in the US. I went to DC for a meeting of the CSIS board and asked two of the respected Republican moderate members, Bill Brock and Bill Cohen, whether any Republican officials would join Senator Romney in supporting Trump's removal. They said they doubted it. He had too tight a lock on the party. They were right.

By November 7, we knew the outcome of the election, though Trump refused to accept the result. Seventeen Republican attorneys general filed a suit before the Supreme Court to overturn the election, but on December 11 the Court rejected it. Earlier, on December 1, the Electoral College met and affirmed that Biden had been elected president. However, Trump continued to reject the results and on, January 6, 2021, he goaded followers to attack the Capitol and try to intimidate outgoing Vice President Pence from certifying the results. It was the first time that an American president had refused to accept the outcome of a legal democratic election. On January 20, Biden was sworn in as scheduled. The institutions had prevailed – just.

President Biden is still a work in progress, and it is too early to assess his record. In his first two years, there were failures, such as the way he handled the withdrawal from Afghanistan, but they were outweighed by successes in passing bipartisan legislation on infrastructure, support for technological investments, and measures to combat climate change. In the 2022 midterm elections, he defied expectations by retaining control of the Senate and only narrowly losing the House. The results were widely interpreted as a rebuff to candidates supported by Trump. Internationally, Biden maintained American alliances and helped organize a response to the Russian invasion of Ukraine, though the ultimate results are yet to be seen.

Signing off

What sort of a world am I leaving to my grandchildren and their "Generation Z"? I tried to examine part of it in my 2015 book *Is the American Century Over?* and concluded that the answer to that question was "no," but that American primacy in this century will not look like the twentieth century. I argued that the greatest danger we face is not that China will surpass us, but that the diffusion of power will produce entropy, or the inability to get anything done.

China is an impressive peer competitor with great strengths but also weaknesses. In assessing the overall balance of power, the US has at least five long-term advantages. One is geography. The US is surrounded by two oceans and two friendly neighbors, while China shares a border with fourteen other countries and is engaged in territorial disputes with several. The US also has an energy advantage, whereas China depends on energy imports. Third, the US derives power from its large transnational financial institutions and the international role of the dollar. A credible reserve currency depends on it being freely convertible, as well as on deep capital markets and the rule of law, which China lacks. The US also has a relative demographic advantage as the only major developed country that is currently projected to hold its place (third) in the global population ranking. Seven of the world's fifteen largest economies will have a shrinking workforce over the next decade, but the US workforce is expected to increase, while China's peaked in 2014. Finally, America has been at the forefront in key technologies (bio, nano, and information). China, of course, is investing heavily in research and development and scores well in the numbers of patents, but by its own measures its research universities still rank behind American ones.

All told, the US holds a strong hand in the great power competition, but if we succumb to hysteria about China's rise or to complacency about its "peak," we could play our cards poorly. Discarding high-value cards – including strong alliances and influence in international institutions – would be a serious mistake. China is not an existential threat to the US unless we make it one by blundering into a major war. The historical analogy that worries me is 1914, not 1941.

My greater concern, however, is about domestic change and what it could do to our soft power and the future of the American century. Even if its external power remains dominant, a country can lose its internal virtue and attractiveness to others. The Roman empire lasted long after it lost its republican form of government. As Benjamin Franklin remarked about the form of American government created by the founders: "A republic if you can keep it." Political polarization is a problem, and civic life is becoming more complex. Technology is creating an enormous range of opportunities and risks that my grandchildren will face as they cope with the Internet of Things, AI, big data, machine learning, deep fakes, and generative bots – to name but a few. And even larger challenges are approaching from the realms of biotechnology, not to mention coping with climate change.

Some historians have compared the flux of ideas and connections today to the turmoil of the Renaissance and Reformation five centuries ago, but on a much larger scale. And those eras were followed by the Thirty Years' War that killed a third of the population of Germany. Today, the world is richer and riskier than ever before. I am sometimes asked whether I am optimistic or pessimistic about the future of this country. I reply, "Guardedly optimistic."

America has many problems – polarization, inequality, loss of trust, mass shootings, deaths of despair from drugs and suicide – just to name a few that make headlines. There is a case for pessimism. At the same time, we have survived worse periods in the 1890s, 1930s and the 1960s (as I described in Chapter 2). For all our flaws, the US is an innovative society that, in the past, has been able to recreate and reinvent itself. Maybe Gen Z can do it again. I hope so. We should be wary of counting too heavily on American exceptionalism, but the reasons for my optimism are described in this account of what it was like to live through the first eight decades of the American century. But to be honest, I cannot be fully sure how much of my optimism rests on my analysis or in my genes.

As a government official, I was privileged to help shape decisions on two major foreign policy issues in this American century: nuclear proliferation and American policy toward Asia. I think they made the world a better place. As a public intellectual, I helped to promote ideas and create and sustain nongovernmental networks to reinforce our democratic alliances. As a teacher and mentor, I was fortunate to work with many wonderful people. As an analyst and writer, I tried to produce and share new ideas such as complex interdependence and soft power, which enhanced our understanding of the world. I also tried to clarify our theories of leadership, to make sense of the nuclear revolution, and to make a small dent in understanding the cyber revolution.

As I have said above, however, the more I learn, the less I know. The numerator grows, but the denominator grows even more rapidly. I have learned that I have lived in a very small corner of the universe, and that *Homo sapiens* is a baffling species. Though I have spent a lifetime following my curiosity and trying to understand us, I do not leave many answers for my grandchildren. The best I can do is leave them my love and a faint ray of guarded optimism.

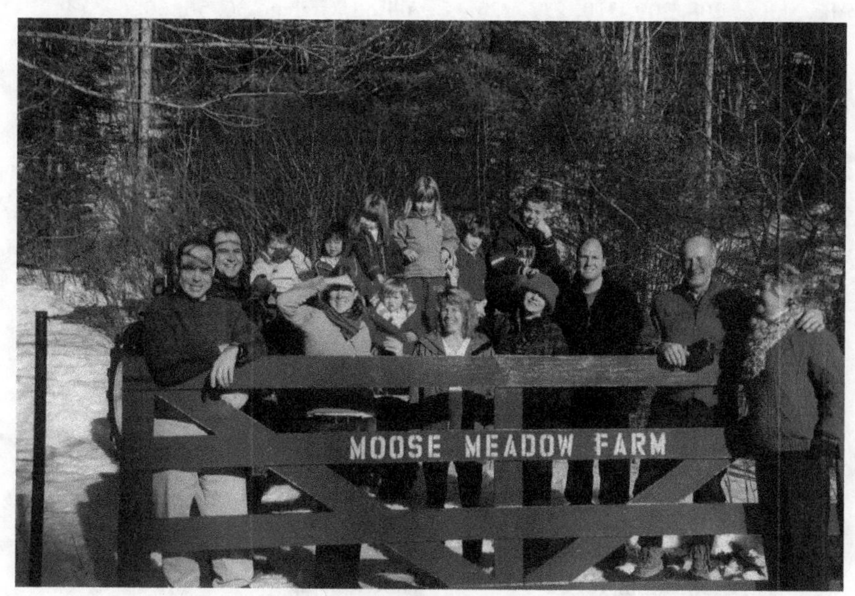

Family Christmas at Moose Meadow Farm, 2004

Index

Page numbers in *italic* refer to images